Project Valuation Using Real Options

A Practitioner's Guide

Project Valuation Using Real Options

A Practitioner's Guide

Dr. PRASAD KODUKULA, PMP

CHANDRA PAPUDESU

Copyright ©2006 by J. Ross Publishing, Inc.

ISBN 1-932159-43-6

Printed and bound in the U.S.A. Printed on acid-free paper
10 9 8 7 6 5 4 3 2 1

Library of Congress Cataloging-in-Publication Data

Kodukula, Prasad.
   Project valuation using real options : a practitioner's guide / by Prasad
Kodukula and Chandra Papudesu.
      p. cm.
   Includes bibliographical references and index
   ISBN 1-932159-43-6 (hardcover : alk. paper)
   1. Real options (Finance). 2. Investments. 3. Project management. I.
Papudesu, Chandra. II. Title.
   HG6042.K62 2006
   658.15′5—dc22   2006005534

Phone: (954) 727-9333
Fax: (561) 892-0700
Web: www.jrosspub.com

TABLE OF CONTENTS

PREFACE

"To invest or not to invest?" is a question pondered every day by business executives all over the world. You may be regularly involved in helping the executives of your organization to answer that very question, and perhaps that is why you are reading this book. We suspect that you belong to one of the following three groups: You are relatively new to real options and excited about learning more, you are intimidated by its complex theoretical groundwork and hoping to find some simple application tools, or you are totally frustrated with it and were just about ready to give up before you came across this book. Whatever group you fall into, believe us, we understand where you are coming from, because we have been through the gamut of those emotions ourselves. But first, let us thank you for reading this book and giving real options a chance — maybe another chance if you are among those who are ready to give up.

A real option is a right — not an obligation — to take an action on an underlying nonfinancial asset, referred to as a *real* asset. The action may involve, for example, abandoning, expanding, or contracting a project or even deferring the decision until a later time. Real options analysis is a tool that helps to quantify the value of an option. It is a relatively new project valuation tool, and we think it is experiencing "growing pains." It is just a matter of time, we believe, before it becomes a standard tool in the valuation toolbox. After all, it took decades for the traditional discounted cash flow analysis to become the corporate standard for project valuation!

WHY WE WROTE THIS BOOK

We wrote this book for several reasons. First, it seemed to us that most of the current books on real options are long on theory and short on application. We repeatedly heard from our clients that there was a strong need for a book that focused on the real world application of real options tools. Second, considering the theoretical complexity involved, many practitioners are taking a "black box" approach to real options solutions, causing resistance from management because of lack of transparency. We wanted to break that black box and walk you through the solution process step by step by holding your hand. We hope that this will help both you and your management understand the tool and its application better and ultimately result in wider acceptance of real options analysis in your organization. Third, most real options books deal with valuation of relatively large strategic initiatives and companies as a whole. We wanted to focus on project valuation rather than company valuation, although the principles are basically the same for both. Finally, most corporate managers and decision makers seem to think that you need a Ph.D. in finance to understand real options. But we disagree, so we wanted to write a book that does not require even an MBA — let alone a Ph.D. — as a prerequisite. We started the book with these goals in mind, which we hope we have accomplished. The real inspiration behind this book is a real options course we presented in spring 2004 for a client. The background research material and the final course content formed the foundation for this book, but the real catalyst in making this book happen is the overwhelming positive feedback we received about the course.

WHO CAN BENEFIT FROM THIS BOOK

We have a broad audience in mind. Corporate executives and senior managers can benefit by understanding the real options principles and the importance of the real options mind-set in the decision process in today's uncertain world. Program and project portfolio managers will be able to select the right tools and techniques and make the real options framework part of the overall valuation and portfolio management methodologies in their organizations. Most important, we wrote the book for the financial analyst — the real practitioner — who needs valuation tools to do his or her job every day. We hope our audience will find the book most valuable in terms of the tools, step-by-step calculations, and the insights presented herein. Finally, we believe that this book presents a solid introduction to real options for any student of business management.

HOW THIS BOOK IS ORGANIZED

The first chapter introduces real options analysis as a project valuation tool, presents the terminology, and draws parallels between real and financial options. The second chapter is a discussion with examples on the three frequently used traditional project valuation tools: the discounted cash flow method, decision tree analysis, and Monte Carlo simulation. Chapter 3 introduces the concept of risk, differentiates market versus private risk, and describes what is known, in financial circles, as the discount rate dilemma (what discount rate to use under what circumstances). This chapter also presents a discussion on the challenges a practitioner faces in applying traditional valuation tools. Chapter 4 focuses on how real options analysis supplements the traditional tools in project valuation. It also shows under what conditions real options offer the greatest benefit over the traditional tools. Chapter 5 presents the methods and computational techniques commonly employed to solve real options problems. The next chapter deals with real world application of real options with a discussion on limitations of current options models and how they can be overcome. It also offers a six-step process to value a project using real options analysis. Chapter 7 includes examples of simple options (expansion, contraction, abandonment, etc.) and step-by-step calculations illustrating how to solve the options problem in each example. Similarly, advanced option (sequential and parallel compound options, rainbow options, etc.) examples and step-by-step solutions for each example are presented in Chapter 8. The last chapter of the book addresses real world issues and the current status of real options applications in the corporate world.

The spreadsheets used in conjunction with the numerous example calculations presented throughout the book as well as the solutions to the problems included at the end of each chapter are available at www.jrosspub.com and www.kodukula.com. Additional information and ancillary material related to real options are also available there.

Prasad Kodukula, Ph.D., PMP
Chandra Papudesu

ACKNOWLEDGMENTS

First and foremost, we want to thank Kasu Sista, a longtime friend of Prasad since his graduate school days, for inspiring us to study and develop a consulting practice in real options. We cannot thank Raghu Saripalli, a real practitioner of valuation tools, enough for his numerous reviews and insights, which were most important in shaping this book. Our special thanks to Raghu Adibhatla for drawing all the figures in the book with so much patience. We would like to acknowledge Ashwin Laheja and Carl Bandy II for their comments on the early drafts of the book. The seeds of the book were planted in the course that we developed for Futoshi Nakamura and his team at Japan Tobacco, who deserve a very special "thank you."

We would like to also thank Drew Gierman, Publisher and Vice President of Sales; Sandy Pearlman, our editor; and the rest of the J. Ross Publishing team for their patience, guidance, encouragement, and fine efforts.

ABOUT THE AUTHORS

Dr. Prasad Kodukula, PMP, is President of Kodukula & Associates, Inc. (www.kodukula.com) and a management teacher, executive coach, and motivational speaker with nearly 20 years of professional experience. He has spoken in 15 countries to a total audience of more than 100,000 people on project management, project portfolio management, and leadership skills. His clients include 20 Fortune 100 companies and the U.S. government. Dr. Kodukula is also co-founder and president of 2Ci (www.constantcompliance.com), where he is involved in developing environmental and homeland security technologies. In 2005, 2Ci received the Innovate Illinois award for being the most innovative small business in the environmental category in Illinois. Dr. Kodukula was recognized by the U.S. Environmental Protection Agency and the Kansas Department of Health and Environment for his outstanding contributions in environmental science and engineering. He holds degrees from the Illinois Institute of Technology, Cornell University, and Rutgers University. He is a contributing author on four books and has co-authored three books and more than 40 technical articles.

Chandra Papudesu, M.S., has more than eight years of application development, project management and consulting experience spanning every phase of the software life cycle. As Director of Software Services at a software product company, he oversees projects for customers in multiple industries including healthcare, retail, pharmacy, and banking.

Mr. Papudesu also served as project manager for a software services and product company, where his team designed and developed custom enterprise software for clients in the energy, banking, and insurance sectors. He holds a bachelor's degree from the Indian Institute of Technology and a master's degree from Massachusetts Institute of Technology, both in engineering.

Web
Added
Value

*Free value-added materials available from
the Download Resource Center at www.jrosspub.com*

At J. Ross Publishing we are committed to providing today's professional with practical, hands-on tools that enhance the learning experience and give readers an opportunity to apply what they have learned. That is why we offer free ancillary materials available for download on this book and all participating Web Added Value™ publications. These online resources may include interactive versions of material that appears in the book or supplemental templates, worksheets, models, plans, case studies, proposals, spreadsheets and assessment tools, among other things. Whenever you see the WAV™ symbol in any of our publications, it means bonus materials accompany the book and are available from the Web Added Value Download Resource Center at www.jrosspub.com and www.kodukula.com.

Downloads available for *Project Valuation Using Real Options: A Practitioner's Guide* consist of assessment tools and solutions to the problems presented in the book.

INTRODUCTION

Thales, a famous Sophist philosopher circa 600 B.C., gazed into the star-studded sky one evening and predicted an outstanding olive harvest the next season. For a small up-front fee, he bought the right from the owners of the olive presses to rent them for the usual rate during the harvest season. If the harvest turned out to be meager, there would be less need for the presses and Thales would not rent them, losing the up-front fee. But if the harvest was bountiful, he would rent the presses at the regular agreed-upon price and turn around and rent them out to the farmers at a significant margin. Sure enough, it was an outstanding harvest, and Thales rented the in-demand presses and made a fortune. He was apparently more interested in proving the wisdom of Sophists than making money, as Aristotle tells this story in *Politics*.

This is one of the frequently cited earliest examples of a real options contract, wherein Thales bought an option — a right, but not an obligation — to rent the presses, the underlying risky asset. This is called a real option, not a financial option, because the underlying asset is a real asset, not a financial asset. Real options evolved from financial options, and therefore the terminology is common to both. Using a simple financial example, let us first introduce the options terminology and draw parallels between commonly known financial options and poorly understood real options.

FINANCIAL OPTIONS EXAMPLE

HiTech* is a publicly held technology company whose stock is selling at $20 per share. The stock price is expected to rise significantly in the near future

---

* The names of all companies used as examples throughout the book are fictitious.

because of the company's innovative products and market demand. At the same time, however, there is also market uncertainty that indicates a possible sharp drop in the stock price. As an investor, you can buy shares of this stock today at $20 per share or instead buy options to buy or sell the stock in the future. An option is a right — not an obligation — to either buy or sell the stock, the underlying asset, at a predetermined cost on or before a predetermined date.

For instance, let us say that you buy one option on the underlying stock of HiTech today at the market price of $2 that gives you a right — without any obligation whatsoever — to buy the stock one year from now at a price of $25. One year from now, if HiTech's stock price drops below $25, you can walk away with no obligation to buy the stock and lose the $2 that you paid to acquire the option. On the other hand, if the stock price goes above $25, to say $35, as a rational investor, you will exercise your option and buy one share of the stock. This would be worth $35, but you pay only the agreed-upon price of $25, thus making a gross profit of $10. Accounting for the initial price of $2 paid to buy the option, your net profit is $8. Thus, using the options approach, you would exercise your option (i.e., buy the stock) only if it goes above your exercise price; otherwise, you would walk away and take your up-front fee as a loss.

In another scenario, you may acquire an option to *sell*. If you believe that the stock price of HiTech will be below $25 a share one year from now, you may buy one option of the stock at the market price of $2 that gives you a right — with no obligation — to sell the stock one year from now at a price of $25 per share. If the stock price is above $25 per share on that day, you will not exercise the option, which expires and becomes worthless. However, if the stock price drops below $25, to say $15, you will exercise your option to sell one share of the stock worth $15 for a price of $25, making a gross profit of $10 and a net profit of $8 after accounting for the initial option price of $2.

In both of the above scenarios, the options approach allows you to take advantage of the payoff when it is positive while limiting the downside risk.

OPTIONS TERMINOLOGY

The first scenario above involves an option to buy and is called a call option. The sell option in the second scenario is called a put option. The price at which the option is exercised is called the exercise price or strike price, which is $25 per share in both cases. A European option has a fixed maturity date, whereas an American option can be exercised on or any time before the option's maturity or expiration date. Therefore, both of the above scenarios involved European options. The commonly used key options terms are summarized in Table 1-1.

Table 1-1.   Options Terminology

- An option is a right — not an obligation — of its owner to buy or sell the underlying asset at a predetermined price on or before a predetermined date.

- A buy option is known as a call option and a sell option as a put option.

- A financial option is a right — not an obligation — to take an action (buy or sell) on an underlying financial asset (e.g., a stock) at a predetermined cost on or before a predetermined date.

- A real option is a right — not an obligation — to take an action (e.g., defer, expand, contract, abandon, stage) on an underlying nonfinancial asset at a predetermined cost on or before a predetermined date.

- The expiration date is the date when the option expires or matures.

- A European option has a fixed date when it can be exercised. An American option can be exercised at any time on or before its expiration date.

- Option price or premium is the price paid to acquire the option.

- The exercise or strike price is the price at which the option owner can buy or sell the underlying asset.

- The call option value (C) at expiration is the maximum of two values: (1) zero and (2) the difference between the underlying asset value (S) at the time when the asset is bought at maturity and the exercise price (X) at maturity:

$$C = \text{Max} [0, S - X]$$

- The put option value (P) at expiration is the maximum of two values: (1) zero and (2) the difference between the exercise price (X) at maturity and the underlying asset value (S) when the asset is sold at maturity:

$$P = \text{Max} [0, X - S]$$

- A call option is in the money if $S - X > 0$, at the money if $S - X = 0$, and out of the money if $S - X < 0$.

- A put option is in the money if $S - X < 0$, at the money if $S - X = 0$, and out of the money if $S - X > 0$.

Figures 1-1 and 1-2 are called payoff diagrams and show the cash payoff of a call and put option, respectively, at expiration. With a call option, if the underlying asset value is less than the strike price at the time of option expiration, the option is considered to be "out of the money" and, rationally speaking, will not be exercised. Thus, your net payoff in this case is negative and equal to the option price, also called the call price. If the asset value exceeds the strike price, the option is "in the money" and, rationally speaking, will be exercised and your gross payoff will be positive. Your net payoff, however, may be positive or negative depending on the call price. When the asset value is exactly equal to the strike price, the option is considered to be "at the money." At this point, your gross profit is zero, but the net profit is negative and is equal to the call price.

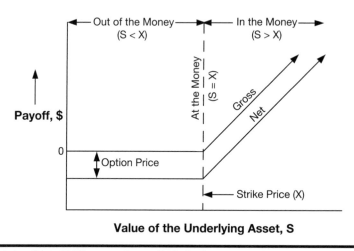

Figure 1-1. Payoff Diagram for a Call Option

As shown in Figure 1-2, the net payoff of a put option remains negative and equivalent to the put price (price paid to buy the option), as long as the underlying asset value at the expiration time remains above the strike price or the option is out of the money. In other words, you lose what you paid for the put. If the asset value is less than the strike price (that is, the option is in the money), the gross payoff is equal to the difference between the strike price and the value

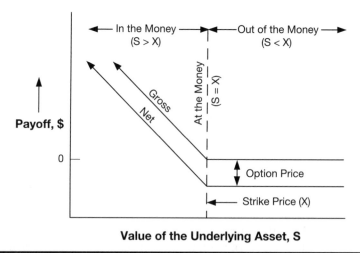

Figure 1-2. Payoff Diagram for a Put Option

of the underlying asset. The net payoff will be negative until the put price is recovered and from that point goes into the positive territory.

FINANCIAL VERSUS REAL OPTIONS

Options can be classified into two broad categories, financial and real, based on whether the underlying asset is a financial or real asset. Financial assets are primarily stocks and bonds that are traded in financial markets. The options for most of these assets are listed on exchanges such as the Chicago Board Options Exchange and the American Stock Exchange. Real assets may include real estate, projects, and intellectual property, most of which are not usually traded. A real option is a right — not an obligation — to take an action on an underlying nonfinancial, real asset. The action may involve, for example, abandoning, expanding, or contracting a project or even deferring the decision until a later time. The real options can be either American, which can be exercised on or before a predetermined expiration date, or European, which can be exercised on a fixed date only. They share the same characteristics as the financial options and, therefore, the same terminology is used. Table 1-2 provides a comparison of financial and real options.

REAL OPTIONS EXAMPLES

In the historic example cited at the outset of this chapter, Thales used a call option, presumably an American one, and exercised it when it was in the money. Let us now review three modern-day examples. To keep the illustrations simple, we will ignore the time value of money.

GeneMiracles is a 21st century biotechnology company that specializes in human genomics. It invented a new technology for which it obtained two patents, based on which it plans to develop a new product. Because the potential market for the product is uncertain, management does not want to commit to fully invest in its development and chooses to create an option to sell the technology if at any time during the development effort it becomes clear that the future payoff on the product would not be favorable. Genes & Foods (G&F) is another biotech company with a market niche in genetically modified foods. It has great interest in GeneMiracles' new technology, which fits very well with its product portfolio. Both companies sign an options contract which allows GeneMiracles to sell its patented technology to G&F for a price of $60 million anytime during the three years of product development time. To acquire this option, GeneMiracles pays G&F $10 million. After completing two years of

Table 1-2. Financial Versus Real Options

	Financial Options	Real Options
Option price	Price paid to acquire the option, which is fixed by the financial markets	Price paid to acquire or create the option, keep it alive, and clear the uncertainty (for instance, price paid to acquire a patent, maintain it, and conduct market research to identify its potential). The option price is not fixed (for example, the price to buy a patent is negotiable).
Exercise price	Price paid to buy/sell the underlying stock; a fixed value defined in the option contract	Cost of buying/selling the underlying real asset (e.g., the cost of commercializing a new technology is a call option exercise price, the underlying asset being the profits from the commercialization; the selling price of abandoned manufacturing assets is a put option exercise price, the underlying asset being the manufacturing assets).
Expiration time	Defined in the options contract and is clearly known	Clearly known in some cases (e.g., leases may be signed on oil fields involving options on drilling) and not so in others (e.g., for technology projects, it depends on the market conditions and competition).
Timing of payoff	Immediately after the options are exercised; basically instantaneous	Often not until some time after the option has been exercised. May be spread over a long period of time. For example, after a decision has been made to commercialize a new technology, the commercialization itself takes months, and the profits from the sales are spread over a period of many years.
Option holder's control on its value over the option's life	None	Proper management action can increase the option value while limiting the downside potential. For example, the holder of a new, novel technology option can invest in developing other complementary technologies, increasing the value of the original option.
Option value as a function of option life	Larger for longer life of a given option	Larger for longer life of a given option, especially related to patents and property with exclusive rights. But with many options, the asset value may be diminished because of entry of competition, thereby bringing the option value down.
Option value as a function of the underlying asset's volatility	Increases	Increases.

Resolution of uncertainty	Uncertainty clears automatically with time; the option holder has to do nothing to clear it	Uncertainty clears through time in some cases. In most cases, the option holder needs to actively invest in clearing the uncertainty, for instance, through market research or pilot testing.
Liquidity and tradability of the option	Liquid and tradable in financial markets	Most often neither liquid nor tradable.
Rationality behind the exercise decision	Mostly rational; dictated by the numerical difference between the underlying asset (e.g., stock) value and the exercise price	Exercise decision may have political and emotional implications (e.g., abandonment of a long-term project with a large team).

development work, based on the most reliable market information, GeneMiracles estimates the net future payoff on the product to be a paltry $50 million. Management therefore exercises its put option by selling the intellectual property to G&F for $60 million.

MoneyMaker Drugs, with healthy cash reserves and good potential for future profitability, is contemplating expanding one of its operations by 50% by possibly acquiring a start-up company. Due to market uncertainty, executive management does not want to commit to the full investment at this point. Therefore, it creates an option to expand anytime over the next two years, which it would exercise by acquiring the start-up for $6 million, if the market uncertainty clears and shows positive results. In return for this option, MMD invests $1 million in the start-up company. At the end of the second year, the market information becomes clear, showing an estimated $10 million payoff due to the planned expansion. At this time, MoneyMaker Drugs exercises its option by acquiring the start-up company and expands the operations. It would have maintained the status quo and not invested in the acquisition if the expected market value of operations expansion had turned out to be less than the exercise price of $6 million.

MobileVDO, a telecom company, paid $20 million to buy a patent for ultrawideband wireless technology that can transfer streaming video at high speeds with minimal power requirements. MobileVDO estimates that it will take another $200 million to develop and commercialize this technology, but there is great uncertainty about the payoff. It therefore plans to wait for the uncertainty to clear before investing in development and commercialization. Buying the patent gives MobileVDO an option to develop and commercialize the technology. In the next three years, if the market uncertainty clears and the payoff from commercialization is expected to be greater than $200 million, MobileVDO would make the investment. It may even fund initial studies such as focused market surveys to clear some of the uncertainty to facilitate a more informed decision. However, if the uncertainty does not clear in a reasonable time, the telecom may let the patent expire.

Table 1-3 analyzes the characteristics of the options available in each example presented above. In every example, the payoff was uncertain and the management decisions were contingent. Therefore, the options approach made sense. But an important question that the decision makers presumably faced was: What is the value of the option? If the value of the option is significant, only then would it make sense to create an option. Otherwise, the decision might as well be made up front, instead of waiting for the uncertainty to clear. The managers created options in every case, because their evaluation presumably showed enough option value to wait until the uncertainty cleared.

Table 1-3. Option Characteristics for the Real Options Examples

Characteristic	GeneMiracles	MoneyMaker Drugs	MobileVDO
Option	To sell the patented technology	To expand operations by 50% by acquiring a start-up company	To launch a new product
Call or put	Put	Call	Call
Expiration time	Three years	Two years	Three years
Price	$10 million	$1 million	$20 million (price of the patent)
Exercise price	$60 million (selling price of the patented technology)	$6 million (cost of acquiring the start-up company)	$200 million (cost of developing and commercializing the technology)
Value of the underlying asset at expiration	$50 million (the expected payoff from the technology)	$10 million (the expected payoff from expansion)	Not known since the option is still active
Option value at expiration	$10 million ($60 million – $50 million)	$4 million ($10 million – $6 million)	Not known since the option is still active

OPTIONS VALUATION

Senior business executives and managers struggle every day in making project investment decisions. The decision may be whether to invest in a new project now or wait a while, or it may be whether to contract, expand, or abandon an ongoing project. The decision makers often are looking for tools that can help them make the right decisions. The most fundamental information needed to make such decisions relates to the value of the project in financial terms. Net present value (NPV) based on discounted cash flow (DCF) analysis is the most commonly used tool today in project valuation. You will invest in a project if the NPV of the project is positive. The universal use of DCF notwithstanding, the technique has certain limitations. The NPV is based on a set of fixed assumptions related to the project payoff (a deterministic approach), whereas the payoff is uncertain and probabilistic. DCF does not take into consideration the contingent decisions available and the managerial flexibility to act on those decisions. For example, the value of the future flexibility to expand, contract, or abandon is not captured by DCF. Furthermore, DCF analysis accounts for only the downside of the risk without considering the rewards. This inherent bias leads to rejection of highly promising projects because of their uncertainty. Many of today's technology projects exhibit such characteristics; therefore, the limitations of DCF are of enormous significance in their valuation.

Real-options-based valuation, referred to as real options analysis (ROA) in this book, offers new ways to address these limitations of DCF. To be sure, ROA is not a substitute for DCF. It is a supplement that fills the gaps that DCF cannot address. ROA uses DCF as a building block and captures the value of the options — expressed as real options value in this book — embedded in growth projects that DCF alone cannot measure. It integrates traditional valuation tools into a more sophisticated framework that provides practicing financial analysts and decision makers with more complete and meaningful information. Whereas real options embedded in projects are implicitly recognized by organizations, the formal valuation using ROA makes them explicit and quantifies their value, thereby helping management make rational decisions.

ROA evolved from financial options valuation, which has been the subject of numerous technical papers and books for decades. The Nobel Prize–winning work of MIT economists Fisher Black, Robert Merton, and Myron Scholes was the foundation of the financial options theory.

In this book, we attempt to briefly describe the theory behind options valuation and focus on how a practicing professional (say, a financial analyst) involved in project valuation can use the options models to calculate the value of different types of project investments. We also compare and contrast the real options approach with the traditional tools of valuation. Furthermore, we discuss the benefits and limitations of ROA in terms of practical application.

PROBLEMS

1-1. Fuel Sells holds several patents related to a new technology that provides power to laptops and cellular devices using fuel cells in lieu of the conventional batteries. The development cost for this technology is expected to be $100 million. If the technology is proven effective, the net payoff over the project's lifetime is estimated at $105 million. Since there is considerable technology as well as market uncertainty, Fuel Sells made an agreement to sell its assets to Cool Buys for $50 million, if the project is deemed unattractive within the next three years. What is the option created by Fuel Sells? Is it a call or a put? What is the strike price? What is the option life?

1-2. Seamless Transitions is contemplating whether to launch within the next three years a new technology that allows seamless transition of networks from landline to cellular so that the same phone handset can be used with both networks. Since there is enormous uncertainty related to this technology, the company decides to conduct a pilot test in a small market before a "full-blown" launch. It initiates a pilot test in a small metropolitan area, which is expected to cost $200 million. If the pilot test proves the project's large-scale commercial viability, the company will launch the seamless technology and its related products in seven major metropolitan areas at an estimated investment cost of $1 billion. What is the option created by Seamless Transitions? Is it a call or a put? What is the price of the option? What is its strike price?

1-3. Priceless Polymers invested $100 million to build a new manufacturing plant, the lifetime payoff from which was expected to be $120 million at the time the project was initiated. Since there was a great deal of uncertainty regarding this estimate, the company decided at the time of project initiation that it would sell its assets for an expected salvage value of $20 million if at any time within the next three years the uncertainty cleared and the expected payoff dropped below the salvage value. At the end of the third year, the market uncertainty cleared and the expected project payoff was estimated to be merely $15 million. The company then sold its assets and terminated the project. What option did Priceless Polymers create to begin with? Was it a call or a put? What was its strike price? What was the option life? What was the option value at the exercise time?

2

TRADITIONAL PROJECT VALUATION TOOLS

The objective of project valuation most often is not only to evaluate a project for its own merit but also to compare how it stacks up against other projects competing for the same investment pool. To maximize returns on their investments, today's corporations — especially their product development and IT organizations — are taking a portfolio approach. The project portfolio is designed to maximize the portfolio value by assessment, prioritization, selection, tracking, and termination/completion of projects based on the strategic goals of the organization and resource availability.

Figure 2-1 presents the Funnel & Filters® model to represent a portfolio of projects. Each project's end-to-end life cycle is characterized by three distinct phases:

- Assessment
- Development
- Production

In the assessment phase, project ideas are initiated and assessed for their merit as well as how they compare with other competing ideas. The ideas go through a filter(s), which helps in selecting those that are deemed worthwhile for investment and reject those that are not. The selected ideas become "formal" projects and enter the next phase. The objective of the development phase is to develop the target product (or service). In this phase, there are additional filters that facilitate management's contingent decisions (defer investment; abandon, expand, contract, or continue the project at the planned scale; etc.) on

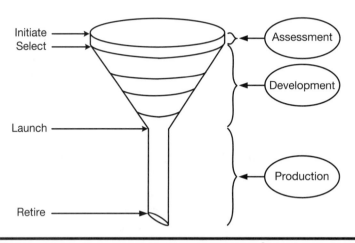

Figure 2-1. Portfolio Management: Funnels & Filters®

the product development. The end of this phase is marked by "launch" of the product associated with the project.

In the third and last phase, if the project results in a product, it will be made, sold, and supported. On the other hand, if the project results in a service offering, this phase may simply involve support only. At the end of the production phase, the product or service becomes obsolete, is no longer sold or supported by the organization, and "retires" from its life cycle. If a product is considered for improvement or enhancement to take a new form or version or if a service is to be expanded or contracted, it is identified as a new project idea and goes through a new life cycle starting at the top of the funnel.

Project valuation is probably the most important part of the selection process, because it assigns a dollar value to the project. In a broad sense, the project value is the net difference between the project revenues and costs over its entire life cycle. If the project's net revenues during the production phase are higher than the investment costs, the project is considered worthy of investment. Several tools are available to calculate the value of the project, and the quality of the valuation is related to the validity of the tools and how effectively they account for three important factors:

1. Cash flow streams (investment costs and production phase costs and revenues) through the entire project life cycle
2. Discount rate used to discount the future cash flows to account for their uncertainty
3. Availability of management's contingent decisions to change the course of the project

PROJECT CASH FLOWS

Project cash flows represent both the benefits and costs of the project. These cash flows should be estimated for the entire project life cycle, including the development and production phases. There are basically two cash flow streams:

- Investment cost
- Net revenues in the production phase

The first cash flow stream typically is comprised of development phase costs and production phase capital costs. The latter, in the case of a product development project, for example, may include building a manufacturing plant and product launch costs. The second stream, commonly referred to as project payoff, is a net cash flow, which is the difference between the revenues and the costs associated with those revenues in the production phase of the project. After accounting for depreciation, taxes, working capital, and so forth, these cash flows are referred to as "free cash flows." (The terms net revenue, payoff, and free cash flows are used interchangeably in this book.) The crux of project valuation lies in estimating these two cash flow streams over the entire project life cycle and discounting them back to today's value using the appropriate discount rate.

DISCOUNT RATE

We all know that a dollar today is worth more than a dollar tomorrow. Discount rate is the rate that is used to convert the future value of the project cash flows to today's value. It is adjusted for the risk perceived to be associated with the project; the higher the risk, the higher the discount rate. The project risk is dictated by the uncertainty of the cash flows, which is discussed in more detail in the next chapter.

CONTINGENT DECISIONS

Most projects involve contingent decisions, where senior management can change the course of the project by deciding whether to defer the investment for a while; abandon, expand, or contract the project; maintain the status quo; and so on. There is great strategic value imbedded in these decisions, which can be taken advantage of only if management recognizes it and is willing to exercise the decisions. To capture the true value of a project in its assessment phase, the value of such decisions must be quantified and captured. Otherwise, a project of great future strategic value may be rejected because it cannot compete with other projects in a portfolio based on its short-term value only.

There are three traditional tools that incorporate some or all of the above three factors into their project valuation calculations:

- Discounted cash flow analysis
- Monte Carlo simulation
- Decision trees

Irrespective of the tool, the building blocks for the calculations are provided by present values of the cash flow streams.

PRESENT VALUE

The methods that the financial analysts use to value projects may range from the simple to the sophisticated, but the building blocks for these methods are the same. Any valuation starts with estimation of development and production phase costs and net revenues (free cash flows) over the project life. Because of the time value of money, each cash flow from the future is converted into today's dollars, using the formula

$$PV = FV/(1 + r)^n \tag{2-1}$$

where FV = future value, PV = present value, r = discount rate per time period, and n = number of the time period.

For the sake of convenience, $1/(1 + r)^n$ is typically calculated as "discount factor" for a given discount rate and time period and is multiplied by the FV to arrive at the corresponding PV.

For example, for an annual discount rate of 10% and a two-year time period, the discount factor is 0.826 [i.e., $1/(1.10)^2$]. If the annual net cash flow on a project is expected to be $1 million two years from now, using six decimal places for the discount factor, the PV will be $826,446 ($1,000,000 * 0.826446). Equation 2-1, which accounts for "discrete" compound discounting, can be rewritten as follows for continuous compound discounting:

$$PV = FV * \exp(-r * n) \tag{2-2}$$

For the above example, Equation 2-2 gives a PV of $818,730, which is lower than but relatively close to the value provided by discrete compound discounting from Equation 2-1.

This principle of PV is used in every project valuation method and is fundamental to any valuation tool, including the traditional tools such as discounted cash flow, Monte Carlo simulation, and decision trees as well as more advanced techniques involving real options.

DISCOUNTED CASH FLOW METHOD

There are literally hundreds of discounted cash flow (DCF) models, but they are all based on the same foundation that simply involves calculation of the *net present value* (NPV) of a project over its entire life cycle, accounting for the investment costs and the production phase free cash flows. If the investment costs are incurred over a short period of time (say, less than a year), there is no need for discounting, but for longer time frames, the investment costs have to be discounted back to today using the PV calculation. Free cash flows typically are realized over a long period of the production phase, which means they have to be discounted back to today using an appropriate discount factor that best represents the risk associated with the project. Most commonly, only one single rate is used to discount all these cash flow streams. In fact, DCF involves the use of only one set of input variables, making it a deterministic method. However, since the input variables rather behave in a probabilistic fashion, a common practice is to conduct a sensitivity analysis by varying these variables to study their impact on the final NPV.

The project NPV is the summation of the PVs of all the cash inflows and cash outflows from the development and production phases of a project:

$$\text{Project NPV} = \text{PV of free cash flows in production phase} \quad (2\text{-}3)$$
$$- \text{PV of investment costs}$$

If the project NPV based on the DCF analysis is greater than zero, the project is considered financially attractive. In other words, if the total PV of expected free cash flows (the project payoff) is greater than the total PV of the investment costs, the project is deemed worthy of investment. Furthermore, in a project portfolio situation, a candidate project's NPV is compared with that of others for project (re)prioritization to facilitate go/no-go decisions. This means that even if a given project is attractive based on its NPV, it may not be selected for investment if there are other competing projects that are even more attractive. In the following simple example, project NPV is first calculated using the DCF method. Then the sensitivity of the NPV to key input parameters is explored. Furthermore, scenario analysis is performed to compare the baseline case with the best and worst cases.

Wireless in Washington (WIW) is a small telecommunications company that has a patent pending for an innovative product that increases the range of wireless hot spots by tenfold compared to the competing technologies. The product has already been rolled out successfully in the Washington, D.C. area, and WIW is now exploring introducing the product in three other major metropolitan markets in the United States. The initial investment cost to launch the product is estimated to be $10 million. The product is estimated to have a lifetime of seven years, by which time newer innovations are expected to take over. A discount rate of 25% is used to reflect the uncertainty of the project cash flows. Table 2-1 presents the steps involved in calculating the project NPV using the DCF method and summarizes the results.

WIW also conducted a sensitivity analysis by varying the initial investment, discount rate, annual cost, and peak annual revenue. Table 2-2 presents the results and Figure 2-2 shows the impact of input variables on the NPV in the form of a so-called "tornado" diagram. (A tornado diagram graphically shows the ranges of NPVs in descending order, starting with the highest range first, where each range represents the NPVs from the change in each of the input variables. The resulting graphic looks like a tornado; hence the name.)

Even with ±20% change in the input variables compared to their "average" estimates, WIW's project NPV is still a positive number, showing that the project is probably a good investment. The sensitivity analysis also shows that the peak annual revenue has the highest impact on the final NPV.

To gain further insight into the problem, WIW also conducted a scenario analysis where best and worst cases were evaluated and compared with the average case. The best and worst scenarios represented 150% ($19.84 million) and 50% ($6.61 million) of the expected total net annual revenues of the baseline case ($13.23 million), respectively. Accounting for the investment cost of $10 million, the project NPV would be $3.23 million, $9.84 million, and –$3.39 million for average, best, and worst cases, respectively.

In the foregoing discussion, the basic principles behind the DCF method were presented using a simple illustrative example. For a detailed analysis of DCF, we suggest a popular and authoritative textbook by Damodaran (2002). However, there are three aspects of DCF evaluation that warrant further discussion:

1. Certain products, especially those in the fast-changing technology and telecommunications areas, may have a limited "shelf" life (as in the WIW example), whereas others may have a longer life; in fact, so long that the cash flow streams may need to be estimated in perpetuity. In the latter case, it is common practice to estimate individual annual cash flows for a period of 7 to 10 years and use a "terminal" value for the

Table 2-1. Discounted Cash Flow Calculations for Wireless in Washington

1. Estimate the investment cost to launch the product today: $10 million.

2. Estimate the annual revenues and annual costs and calculate the annual net cash flows for the expected project life cycle. The net revenues are expected to increase and reach a peak for years 3 through 5 and decline thereafter (see the table below).

3. Choose a discount rate for the entire project life that reflects the risk associated with the project: 25% (based on management's decision).

4. Calculate the PVs of each annual net cash flow by discounting the future values by 25%. To do so, multiply the cash flow by the corresponding discount factor. (The discount factor is $[1/(1 + r)^n]$ based on Equation 2-1.) For example, PV of the net cash flow for year 1 is:

$$(\$1 \text{ million} * 0.8) = \$0.8 \text{ million}$$

5. Add the PVs of all the annual net cash flows for the entire project life cycle: $13.23 million.

6. Calculate the project NPV by subtracting the investment cost from the sum of the PVs of the annual net cash flows:

$$(\$13.23 \text{ million} - \$10 \text{ million}) = \$3.23 \text{ million}$$

		Year						
	0	1	2	3	4	5	6	7
Investment cost	−$10.00							
Annual revenue		$3.00	$6.00	$10.00	$10.00	$10.00	$6.00	$5.00
Annual cost		$2.00	$2.50	$3.00	$3.00	$3.00	$2.50	$2.50
Annual net cash flow		$1.00	$3.50	$7.00	$7.00	$7.00	$3.50	$2.50
Discount rate	25%	25%	25%	25%	25%	25%	25%	25%
Discount factor[a]	1	0.8	0.64	0.51	0.41	0.33	0.26	0.21
PV of annual cash flow	−$10.00	$0.80	$2.24	$3.57	$2.87	$2.31	$0.91	$0.53
PV of net annual cash flow	$13.23							
NPV	$3.23							

Note: All dollar values are in millions. For the sake of simplicity, free cash flow calculations are ignored (that is, additional capital expenses, depreciation cash backs, taxes, working capital needs, etc. are not considered) and the terminal value is assumed to be zero.
[a] $1/(1 + 0.25)^n$, where n is the year number.

remainder of the project life. The three most common methods to estimate the terminal value are briefly discussed in Table 2-3.

2. To keep the WIW example simple for the purpose of illustration, we did not show how the project revenues and costs were obtained over the project lifetime, nor did we calculate free cash flows accounting for interest, taxes, depreciation, etc. Two of the models that are commonly used to estimate the project revenues from one time period to the next

**Table 2-2. Discounted Cash Flow Sensitivity Analysis for
Wireless in Washington**

1. Start with the base case represented by the "average" input variables as shown in Table 2-1: Project NPV = $3.23 million.

2. Increase the capital cost by 20% ($10 million * 1.2 = $12 million) keeping the other variables the same, and recalculate the project NPV: $1.23 million.

3. Calculate the percent change in the NPV compared to the base NPV: −62% [($1.23 million − $3.23 million)/$3.23 million].

4. Decrease the capital cost by 20% ($10 million * 0.8 = $8 million) keeping the other variables the same, and recalculate the project NPV: $5.23 million.

5. Calculate the percent change in the NPV compared to the base NPV: 62% [($5.23 million − $3.23 million)/$3.23 million].

6. Similarly, change the discount rate, peak annual cost, and peak annual revenue by ±20%, one at a time, keeping the rest of the input variables the same as in the base case, and recalculate the NPV and % NPV change for each case.

	Variable		NPV	% NPV Change
Investment cost	Base	$10	$3.23	
	+20%	$12	$1.23	−62%
	−20%	$8	$5.23	62%
Discount rate	Base	25%	$3.23	
	+20%	30%	$1.49	−54%
	−20%	20%	$5.37	67%
Peak annual cost	Base	$3	$3.23	
	+20%	$3.6	$2.48	−23%
	−20%	$2.4	$3.98	23%
Peak annual revenue	Base	$10	$3.23	
	+20%	$12	$5.73	77%
	−20%	$8	$0.73	−77%

over the project life are time series and constant growth rate. With the former model, it is assumed that the revenue for each time period is based on the preceding one, whereas with the latter model, as the name implies, a constant growth rate is assumed relative to the revenues. A detailed cash flow analysis would involve estimates of, among other things, the number of product units expected to be sold during each year, unit price of the product, fixed and variable costs, and so on. Table 2-4 provides a sample generic example where such details are used in the DCF calculation.

3. Although sensitivity and scenario analyses help us gain better insight into the DCF results, their effectiveness is limited because you can only

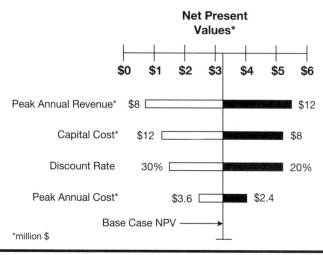

Figure 2-2. Tornado Diagram: Effect of Input Variables on Net Present Value

run so many scenarios without the use of more sophisticated tools involving computers. One such tool is called Monte Carlo simulation, which is discussed next.

MONTE CARLO SIMULATION

The Monte Carlo method, named after the famous gambling city in Monaco, involves simulation of thousands of possible project scenarios, calculation of the project NPV for each scenario using the DCF method, and analyzing the probability distribution of the NPV results. The appropriate discount rate should be used in discounting the cash flows to reflect their uncertainty. This method can be used in many different ways. In the most common approach, each project scenario is created by taking a random value for each one of the input parameters of the DCF method and solving for the NPV. Two basic steps are involved in such a calculation:

1. Define the probability distribution of each input variable (investment cost and revenues/costs for each selected time interval during the production phase, etc.) that dictates the free cash flows by identifying its average value and standard deviation of the distribution. This is typically done by using historical data. If there is no history on the data of an input variable to estimate its standard deviation, optimistic and pessimistic estimates which correspond to approximately 1% and 99% probabilities

Table 2-3.   Models to Calculate the Terminal Value in Discounted Cash Flow Analysis

Liquidation	In this approach, you assume a certain number of years for the product (or service) "shelf life" at the end of which the product becomes obsolete and is no longer made, marketed, sold, and supported. The sale price of the project assets at this point, if sold to the highest bidder, will represent the liquidation value of the project. Sometimes, the project may yield a negative cash flow for the terminal value if it involves cost burden such as environmental cleanup.
Multiple approach	In this approach, first you select the year when you want to apply the terminal value. Then you multiply the expected project cash flow for that year by a number that represents the cumulative expected cash flows for the rest of the project life following that year. For example, assume that a project's cash flow is calculated to be $100 million for year 7 where you want to estimate the terminal value. Assuming the multiplier is 3.0, the terminal value for the project is $300 million. The multiplier is typically obtained by historical information related to comparable products/services and management judgment.
Constant growth model	Using this model, it is assumed that, beyond the terminal year, the cash flows will grow at a constant growth rate in perpetuity.
Comparison of models	The liquidation approach can be used when a project is known to have a finite life. If the project is supposed to generate cash flows forever, the latter methods are more appropriate. The biggest drawback of the multiple approach is that it is subjective and does not provide an estimate of the intrinsic value of the project. The constant growth model is based on fundamentals and provides more accurate valuation. While these models are commonly used in DCF valuation of companies as a whole, we believe, in the context of projects, the terminal value is more meaningful in terms of the liquidation value rather than perpetual cash flows. In today's hyper-competitive environment, the cash flow growth rate is expected to decline considerably after a few years of product introduction. Furthermore, the rate of return in the later years is lower than is expected by the investors and adds very little value to the project. Therefore, we believe that for project valuation, it is sensible to estimate the individual annual cash flows over an expected project lifetime and add the liquidation value as part of the DCF valuation ignoring any "residual" cash flows over longer periods of time.

Table 2-4.   Generic Discounted Cash Flow Example on Free Cash Flows

				Year				
	0	1	2	3	4	5	6	7
Price per unit		$1,200	$1,400	$1,400	$1,400	$1,400	$1,200	$1,000
Number of units sold		10,000	15,000	16,000	17,000	18,000	16,000	15,000
Gross revenue		$12,000,000	$21,000,000	$22,400,000	$23,800,000	$25,200,000	$19,200,000	$15,000,000
Cost of sales		$400	$400	$400	$400	$400	$400	$400
Variable cost		$4,000,000	$6,000,000	$6,400,000	$6,800,000	$7,200,000	$6,400,000	$6,000,000
Fixed cost		$3,000,000	$3,000,000	$3,000,000	$3,000,000	$3,000,000	$3,000,000	$3,000,000
Total cost		$7,000,000	$9,000,000	$9,400,000	$9,800,000	$10,200,000	$9,400,000	$9,000,000
Gross profit		$5,000,000	$12,000,000	$13,000,000	$14,000,000	$15,000,000	$9,800,000	$6,000,000
Less depreciation		$1,000,000	$1,000,000	$1,000,000	$1,000,000	$1,000,000	$1,000,000	$1,000,000
Earnings before interest and taxes (EBIT)		$4,000,000	$11,000,000	$12,000,000	$13,000,000	$14,000,000	$8,800,000	$5,000,000
Tax rate		40%	40%	40%	40%	40%	40%	40%
Less taxes		$1,600,000	$4,400,000	$4,800,000	$5,200,000	$5,600,000	$3,520,000	$2,000,000
Earnings after taxes		$2,400,000	$6,600,000	$7,200,000	$7,800,000	$8,400,000	$5,280,000	$3,000,000
Plus depreciation		$1,000,000	$1,000,000	$1,000,000	$1,000,000	$1,000,000	$1,000,000	$1,000,000
Free cash flows		$3,400,000	$7,600,000	$8,200,000	$8,800,000	$9,400,000	$6,280,000	$4,000,000
Risk-adjusted discount rate		20%	20%	20%	20%	20%	20%	20%
Discount factor		0.83	0.69	0.58	0.48	0.40	0.33	0.28
PV of cash flows		$2,833,333	$5,277,778	$4,745,370	$4,243,827	$3,777,649	$2,103,159	$1,116,327

PV of all cash flows	$24,097,444
Project investment	$15,000,000
Project NPV	$9,097,444

may be provided based on management's judgment. With these esti-mates, standard deviation of the distribution of that input variable can be calculated with the help of standard normal frequency distribution tables or appropriate commercial software.

2. Draw one value for each input parameter from within its distribution and estimate the NPV using the DCF method. Repeat this process thousands of times using a commercially available program such as @Risk® or Crystal Ball®.

Table 2-5 shows a summary of the results from Monte Carlo simulations used to calculate the value of a project with the above approach. In this example, the investment cost is assumed to be deterministic and the risk-adjusted discount rate is kept constant for all the simulations. Probability distribution character-istics of the key input parameters presumably are estimated from historical information. Figure 2-3A presents the "point" probability distribution of the final NPVs calculated from the simulation, whereas the cumulative probability distribution is presented in Figure 2-3B. The second figure shows that the probability that the project NPV is greater than zero is 80%. Such information is extremely valuable not only in evaluating the merit of a given project but also in comparing it with projects (especially with the same NPV) competing for investment from the same pool.

In another approach based on the Monte Carlo simulation, you may start with an expected average project NPV calculated by the DCF method using one

Table 2-5. Monte Carlo Simulation Summary

		Years				
		0	1	2	3	4	5
Simulation inputs							
Investment cost		$10					
Base case annual costs			$3	$3	$3	$2	$2
Base case annual revenues			$5	$7	$10	$10	$5
Risk-adjusted discount rate	25%						
Standard deviation of annual costs	20%						
Standard deviation of annual revenues	30%						
No. of simulations run	1,000						
Simulation results							
Base case NPV	$2						
Average of simulated NPVs	$2						
Standard deviation of simulated NPVs	$3						

Note: All dollar values are in millions. For the sake of simplicity, investment cost is fixed, straight (rather than free) cash flows are used, and terminal value is ignored.

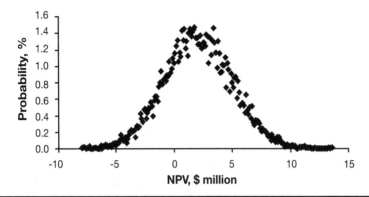

Figure 2-3A. "Point" Probability Distribution of Project Net Present Value Based on Monte Carlo Simulation

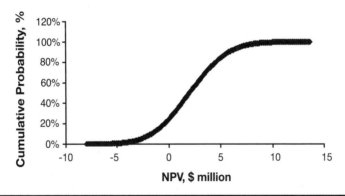

Figure 2-3B. Cumulative Probability Distribution of Project Net Present Value Based on Monte Carlo Simulation

set of input values and conduct thousands of simulations around it. This requires definition of the probability distribution of the average NPV as represented by its expected variance or standard deviation. Since this information is normally unavailable, worst and best case scenarios (corresponding to 1% and 99% confidence levels) are estimated by management to represent the lowest and highest ends of the NPV distribution. As mentioned before, standard deviation can be calculated from this information using the standard normal frequency distribution tables or appropriate commercial software.

Monte Carlo simulation provides additional value compared to the deterministic DCF approach, because it takes into account the uncertainty of the input variables. However, the major challenge with this method lies in the estimation of the distributions of the input variables. It is common practice to first calculate the project NPV using the deterministic DCF method, conduct sensitivity analysis, identify two or three input variables that have the highest impact on the NPV, and then conduct simulations by focusing on those variables.

DECISION TREE ANALYSIS

Decision trees have been used for nearly a half century in the decisions analysis science and are considered effective tools in valuation of projects that involve contingent decisions. A decision tree shows a strategic road map, depicting alternative decisions, their costs, their possible outcomes (for example, success versus failure), and probability and the payoff of the outcomes. Decision trees are also called decision flow networks and decision diagrams. The project NPV is calculated by using the "expected value" (EV) approach. The EV of an event is simply the product of its probability of occurrence and its outcome commonly expressed in terms of its cash flow value. The probabilities used in decision tree analysis (DTA) are subjective and one of the most important inputs in the valuation process. Two classic examples are presented below, the first from the oil industry and the second from product development, to illustrate DTA.

Example 1: Drills for Thrills

Drills for Thrills is a small oil company that needs to decide today whether to invest $40,000 to drill on a site before its option expires or abandon the project altogether. It does not know whether the well will turn out to be dry, wet, or a gusher. To reduce the risk of its decision, the company can get more information about the site by taking seismic soundings at a cost of $5,000. The soundings are expected to disclose the geological characteristics of the terrain below. If the site has "no structure," the well is expected to yield less oil as opposed to "closed structure." Figure 2-4 presents a decision tree for this problem depicting the decision points, decision alternatives, cost of the decisions, possible outcomes, probabilities of the outcomes, and the payoff related to each outcome. The payoff values are expected free cash flows calculated using the DCF method. Table 2-6 summarizes the results and calculations involved in solving the decision tree. The solution to the decision tree involves calculation of EV at each decision point and folding of the EVs from the extreme right of the decision tree into the preceding decision point and on toward the left.

The solution suggests that Drills for Thrills first conduct initial sounding tests before drilling, because the expected NPV of the seismic testing decision

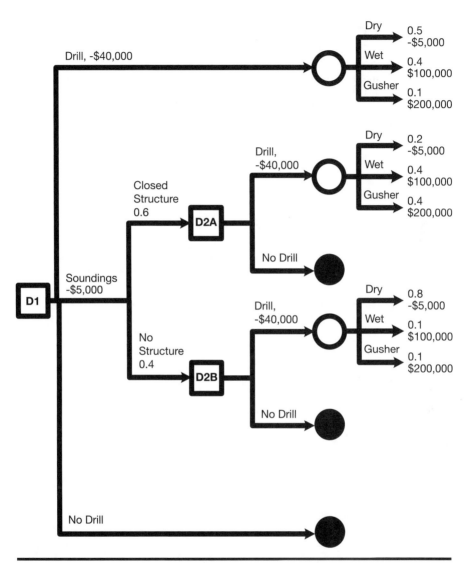

Figure 2-4.   Decision Tree for Drills for Thrills

at this point is higher than that of the drill or no-drill alternative. If the test results show a closed structure, the decision would be to drill because of its higher expected NPV compared to its no-drill counterpart. In the case of no structure, however, the expected NPV of the no-drill decision is higher than the drill alternative; therefore, abandoning the project would be the right decision.

Table 2-6. Decision Tree Calculations for Drills for Thrills

1. Starting at the far right decision nodes (D2A and D2B) of the decision tree in Figure 2-4, for each decision alternative, calculate the EV of each outcome by multiplying the value of the outcome by its probability.

   At D2A, for the drill alternative, the EVs are:

$$\text{Dry} = 0.2(-\$5,000) = -\$1,000$$
$$\text{Wet} = 0.4 * \$100,000 = \$40,000$$
$$\text{Gusher} = 0.4 * \$200,000 = \$80,000$$

   At D2B, for the drill alternative, the EVs are:

$$\text{Dry} = 0.8(-\$5,000) = -\$4,000$$
$$\text{Wet} = 0.1 * \$100,000 = \$10,000$$
$$\text{Gusher} = 0.1 * \$200,000 = \$20,000$$

   For the no-drill decision, EV is zero at both the D2A and D2B nodes.

2. Calculate the expected NPV based on the combined EV for all the outcomes at the far right decision nodes (D2A and D2B) for the drill and no-drill decisions. For the drill decision, this would be the sum of the EVs of each outcome at a given node and the cost of drilling ($40,000).

   At D2A, expected NPV = -$1,000 + $40,000 + $80,000 - $40,000 = $79,000
   At D2B, expected NPV = -$4,000 + $10,000 + $20,000 - $40,000 = -$14,000
   For the no-drill decision at both D2A and D2B nodes, NPV = $0

3. Identify the decision choice at the far right decision nodes (D2A and D2B) by selecting the decision with the highest expected NPV. At D2A, the expected NPVs for the drill and no-drill alternatives are $79,000 and $0, respectively; therefore, the choice will be to drill. At D2B, the expected NPVs are -$14,000 and $0 for the drill and no-drill alternatives, respectively, so the decision will be not to drill.

4. Moving left to the next decision node (D1) on the tree, calculate the EVs of the outcomes for each decision. At D1, there are three alternatives, namely, drill, test for soundings, and no drill.

   For the drill decision, the EVs of each outcome are:

$$\text{Dry} = 0.5(-\$5,000) = -\$2,500$$
$$\text{Wet} = 0.4 * \$100,000 = \$40,000$$
$$\text{Gusher} = 0.1 * \$200,000 = \$20,000$$

   For the test for soundings decision, there are two outcomes:

$$\text{If it is a closed structure, EV} = 0.6 * \$79,000 = \$47,400$$
$$\text{For no structure, EV} = 0.4 * \$0 = \$0$$

   For the no-drills decision, EV = $0.

5. Calculate the expected NPV at D1 for each alternative decision by adding the EVs of all the outcomes related to that alternative, including the cost associated with that decision.

   For drilling, expected NPV = -$2,500 + $40,000 + $20,000 - $40,000 = $17,500
   For soundings, expected NPV = $47,400 + $0 - $5,000 = $42,400
   For no-drill option, expected NPV = $0

6. Identify the decision choice by selecting the decision with the highest NPV. Comparing the three expected NPVs ($17,500 for drilling, $42,400 for test for soundings, and $0 for no drill), the decision would be to test for soundings at D1.

Table 2-6.   Decision Tree Calculations for Drills for Thrills (continued)

Decision Point	Alternatives	Expected NPV Calculations	Expected NPV	Choice
D2A	Drill	0.2(–$5,000) + 0.4($100,000) + 0.4($200,000) – $40,000	$79,000	Drill
	No drill	$0	$0	
D2B	Drill	0.8(–$5,000) + 0.1($100,000) + 0.1($200,000) – $40,000	–$14,000	No drill
	No drill		$0	
D1	Drill	0.5(–$5,000) + 0.4($100,000) + 0.1($200,000) – $40,000	$17,500	Seismic soundings
	No drill	$0	$0	
	Seismic soundings	0.6($79,000) + 0.4($0) – $5,000	$42,400	

Example 2: TerminaTerror

TerminaTerror is a start-up company involved in developing technologies for homeland security applications. One of its new patent-pending products is an early warning system that detects poison that may have been introduced by terrorists into municipal drinking water supplies and distribution systems. The technical effectiveness of the product first has to be proved through development effort, which is expected to cost $1 million and take one year. Successful development will be followed by commercialization of the technology, which is estimated to take an additional year and cost $2 million at that time. DCF analysis shows a project payoff of $15 million (year 2 dollars) over the project horizon. Although this payoff is attractive compared to the investment costs, TerminaTerror is not certain about the technical and commercial success of the project, because the respective success probabilities are estimated to be 0.5 and 0.7. Therefore, the company uses DTA to facilitate the go/no-go decisions for the two phases of the investment.

Figure 2-5 shows the decision tree with different decision paths, outcomes, and costs and payoffs associated with different paths. The decision nodes are not explicitly shown in this diagram, as they were in the previous example, but the success path implicitly represents a "go" decision to the next project phase, while the failure path indicates project abandonment. Assuming a discount rate of 10%, the steps involved in solving the decision tree and the solution are outlined in Table 2-7. The results show that the project's expected NPV today is $2.43 million. This is a relatively high positive NPV, suggesting that the project is investment worthy.

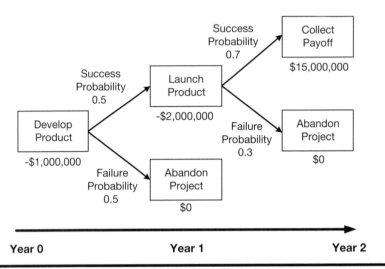

Figure 2-5.   Decision Tree for TerminaTerror

Table 2-7.   Decision Tree Calculations for TerminaTerror

1. Starting at the far right of the decision tree (Figure 2-5), calculate the EV of the payoff at year 2 considering the mutually exclusive outcomes related to the product launch:

> For the success outcome, EV = 0.7($15.0 million) = $10.5 million
> For the failure outcome, EV = 0.3($0) = $0

2. Add the EVs of the two outcomes:

> Total EV at the end of year 2 = $10.5 million + $0 = $10.5 million

3. Calculate the PV of the payoff at year 1 by discounting the total EV of year 2 using a discount rate of 10%:

> Payoff PV at year 1 = ($10.5 million)/(1 + 0.1) = $9.55 million

4. Calculate the NPV of the project at product launch at year 1 by subtracting the launch cost from the payoff PV:

> $9.55 million − $2.0 million = $7.55 million

5. Calculate the EV of the payoff at year 1 of considering the mutually exclusive outcomes related to the product development:

> For the success outcome, EV = 0.5($7.55 million) = $3.77 million
> For the failure outcome, EV = 0.5($0) = $0

6. Add the EVs of the two outcomes:

> Total EV at the end of year 1 = $3.77 million + $0 = $3.77 million

7. Calculate the PV of the project payoff at year 0 by discounting the total EV of year 1 using a discount rate of 10%:

Table 2-7.   Decision Tree Calculations for TerminaTerror (continued)

Payoff PV at year 0 = ($3.77 million)/(1 + 0.1)^1 = $3.43 million

8. Calculate the NPV of the project at year 0 by subtracting the development cost from the payoff PV:

$3.43 million − $1.0 million = $2.43 million

Input Values		
Discount rate	10%	
Development cost	$1,000,000	
Probability of technical success	0.5	
Launch cost	$2,000,000	
Probability of commercial success	0.7	
Payoff at successful launch	$15,000,000	
Launch Phase		
Project EV at year 2	0.7($15,000,000) + 0.3($0) =	$10,500,000
PV at year 1	$10,500,000/(1 + 0.1)^1 =	$9,545,455
Less launch cost		−$2,000,000
Project NPV at year 1	$9,545,455 − $2,000,000 =	$7,545,455
Development Phase		
Project EV at year 1	0.5($7,545,455) + 0.5($0) =	$3,772,727
PV at year 0	$3,772,727/(1 + 0.1)^1 =	$3,429,752
Less development cost		−$1,000,000
Project NPV at year 0	$3,429,752 − $1,000,000 =	$2,429,752

Best, Worst, and Most Likely Cases

Using the decision tree results, you can also gain further insight by considering the best, worst, and most likely case scenarios for the above two examples. Best case represents the scenario where only the best outcomes are experienced and worst case represents the scenario with only the worst outcomes by following the rational decisions shown by the DTA. Therefore, for Drills for Thrills, the former involves seismic testing followed by drilling the site for oil today that results in a gusher or a dry well representing the best and worst cases, respectively. In the case of TerminaTerror, the best case is where both the product development and commercialization efforts are successful, while the worst case involves successful development followed by commercial failure. The most likely case for both examples is represented by the project's expected NPV today, which corresponds to decision node 1 in the decision tree or decision at time = 0. The results from this analysis are summarized in Table 2-8. The advantage of the scenario analysis is that it gives you a perspective on the relative upside and downside to the project. If the most likely NPV is close to the best case and is significantly higher than the worst, there

Table 2-8. Expected NPV: Best, Worst, and Most Likely Case Scenarios for Decision Tree Examples

Scenario	Example 1 Drills for Thrills	Example 2 TerminaTerror, Inc.
Best	$155,000	$9.58 million
Worst	−$50,000	−$2.82 million
Most likely	$42,400	$2.43 million

is an excellent chance of success and vice versa. The scenario analysis provides a simple summary of the decision tree calculations that management can easily understand.

In the two examples presented above, the principles behind the analysis are the same. The expected NPVs of all the decision alternatives at a given node are compared, and the decision with the highest NPV is selected. The expected NPV of a given decision is the sum of EVs of the corresponding outcomes, and the EV of a given outcome is the product of the probability of the outcome and the payoff associated with it. The payoff is derived from the cash flows associated with that outcome and is calculated using the DCF method where the discount rate is not adjusted for risk. The reason for not adjusting the discount rate is that the risk is already accounted for by the EV calculation, where the cash flows are multiplied by their corresponding probabilities. For example, in the case of TerminaTerror, the risk related to the $15 million payoff is accounted for by multiplying it by its probability of 0.7.

While the principles behind the decision analysis are the same for the examples illustrated above, one key difference is that part of the overall investment cost in the TerminaTerror example needs to be discounted, whereas it is not necessary for the other example. With the latter, the investment cost is assumed to be incurred at time zero and the contingent decisions and the associated investment costs at approximately the same time or shortly thereafter. This results in a decision tree that does not extend far into the future. However, the length of the decision tree in the TerminaTerror example is two years, which means that the cash flows within the decision tree must be discounted accordingly. The discount rate to be used depends on the nature of the risk inside the decision tree, which is discussed in more detail in the next chapter.

Another minor difference between the two examples is that the decision tree for Drills for Thrills explicitly shows the decision nodes, whereas the tree for the other example does not. The decisions are implied in the second example (TerminaTerror) in the sense that if it is a success outcome (which is presumably decided by some criteria), you will decide to take the project to the next phase; if not, you will abandon the project. Therefore, the decision nodes are not shown explicitly.

As illustrated above, decision trees offer additional information and insight into the project decision process compared to the DCF method alone when contingent decisions are involved. DTA is not an alternative to but an extension of the DCF method. In fact, the payoffs for different outcomes used in the DTA are derived based on the DCF analysis in the first place. The final project expected NPV is calculated based on this payoff by incorporating contingent decisions at various decision nodes in the future. This is where DTA adds value, because DCF assumes a fixed path and does not account for management's contingent decisions. The major drawbacks of decision trees, however, lie in estimating the probabilities of the decision outcomes and selecting an appropriate discount rate inside the decision tree when the tree is extended for more than a year or so, that is, when the cash flows inside the tree are realized over a long period of time. The outcome probabilities are subjective and should be estimated by subject matter experts. The impact of these probabilities on the NPV of a project can be analyzed by sensitivity analysis. Such analysis can also be applied to the other input variables of the decision trees, including the discount rate. The discount rate to be used inside the decision tree relates to the risk associated with the cash flows inside the decision tree. The question of what discount rates to use in the decision tree (and also DCF analysis) is the focus of the first part of the next chapter. In that chapter, we will also discuss the limitations of the DCF and DTA methods in more detail and introduce real options analysis as a more sophisticated tool for practitioners involved in project valuation.

PROBLEMS

2-1. Gadgets & Gizmos recently developed a special kitchen appliance for physically handicapped people and estimated the following cash flows for the product:

	Year					
	0	*1*	*2*	*3*	*4*	*5**
Investment (million)	$20					
Revenues (million)		$15	$20	$25	$22	$52
Cost (million)		$6	$7	$9	$8	$15

* Terminal value.

Ignoring the capital expenses, depreciation, cash backs, taxes, working capital needs, etc., calculate the NPV of the project using a risk-adjusted discount rate of 20%.

2-2. For the above problem, calculate the sensitivity of the NPV to the input parameters by varying the investment cost, peak annual revenue, peak annual cost, terminal value, and the discount rate by ±25%. Show the results in the form of a tornado diagram.

2-3. For the same project, estimate the variability (the standard deviation) of the expected project NPV using Monte Carlo simulation. Use a standard deviation of 15% for the annual costs and 30% for the annual revenues.

2-4. RoboTechs is interested in developing and commercializing "robotic wait-ers" that can serve food and beverages in restaurants and at cocktail parties. The development effort to prove the technical effectiveness of the product is estimated to cost $1 billion and take four years, while the project launch is expected to cost $300 million. The estimated project NPV is $6 billion, and the probabilities of technical and commercial success are believed to be 0.8 and 0.4, respectively. Based on DTA, would your decision be in favor of investment? (Use a discount rate of 8% inside the decision tree in your DTA calculations.)

3

CHALLENGES WITH TRADITIONAL TOOLS

The traditional valuation tools, including the discounted cash flow (DCF) method and decision tree analysis (DTA), have been employed for several decades in valuation of projects. Although these tools have been effective for many applications, they pose certain challenges under specific conditions. The objective of this chapter is to discuss the challenges and address why a more sophisticated technique is needed. In order to recognize and appreciate the challenges, it is important first to understand risks and how they are accounted for in the DCF and DTA methods. Therefore, this chapter is divided into three major sections. The first section introduces the concept and definition of risk and types of risks; the second deals with the so-called discount rate dilemma, namely, what discount rates to use in DCF and DTA calculations to account for the risks related to the project under scrutiny; and the last section discusses the challenges of the traditional tools.

RISKS

Business is basically about taking risks. The common notion is that the higher the risk one is willing to take, the higher the returns. But it is the *possibility* of higher returns, obviously not *guaranteed* higher returns. Risk, in a layperson's view, is entirely negative, but in business it includes both negative and positive outcomes. It relates to the variance of real outcomes around the expected outcome. The greater this variance, the higher the risk is perceived to be.

A banker would approve a loan only when he or she fully expects the borrower to pay back the entire loan and the agreed-upon interest. If someone has a poor credit history, the chances of loan default are higher, so a higher interest rate (i.e., higher returns for the bank) will be charged for higher risk the bank is willing to take.

An investor interested in funding a large development project considers the same principle. If the chances of success are lower on the project, the investor would account for a risk "premium" on his or her investment. Risk premium corresponds to the incremental return one would expect on a risky asset compared to a risk-free asset such as a U.S. Treasury bill and is proportional to the risk involved.

Whereas the banker and investor may consider their respective endeavors particularly risky, the loan borrower and the project manager may have an opposite view. Furthermore, an outside third party may have a totally different perspective. Notwithstanding this relative nature of risk, risk in an investment is always perceived through the eyes of the investor. The investor presumably looks at the risk from the standpoint of what the market is willing to bear. This principle basically dictates what discount rate should be used in discounting the future cash flows in project valuation using DCF analysis. Qualitatively speaking, the higher the perceived risk is, the higher the discount rate. But the challenge for the practitioner is to decide on what exact rate to use in the DCF calculations. This warrants a clear understanding of the basics of risks.

Definition of Risk

Let us say that, as an investor, you buy a two-year U.S. Treasury bill with a 5% expected return. This is considered a riskless investment, because it is guaranteed by the full faith and credit of the U.S. government. Therefore, the bill is default free and you are guaranteed a 5% return for the two-year holding period, wherein the actual return is the same as the expected return. Figure 3-1 shows the probability distribution of the actual return of this investment. It is a straight line, because it is deterministic.

In contrast, let us say you buy stock in a publicly traded company and are expecting, based on your research, a 20% return over a one-year holding period. But the actual return on this investment will most likely be either higher or lower than what you expect. The probability of the actual return may follow a distribution as shown in Figure 3-2. The shape of the curve may take even different forms (Figure 3-3), showing either positive (curve A) or negative (curve B) skewness at either end. Other types of distribution are also possible, albeit rare.

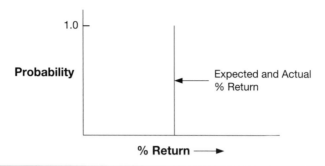

Figure 3-1. Probability Distribution of Return on a U.S. Treasury Bill

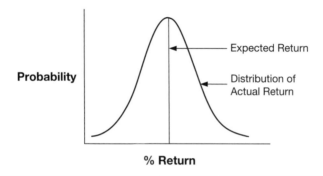

Figure 3-2. Probability Distribution of Return on a Stock

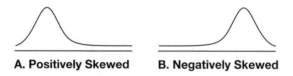

Figure 3-3. Probability Distribution of Returns: Normal Distribution with Skewness

As in stock returns and the corresponding asset values, the distribution of payoff from a project investment also is probabilistic rather than deterministic. To gain better insight into how the actual payoff may vary in relation to the expected value, which basically dictates the risk level of the project, let us examine the meaning of the different shapes of the probability distribution curves and their characteristics in statistical terms:

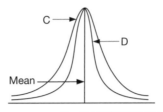

Figure 3-4. Probability Distribution of Returns: Normal Distribution; Same Mean and Different Variances

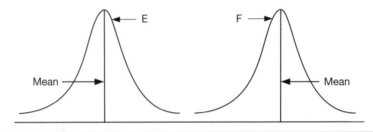

Figure 3-5. Probability Distribution of Returns: Normal Distribution; Different Means and Same Variance

1. The thickness of each curve represents the variance or the standard deviation of the distribution. (In statistical terms, standard deviation is the square root of the variance.) The thicker the curve is, the higher the variance. Curves C and D in Figure 3-4 have the same mean, but curve C has a larger variance. In contrast, curves E and F in Figure 3-5 have different means but the same variance.
2. A distribution may exhibit skewness either positively or negatively, as shown in Figure 3-3. Curve A is positively skewed, showing that there is higher probability of large returns than small returns; curve B is the opposite. If there is no skewness, as in curves C through F, the distribution is symmetrical and considered "normal."

An important challenge a practitioner faces in making the DCF calculations is to forecast the likely distribution, which represents the risk level, of the payoff over the project life cycle, so that an appropriate discount rate may be used. This discount rate also depends on the type of risk involved.

Types of Risks

In the finance world, risks are broadly classified as market risks and private risks. Although experts differ in exact definition of these risks, it is generally accepted that risks that can be captured in the value of a traded security are market risks and all the others are private risks (Amram and Kulatilaka, 2000). For example, oil price fluctuations are market risks, because they are captured in the value of oil futures contracts which are traded in financial markets.

In a broad sense, a practitioner can consider the market risk of a project to be due to the volatility of its expected future payoff (the net cash flow) driven by the market forces, such as market demand, competition, and so on. The private risks are related to the efficiency of an organization in completing the project as well as the effectiveness of the technology related to the project. For example, the private risk of developing a new drug includes how well the drug maker can take the project to completion through the required phases of testing as well as the efficacy of the drug molecule in curing the target disease. In project valuation, it is important to recognize and differentiate private risks from market risks for two major reasons:

1. Financial option pricing models are based on the premise that the market risk of an underlying asset is captured by a traded security. Therefore, at a philosophical level, the validity of the application of these models to real options valuation may be questionable, if there is no traded security corresponding to the uncertainty of the underlying asset.

2. Investors are willing to pay a risk premium for the market-driven risks but not for the private risks. This means that, at a more practical level, the rate used to discount the cash flows is dictated by the type of risk associated with a given cash flow.

The validity and limitations of real options valuation using the financial options pricing models are discussed in more detail in Chapter 6. In the following sections, we identify areas where many practitioners face the "discount rate dilemma" (what discount rates to use under what circumstances) and discuss common practices in calculating the discount rates.

DISCOUNT RATE DILEMMA

Every project valuation method is in some way built on net present value (NPV) calculations, and every NPV calculation requires a discount rate. One of the biggest dilemmas a practitioner faces is what discount rate to use in the NPV calculations. Two important factors determine the discount rate for a given cash flow stream:

- Magnitude of risk (cash flow uncertainty)
- Type of risk (private risk versus market risk)

In determining the discount rate to be used on a given cash flow stream, the first consideration should be whether there is uncertainty associated with that cash flow stream. Irrespective of whether the cash flow is influenced by private or market risk, no uncertainty means no risk; therefore, an investor will not pay a risk premium for the investment. This means that if there is no uncertainty at all on a cash flow stream, the appropriate discount rate is a risk-free rate.

If there is uncertainty associated with a cash flow stream, the next consideration is whether that stream is influenced by private or market risk. If it is influenced by private risk, the investor will not pay a risk premium for the ineptness of the organization in completing the project or the ineffectiveness of the technology involved. On the other hand, if a cash flow is subject to market risk, one would account for it in some fashion — most commonly by adjusting the discount rate.

There seems to be some confusion in the finance community as to how to determine the appropriate discount rate for a given cash flow stream and valuation method. This is most likely due to the lack of agreement in the community on one set of guidelines. Keeping this in mind, we address below seven questions that practitioners often face.

1. If there is no uncertainty — that is, no risk — associated with a cash flow stream, what is the appropriate discount rate?
As mentioned in the preceding section, if there is no uncertainty associated with a cash flow stream, it means that there is no risk associated with it. Therefore, a risk-free interest rate should be used to discount such cash flows. Risk-free interest rate corresponds to a riskless investment. It is earned by assets that are considered entirely creditworthy during the life of the investment. The interest rate paid by the U.S. Treasury is considered risk free and hence used as the benchmark risk-free rate. In dealing with project investments, it is almost impossible to find cash flow streams with absolutely no uncertainty. Therefore, the question of what discount rate is appropriate for a cash flow stream with no uncertainty may only be academic.

2. Is it private or market risk influencing a given cash flow stream?
This question is probably best answered in the context of different types of cash flow streams versus the risks they are influenced by. In Chapter 2, we identified two broad cash flow streams that are common to most projects. Taking a product development project as an example, let us examine these cash flows and identify the types of risk they are influenced by.

1. **Investment cost** — This consists of development cost and production phase capital cost. The former typically includes R&D and design. Or-

ganizations are expected to estimate these costs with very little uncertainty. Successful completion of development phase activities is primarily influenced by the efficiency of the organization, which is not subject to the market forces. Furthermore, with development of new technologies (including drugs), project success is also determined by the effectiveness of the technology, which is also not subject to the market forces. Therefore, the development phase cost is considered to be controlled by private risk but not market risk. The second investment cost, production phase capital, typically includes building a manufacturing plant, launching a product with a massive marketing campaign, etc. An organization is expected to be able to estimate this cost also with very little uncertainty. This cost is not influenced by the market forces and is subject to private risk only, because it is primarily based on how efficiently the organization can bring this phase of the project to completion.

2. **Production phase free cash flows** — These are the net revenues calculated from the expected future revenues and costs associated with the product (or service offering) in its production phase. In principle, these cash flow streams are considered by both academics and practitioners to be influenced by market risk only, because the uncertainty of the cash flows is primarily dictated by the market forces. However, some disagreement seems to emerge regarding the source of the risk for the costs and the discount rate to be used to discount them. This is discussed in more detail under question 5.

3. If the cash flow stream is dictated by private risk, what is the appropriate discount rate?

As discussed above, the cash flow streams that are subject to private risk basically include the initial development investment and the subsequent production phase capital costs. Many academics argue that if a cash flow stream is strictly subject to private risk and not influenced by market forces, a risk-free rate should be used. Theoretically, this may make sense; however, there are two important practical considerations: First, in the real world it may be difficult to completely differentiate the private risk from the market risk. For example, it may be argued that the development and capital costs cannot be estimated with any certainty because of today's fast-changing market forces that are directly influencing these costs irrespective of the private risks. Second, any project investment requires capital, and organizations have to pay a cost to obtain that capital. Therefore, for discounting the cash flows that are subject to private risk, practitioners use a rate that is either slightly higher than the risk-free rate or a rate that is commensurate with the organization's weighted average cost of capital, which represents risk of "business as usual."

Weighted Average Cost of Capital

Cost of capital represents the cost of financing an organization's activities, which is normally done through some combination of debt and equity. Since debt and equity carry different costs of capital, a weighted average is required. The weighted average cost of capital (WACC) of different cost components of issuing debt, preferred stock, and common equity is:

$$\text{WACC} = W_d C_d (1 - t) + W_p C_p + W_e C_e \tag{3-1}$$

where W represents the respective weights; C is the cost corresponding to debt (d), preferred stock (p), and common equity (e); and t is the effective corporate tax rate. Table 3-1 presents an example to illustrate the calculation of WACC.

Although the WACC characterizes the cost of capital at the organizational level, it can be used as a proxy to represent the private risks related to project investment costs.

Table 3-1.   Calculation of Weighted Average Cost of Capital

BioTechno is launching a major initiative for which it needs $100 million in capital. It decides to raise the required capital using both debt ($50 million in bonds payable at 7% interest) and equity ($10 million in preferred stock at 8% return and $40 million in common stock at 11% return). The corporate tax rate is 40%. The WACC can be calculated as follows:

1. Calculate the percentage (weight) of each capital component relative to the total capital:

Bonds payable = $50 million/$100 million = 0.5
Preferred stock = $10 million/$100 million = 0.1
Common stock = $40 million/$100 million = 0.4

2. Given 7% interest on the bond, compute the effective interest rate accounting for the tax rate of 40%:

$0.07 * (1 - 0.40) = 0.042$

3. Calculate the weighted cost of capital for each capital component by multiplying the cost of capital by its respective weight:

Bonds payable = 0.5 * 0.042 = 0.021
Preferred stock = 0.1 * 0.08 = 0.008
Common stock = 0.4 * 0.11 = 0.044

4. Add all the above costs of capital to obtain the WACC:

$0.021 + 0.008 + 0.044 = 0.073$

4. If a cash flow stream is influenced by market risk, what is the appropriate discount rate when using the DCF method?

The academics as well as the practitioners agree that in order to account for higher market risks, a proportional risk premium should be added to the risk-free rate. Because investors expect higher returns for taking higher risks, it is only reasonable to discount the market-driven project cash flows at a rate that is defined by the risk level of the project. Since it is difficult to objectively quantify project risk, most of the approaches to determine the risk-adjusted discount rates are subjective or semi-quantitative at best. Typically, a project, a portfolio of projects, a security, a portfolio of securities, or even an organization as a whole that has a risk profile similar to the candidate project is used as a proxy to estimate the risk-adjusted discount rate. The idea is that if you can find a proxy that has the same (or multiple of) cash flows expected from the project under evaluation, you can use the proxy's annual returns as the discount rate to discount the project cash flows. There are many different ways to determine this rate; a few common methods are presented below.

Capital Asset Pricing Model

The most widely used method to estimate a publicly traded company's cost of equity is the capital asset pricing model (CAPM). According to this model, the expected return of a security equals the risk-free rate plus a risk premium. The risk premium itself is defined as the product of β (a measure of risk specific to the security) and the difference between the overall market return and the risk-free rate.

$$r_a = r_f + \beta_a(r_m - r_f) \tag{3-2}$$

where r_a = expected return of security a, r_f = risk-free rate, r_m = expected market return, and β_a = beta of security a.

By definition, the beta value for the overall market is 1.0. Stocks that are more volatile than the market have a beta value greater than 1.0 and, therefore, are expected to provide higher returns than the market. Similarly, stocks that are less volatile than the overall market have a beta value less than 1.0 and are expected to provide lower returns than the market. Using this principle, projects can be assumed to have equivalent betas corresponding to their risks. Since no betas are available for projects, the idea is that betas for equivalent securities can be used as proxies with the CAPM model to calculate the expected return of the project which would serve as the discount rate.

In using CAPM, you look for a publicly traded security — a twin security — that is believed to have the same risk profile as the project under consideration. A company is believed to have the same risk if its expected cash flow profiles are the same as or multiples of the project cash flows. Since the beta values for publicly traded companies are readily available, those beta values can be used to calculate the expected return using the CAPM equation. This expected return is considered to represent the risk associated with the project and is, therefore, used as the discount rate to discount the project cash flows. A variation of this approach uses the reciprocal of the price-to-earnings ratio of the twin security to calculate the expected return.

When using the CAPM/twin security approach to determine the risk-adjusted rate, it is recommended that you use a twin security of a company that does not have large debt (i.e., not leveraged). Projects are not leveraged; therefore, unleveraged companies serve as better proxies than leveraged ones. If you cannot find an unleveraged security, we recommend adjusting beta for leverage in the CAPM calculation. Furthermore, a twin security does not need to be a single security; it can also be a portfolio of securities with similar risk profile as the candidate project.

WACC-Based Discount Rates

CAPM is a market-based approach to calculate the risk-adjusted discount rate and is consistent in addressing the market risk associated with the project net revenues. However, it may be difficult to find a twin security comparable to the project under scrutiny. A more common and easier method, and one that is not so much market based as operational, is to use the organization's cost of capital or WACC as the benchmark discount rate and adjust it in proportion to the expected risk of the project. In this approach, the project risk is evaluated using established risk assessment methodologies, and a risk rating is assigned to the project. If the risk is relatively low and the project represents "business as usual," WACC is used as the discount rate, but for higher risk projects, higher rates are used as the risk rating increases.

A risk rating scale can be simplified further for operational purposes by dividing the projects into certain risk groups and assigning corresponding risk-adjusted discount rates. Canada et al. (1996) cite a major industrial firm that uses the following discount rates depending on the project's risk level:

- High-risk projects (e.g., new products, new business, acquisitions, joint ventures): 40%
- Moderate-risk projects (e.g., capacity increase to meet forecasted sales): 25%
- Low-risk projects (cost improvements, make versus buy, capacity increase to meet existing orders): 15%

Although the authors do not specifically identify the WACC, presumably it is less than but close to 15%, representing risk of "business as usual."

Hurdle Rate

In lieu of the risk-adjusted discount rates, corporations often use benchmarks commonly referred to as hurdle rates or minimum acceptable rates of return, especially when several projects are competing for funding from the same pool of investment dollars managed under a portfolio. These rates are usually set by the corporate finance department at levels higher than the WACC and are dictated by the current and near-term economic conditions. The hurdle rate is sometimes represented by the so-called opportunity cost.

Opportunity Cost

Opportunity cost represents the rate of return that would have been earned by selecting an alternate project rather than the one under consideration. It accounts for capital rationing, which means that there is a limitation of funds relative to prospective projects to use the funds.

To calculate the opportunity cost, first the prospective projects are ranked according to their expected rate of return, with the project with the highest return at the top. Then the available funds are allocated, starting with the first project on the list until the funds are exhausted. The rate of return of the last project for which full investment is available is called the opportunity cost.

If only a fraction of the total investment needed for the next project on the list is available, it either can be used to fund the initial phase of that project, kept as a reserve for the entire portfolio of projects, or used for some other purpose. Table 3-2 provides an example to illustrate the opportunity cost.

5. Should the risk premium be different for cash inflows versus cash outflows?

Of the two cash flows identified as fundamental to project valuation — investment cost and production phase net revenue — the former as well as the cash outflow component of the latter are subject to private risk. As discussed earlier under question 3, whereas many academics believe that these cash outflows should be discounted at a risk-free rate, practitioners use either WACC or a rate that is slightly higher than the risk-free rate. However, there is general agreement that the cash inflows are typically uncertain and driven by market risk and therefore should be discounted in accordance with their risk level by adding a risk premium.

Table 3-2. Calculation of Opportunity Cost

One of the divisions of BioRobotics has a pool of $30 million allocated for a portfolio of development projects. The six candidate projects under evaluation are ranked in the table below based on their expected rates of return, starting with the highest. The expected returns and investment costs are also provided. Calculate the opportunity cost for this portfolio as follows:

1. Allocate funding for each project starting at the top of the list, and calculate the funds remaining for the rest of the projects.
2. Select the last project for which investment dollars are available: Project ABC. The expected rate of return for this project, 30%, is the opportunity cost.

Project ID	Rate of Return	Investment (in Millions)	Funds Remaining for the Project
PDQ	50%	$5	$30
XYZ	40%	$15	$25
ABC	30%	$10	$10
KLM	25%	$5	$0
RST	20%	$10	$0
JGZ	15%	$10	$0

6. What is the appropriate discount rate to discount the cash flows in Monte Carlo simulation?

Monte Carlo simulation typically involves the calculation of the project NPV using the DCF method thousands of times with different values for the input variables keeping the discount rate constant. Whereas the commonly used simplistic DCF method is deterministic, the overall simulation is probabilistic, resulting in a probability distribution of the expected NPV. Since each individual simulation is deterministic by itself, the discount rate used in discounting the cash flows should be adjusted for risk just as with the DCF method.

7. What is the appropriate discount rate to discount the cash flows when using decision trees?

In DTA, you start with the present values of expected project free cash flows at the extreme right of the tree and fold them back into the decision tree, moving all the way to the left (that is, time zero) to account for the contingent decisions and outcome probabilities. If the decision tree is relatively long in its time length, the cash flows must be discounted as you fold them back toward time zero (see the TerminaTerror example in Chapter 2); hence the question of what the appropriate discount rate is.

Inside the decision tree, the contingent decisions are related to cash flows driven by private risk; therefore, academics suggest that they be discounted by a single risk-free rate. Furthermore, their argument goes, even that private risk is presumably removed through the probabilities used in calculating the present values of the cash flows. For instance, in the case of the TerminaTerror example in Chapter 2, the project payoff is multiplied by 0.7 and 0.5 at different time intervals to account for the success probabilities of product launch and product development, respectively. Many practitioners, however, believe that the WACC is a better representative of the risks inside the decision tree for three key reasons. First, the outcome probabilities do not truly account for all the risks. Second, it is difficult to completely separate private risks from market risks associated with investment cash flow streams inside the decision tree. Some of the risks that are believed to be private can, in reality, be market driven. Third, there is uncertainty associated with the investment-related cash outflows, which, as mentioned earlier, can be due to not only sloppy cost estimation practices and poor project management practices but also market forces.

Using the WACC as the only discount factor across the entire decision tree has some limitations in itself. As you move from the left to the right of the decision tree, the success probability of the project increases and the risk decreases; therefore, a decreasing discount factor would be more appropriate as you move toward the right than a single factor across the tree. It becomes entirely subjective at this point as to what the appropriate discount factor is for the decision trees. As a middle of the road approach, we recommend a single discount factor that is slightly higher than the risk-free rate and lower than the WACC for the entire decision tree.

Discount rate dilemma is a common challenge the practitioners face in valuation, irrespective of the method used. There are other challenges and limitations the valuation methods pose, as discussed below.

DISCOUNTED CASH FLOW METHOD

DCF is a well-established technique that has been used successfully for several decades in valuation of projects as well as organizations as a whole. The theory behind the technique is sound, and the results are as good as the input data — as is true, for that matter, for any model. DCF is effective in many scenarios that are applicable to project investment decisions often faced by upper management. However, it does fail to capture certain realities of today's corporate world. Some of its major limitations include:

1. DCF takes a deterministic approach based on a single set of input values. Using one value for each of the two cash flow streams in Equation 2-3,

a total NPV is calculated for the entire project. In the real world, however, there is uncertainty with the cash flows, and therefore they are rather probabilistic. Adding sensitivity analysis to the DCF method through studying different scenarios may give more insight about the uncertainty, but still each scenario is based on a fixed path outcome.

2. DCF assumes a fixed path for the project outcome, which does not take into account management's flexibility to change the course of the project. Today's projects involve many contingent decisions. You may expand a project if the initial results are extremely favorable. In the case of the opposite outcome, you may contract it or even abandon it. The value of these contingent decisions is not captured in the DCF analysis, because the project is assumed to take a predetermined path. The value of a project, in fact, may be greater than the NPV of the expected cash flows, if the cash flows are contingent on future decisions. In the case of Wireless in Washington, for example, DCF analysis assumes that after the product has been developed, the company *will* launch the product at the scale corresponding to the assumed cash flows. But what if the market conditions change at the time of the launch, and you want to delay, contract, or expand the launch? The additional value created because of these contingent actions is not captured in DCF.

3. To account for the risk associated with the project payoff, DCF discounts the cash flows at a higher rate by adding a risk premium to the risk-free rate. The higher the risk is, the higher the risk premium added. This means only the downside of the risk is accounted for, with no consideration for the rewards. Based on the risk principles, as the downside risk increases, the upside potential also increases. But if the discount rate is increased with an increase in risk, the upside potential is ignored even more. This inherent bias may result in rejection of potentially highly successful projects just because of their high uncertainty.

MONTE CARLO SIMULATION

Monte Carlo simulation is an extension of but not a substitute for the DCF method. Whereas DCF takes one set of input parameters and calculates one project NPV, Monte Carlo simulation makes the exact same calculation thousands of times by just changing the input parameters each time. The simulation results show a distribution of the project payoff, with the "average" case representing the NPV based on the DCF method. Whereas the simple DCF method is deterministic, Monte Carlo simulation results in a probability distribution of the possible project NPVs. Simulation has the same drawbacks as the DCF method. It does not take into account the contingent decisions and their impact on the project valuation.

DECISION TREE ANALYSIS (DTA)

DTA is a more sophisticated tool than DCF and offers value when a project is multistage and contingent decisions are involved. It differs from DCF in the sense that, to account for market risk, it uses probabilities of outcomes rather than risk-adjusted discount rates. Although DTA accounts for contingent decisions, it faces its own limitations:

1. DTA may include decisions related to both private and market risks. To account for these risks, probabilities of success are used on the decision outcomes. For example, for the TerminaTerror project depicted in Figure 2-5, the probabilities of technical success (private risk) and commercial success (market risk) are estimated to be 0.5 and 0.7, respectively. These are subjective estimates, and the critics claim that the analysts and management can pick numbers to skew the decision in their favor.
2. There is no consensus in the finance community on what is the most appropriate discount rate to discount the cash flows inside the decision tree. As discussed earlier, this is primarily because of decreasing risk as you move from the left to the right side of the tree. While a decreasing discount rate across the tree in that direction seems to hold some rationality, it becomes subjective as to what the appropriate rate would be at a given decision node. Furthermore, there is no agreement within the finance community as to whether it is completely the private risk that controls the cash flows inside the tree, making it difficult to select an appropriate discount rate.

NEXT LEVEL OF PROJECT VALUATION

In view of the limitations discussed above, real options analysis (ROA) offers a new approach to project valuation. ROA is not a substitute for any of the three methods discussed in this chapter. It uses DCF as a building block and allows you to integrate decision trees, as necessary, into a sophisticated framework that provides analysts and decision makers with more meaningful information. Simulations can also be used to solve options problems and integrated as part of the overall solution methodology. The next chapter discusses why the real options approach is superior, and the subsequent chapters deal with ROA calculations and real world applications.

PROBLEMS

3-1. Pervasive Plastics is launching a new major project which requires an investment of $350 million to be obtained through debt and equity financing. Corporate bonds worth $250 million will be sold at a 6% interest rate, whereas the rest of the capital will be obtained by raising an equal amount of preferred and common stock at an expected 9 and 12% return, respectively. What is the weighted average cost of capital for this project?

3-2. What is the opportunity cost for the following portfolio of projects, if the available capital investment pool is $150 million?

Project No.	Required Investment (Millions)	Expected Rate of Return (%)
1	$20	31
2	$25	18
3	$22	3
4	$35	7
5	$61	22
6	$17	26
7	$11	8
8	$31	9

3-3. Sun 'n Fun Clothing has several patents pending on its new technology related to solar-panel-equipped military clothing, which eliminates the need for troops in the field to carry heavy batteries required for various equipment. The start-up is considering launching the products only if there is enough demand once the technology is proven effective. While the company has relatively accurate projections of the investment cost, there is uncertainty related to the revenues and cost of production. Identify the type of risk — private or market — that applies to the following cash flow streams:

■ Technology development cost
■ Product launch cost
■ Annual revenues
■ Annual costs of production

3-4. If the weighted average cost of capital for Sun 'n Fun is 12% and the risk-free rate for the next five years is 5%, what discount rates would you use for the above cash flow streams for discounted cash flow and decision tree analyses?

4

REAL OPTIONS ANALYSIS: THE NEW TOOL

The discounted cash flow (DCF) method and decision tree analysis (DTA) are standard tools used by analysts and other professionals in project valuation, and they serve the purpose very well in many applications. However, as discussed in the previous chapter, these tools have certain limitations. For example, if there is large uncertainty related to the project cash flows and contingent decisions are involved, where mangers have flexibility to change the course of the project, some of the value is not accounted for by these tools. In this chapter, we demonstrate how that additional value can be captured by real options. We also compare and contrast real options analysis (ROA) with DCF and DTA.

HOW IS REAL OPTIONS ANALYSIS DIFFERENT?

Let's start with a simple example to illustrate how the real options approach is different. You have a chance to invest $100 in a project. The payoff is expected to be between $60 and $160 with an average of $110. The DCF analysis, which does not account for the uncertainty, will put the net present value (NPV) at $10. Assume that this return does not meet your corporate standard; therefore, your decision will be not to invest in the project. But what if an initial small investment (say $10) will help settle the uncertainty and give you an option to fully invest in the project at a later date only if the return is favorable but abandon it otherwise? You are likely to accept this idea. When the uncertainty clears over time and the return is expected to be favorable (let's say $160), you will invest. If the return is expected to be unfavorable, you will walk away from the project. Thus, by considering the uncertainty and accounting for the managerial flexibility, you are able to make the right decisions to minimize losses and maximize returns. ROA helps you quantify the value added to the project due to the option.

A DEFERRAL OPTION

Using a more rigorous example below, we first demonstrate the value added to the project because of a deferral option, where you have a choice between investing in a project today with uncertain future cash flows and deferring the decision until next year, by which time the uncertainty is expected to clear. (This example follows that of Dixit and Pyndick, 1994.) Then we show how the option value increases as the payoff uncertainty increases.

You have a chance to invest $100 in a project today that is estimated to yield a return of $125 one year from now with a 50-50 chance that it may go up to $170 (good case) or down to $80 (bad case). But you also have the choice to defer the decision for a year, by which time the uncertainty about the payoff is expected to clear.

As shown below, using the standard DCF method with a discount rate of 15%, the project value today (time = 0), represented by its NPV, is $9. Assuming that this return is acceptable, you may want to invest in it.

$$\text{Time} = 0 \qquad \text{Time} = 1 \text{ year}$$
$$-\$100 \qquad\qquad \$125$$
$$\text{Discount Rate} = 15\%$$

$$\text{NPV} = \frac{\$125}{(1 + 0.15)^1} - \$100$$

$$= \$109 - \$100$$

$$= \$9$$

As mentioned, there is also a mutually exclusive alternative of deferring the decision until one year from now, by which time the uncertainty of the cash flows is expected to clear. Let's calculate the value of the project at that time for the good and bad cases (each with a probability, P, of 0.5), assuming the same conditions, so you can decide whether it will be to your advantage to wait for a year.

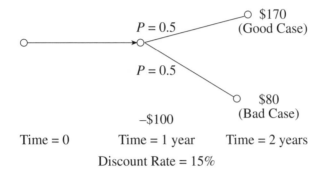

The expected NPV for the good case is:

$$0.5 \left[\frac{-\$100}{(1 + 0.15)^1} + \frac{\$170}{(1 + 0.15)^2} \right] = \$21$$

The expected NPV for the bad case is:

$$0.5 \left[\frac{-\$100}{(1 + 0.15)^1} + \frac{\$80}{(1 + 0.15)^2} \right] = -\$13$$

In summary, the expected NPVs for the good and bad cases are $21 and –$13, respectively. Therefore, after one year, if it turns out to be the good case, you will invest in the project, but if it turns to be the bad case, you will not. Thus the decision to defer for one year is worth $21 today. However, the decision to invest now is worth only $9, as shown by the DCF method. Therefore, the value added because of the option to defer is the difference between the two alternatives: $21 – $9 = $12.

Effect of Uncertainty

In the above example, let's say that the net project cash flow is still expected to be $125 but with an increase in the uncertainty. What would be the effect on the option value if the payoff is expected to go up to $200 (good case) or down to $50 (bad case) with a 50-50 chance?

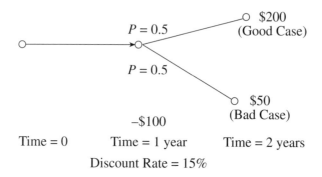

The expected NPV for the good case is:

$$0.5 \left[\frac{-\$100}{(1 + 0.15)^1} + \frac{\$200}{(1 + 0.15)^2} \right] = \$32$$

The expected NPV for the bad case is:

$$0.5 \left[\frac{-\$100}{(1 + 0.15)^1} + \frac{\$50}{(1 + 0.15)^2} \right] = -\$25$$

You would exercise your deferral option for the good case (NPV = $32), whereas you would let the option expire for the bad outcome (NPV = –$25). Even with the higher uncertainty in this scenario, the NPV calculated by DCF is still $9; therefore, the value added to the project when the deferral option is considered is $32 – $9 = $23. In the first scenario with lower uncertainty, the additional value was only $11. This shows that the option value increases with uncertainty.

DISCOUNTED CASH FLOW VERSUS REAL OPTIONS

Whereas DCF is a deterministic model, ROA accounts for the change in the underlying asset value due to uncertainty over the life of a project. In the above example, to keep it simple, we considered only two possible outcomes to represent the uncertainty. But there can be a range of possible outcomes over the life of a project, with the uncertainty increasing as a function of time. As a result, the range of asset values would take the shape of a curve, called the "cone of uncertainty" (Figure 4-1). ROA accounts for this whole range of uncertainty using stochastic processes and calculates a "composite" options value for a project, considering only those outcomes that are favorable (i.e., options are

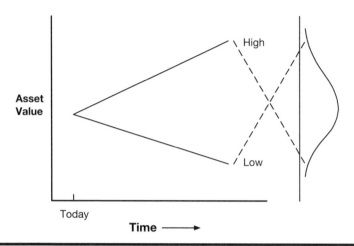

Figure 4-1. Cone of Uncertainty

exercised) and ignoring those that are not (letting the options expire). This assumes that the decision makers will always take the value-maximizing decision at each decision point in the project life cycle.

DCF accounts for the downside of a project by using a risk-adjusted discount rate. ROA, on the other hand, captures the value of the project for its upside potential by accounting for proper managerial decisions that would presumably be taken to limit the downside risk. Table 4-1 summarizes the major differences between DCF and ROA.

DECISION TREE ANALYSIS VERSUS REAL OPTIONS ANALYSIS

Both DTA and ROA are applicable when there is uncertainty about project outcomes and opportunity for contingent decisions exists. There are two basic differences between them:

1. As discussed in Chapter 3, DTA can account for both private and market risks, but ROA addresses only the market risk. The solutions to real options problems will not be valid for private risk, because the theoretical framework behind the solution development does not apply to it.
2. DTA accounts for the risks through probability of project outcomes. While it basically considers only two, three, or a few mutually exclusive possible outcomes, ROA accounts for a wide range of outcomes. This

Table 4-1. Discounted Cash Flow and Real Options Analysis Comparison

Discounted Cash Flow	Real Options Analysis
All or nothing strategy. Does not capture the value of managerial flexibility during the project life cycle.	Recognizes the value in managerial flexibility to alter the course of a project
Uncertainty with future project outcomes not considered. *N/y [relative to point I]*	Uncertainty is a key factor that drives the option's value.
Undervalues the asset that currently (or in the near term) produces little or no cash flow.	The long-term strategic value of the project is considered because of the flexibility with decision making.
Expected payoff is discounted at a rate adjusted for risk. Risk is expressed as a discount premium.	Payoff itself is adjusted for risk and then discounted at a risk-free rate. Risk is expressed in the probability distribution of the payoff.
Investment cost is typically discounted at the same rate as the payoff, that is, at a risk-adjusted rate.	Investment cost is discounted at the same rate as the payoff, that is, at a risk-free rate.

makes a difference in the discount rate used to discount the cash flows. As discussed in Chapter 3, there is no general agreement in the finance community on what the most appropriate discount rate is for decision trees, whereas a risk-free rate is established to be appropriate for ROA. The drawback with DTA is that probabilities of outcomes have to be estimated, which involves subjectivity.

In the absence of market risks, DTA is more appropriate for project valuation, but ROA is a better tool when such risks exist. The real options approach is not a substitute for but rather a supplement to decision trees. When there are contingent decisions involved and both private and market risks exist, both tools can be integrated into a framework that can offer the highest value to the analyst and the decision maker.

WHEN IS REAL OPTIONS ANALYSIS MOST VALUABLE?

ROA is most valuable when there is high uncertainty with the underlying asset value and management has significant flexibility to change the course of the project in a favorable direction and is willing to exercise the options. When there is little uncertainty and not much room for managerial flexibility, the real options approach offers little value (Figure 4-2).

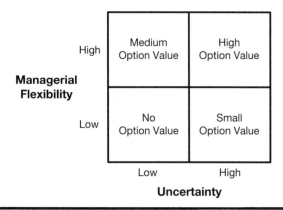

Figure 4-2.   When Does Real Options Provide Value?

ROA does not provide much value in investment decisions on projects with very high NPVs, because the projects are already attractive for investment and the additional value that may be provided would not change the decision. Similarly, on projects with very low NPVs, the additional value provided by real options would most likely be so negligible that the investment decision would still be a "no go." As illustrated in Figure 4-3, real options offer the greatest value on projects with an NPV close to zero (either positive or negative) and high certainty.

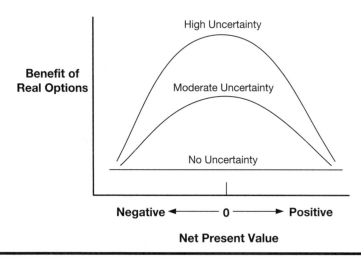

Figure 4-3.   Benefits of Real Options Analysis Relative to Net Present Value

WHY IS REAL OPTIONS ANALYSIS VALUABLE?

A project with a high option value reflects high market uncertainty and high upside potential. More information may be obtained about such a project to study and resolve the uncertainty to facilitate the future contingent decisions. Instead of making a full-blown investment in a project or committing to it, you may conduct a market survey or execute a product rollout in a limited test market to resolve the uncertainty first. If the results are favorable, you would move forward with the full-scale project or even scale it up, thus taking advantage of the upside potential of the project. On the other hand, in the case of unfavorable results, you may scale down or abandon the project altogether, thereby limiting your losses to the small investment made to resolve the uncertainty.

Small investments made to clear market uncertainty are called active learning. You may also decide not to invest at all and let time take its course to resolve the uncertainty, which may occur due to changes in market conditions. This is known as passive learning.

Resolution of market uncertainty is necessary but not sufficient to capture the true options value, if the private uncertainty related to the technology effectiveness is high. Resolution of such private uncertainty requires active up-front investment. For example, a prototype may need to be built to demonstrate that the technology works, or a drug must pass clinical trials to prove its effectiveness.

Whereas DCF provides a fixed path for investment decisions, ROA offers a strategic map that outlines the contingent decisions, especially those related to private and market uncertainties. ROA will help you evaluate possible alternatives, so you can take advantage of the potential project payoff while minimizing the downside. ROA is not a substitute for but rather an extension of the DCF method. Every real option valuation starts with the underlying asset value, which is the expected payoff calculated using the DCF method, where risk premium is added to the discount rate to account for the uncertainty. Adjustments are then made to this value, taking into consideration the contingent decisions. ROA thus takes the DCF to the next level, making it a more sophisticated tool. It captures the additional value created by the options embedded in a project when the payoff uncertainty is high.

ROA offers valuable information for go/no-go decisions based on evaluation of projects not only for their own merit but also for their relative merit against other competing projects in a portfolio. When the option value is significant, less attractive projects ranked lower based on DCF alone can move higher on the ranking scale and receive approval for investment, bumping other projects. ROA can become a "tie breaker" where two or more competing projects have similar NPVs.

ROA, in lieu of the DCF method, should not be construed as a means to justify projects that should be turned down in the first place. If a project has a very high negative NPV, it probably should be rejected. Trying to justify such a project using real options would be a meaningless exercise.

When both market risks and private risks exist as well as opportunities for contingent decisions to change the future course of the project, ROA in combination with DTA can provide better valuation. ROA is not a substitute for either DCF or DTA. It supplements and integrates the traditional tools into a more sophisticated valuation technique.

TYPES OF OPTIONS

Options can be grouped into two basic categories: simple options and compound options. An example of a simple option is a deferral option (discussed earlier in this chapter), where you have the right to delay a project. This option exists on every single project. Option to expand is another common example, where you have the right to expand a project through additional future investments. Both of these are American call options, where the option can be exercised on or at any time before the expiration date and you acquire the right to invest (buy) in the project. Option to contract involves the right to scale back on a project by selling some of the assets when market conditions are not favorable to you. Option to abandon, which exists on every project, gives you the right to sell off all the assets and totally terminate the project. Options to contract and abandon are American put options, where you can exercise the option on or before its expiration date by selling your project assets.

Chooser option is an option that gives you the right to choose from a variety of options, including deferral, expansion, contraction, and abandonment. With a switching option, you have the right to switch between two modes of operation; an example would be switching between natural gas and fuel oil for boilers at a manufacturing facility. Chooser and switching options include both American calls and puts.

The value of a compound option depends on the value of another option rather than the underlying asset value. Compound options are common in many multiphase projects, such as product and drug development, where the initiation of one phase of the project depends on the successful completion of the preceding phase. For example, launching a product that involves a new technology requires successful testing of the technology; drug approval is dependent on successful Phase II trials, which can be conducted only after successful Phase I tests. With compound options, at the end of each phase, you have the option to continue to the next phase, abandon the project, or defer it to a later time.

Each phase becomes an option that is contingent upon the exercise of earlier options. For phased projects, two or more phases may occur at the same time (parallel options) or in sequence (staged or sequential options). These options are mostly American with the right to buy (call) or sell (put).

A compound option can be called a learning option if it involves resolution of either private or market uncertainty. For example, in the case of a product development project, a pilot test planned to resolve the technological (that is, private) uncertainty (predecessor option of a sequential compound option) leading the way to the product launch (successor option of a sequential compound option) would be considered a learning option.

Similarly, an initial market test performed to clear the market uncertainty is also called a learning option. In this case, the market test is the first and the product launch is the second sequential option. Organizations often do not commit full investments up front on large projects in order to take advantage of the compound options embedded in them. The initial phases of the project are used as the predecessor options for later phases of the project. For example, you may not start the construction of a chemical plant until the design/engineering work is complete, which you may not commence until the required permits are obtained. The idea is to watch for the uncertainty to clear as you go through the project phases and make go/no-go decisions on each phase accordingly. This is considered passive learning since it does not involve up-front investments exclusively made for the uncertainty to clear. Therefore, such options are not considered learning options. Thus, learning options are not different types of options per se, but are simply part of compound options that help clear uncertainty through active learning.

There is another group of options called rainbow options, which may be either simple or compound. Options for which multiple sources of uncertainty exist are called rainbow options. The uncertainty may be related to one or more of the input parameters used in options valuation or to the individual components that make up an input parameter, or there may be changes in the uncertainty itself over the option lifetime.

Examples of Different Types of Options

Option to defer — EnergyNow has acquired a 20-year lease for an oil field. It will cost $100 million to develop this oil field for extraction. Based on the estimate of the oil reserves and the current oil price, the DCF analysis based on a risk-adjusted discount rate shows a negative NPV for the project. But oil prices are highly volatile and may go up in the future. Therefore, based on the high options value of the project, EnergyNow decides to defer the exploration project until the market price of oil becomes favorable.

Option to expand — TaxTricks, a highly profitable tax-related software development company, is interested in expanding rapidly into other financial areas. The company has healthy cash reserves and can easily afford to acquire a small company that provides synergy to its current portfolio of products. But the current uncertainty shows a high value for the option to expand, which helps TaxTricks chart out a strategic map for future growth.

Option to contract — Super Shrinkers has been a very successful company focused on drugs for niche population groups. Due to changing and uncertain demographics, the market demand for its products is shrinking, and the company is evaluating an option to contract its operations in the near future through outsourcing and internal cost reduction.

Option to abandon — RoboPharms is a manufacturing firm that supplies drug-making equipment to pharmaceutical companies. It is concerned that it may have to close one of its major plants due to competitive market conditions. There is a great deal of uncertainty about the fate of this industry, especially due to potential new international trade legislation that would go into effect in the near future. Senior management feels that the uncertainty will clear in the next two years, allowing additional time to make a better informed decision using an option to abandon.

Option to choose — Choose 'n Chase Autos is an automobile manufacturer faced with the realities of today's globalization. It has to make a difficult choice between four strategies: continuation of the status quo, expansion, contraction, or total abandonment of some of its manufacturing operations. It uses a chooser option to optimize its decision and make the right choice.

Parallel compound option — BigWig Pharma is going through the final phase of human trials for a new drug and preparing the application package for FDA approval. Upon approval, the company will launch the drug with a marketing campaign. FDA approval provides BigWig an option to launch the drug, and successful completion of human trials provides an option to apply for the approval; hence this is an option on an option. Because both options are active simultaneously, this is called a parallel compound option.

Sequential compound option (option to stage) — Creative Chemicals is considering investment in a new plant to manufacture a chemical called creatin. Because of the market uncertainty regarding the profitability of creatin, the company uses an options approach to facilitate a go/no-go investment decision. The project is divided into three phases: permitting, design/engineering, and construction. Before constructing the plant, the design/engineering phase must be completed, before which the company must obtain permits. Thus, the project involves a phased investment and is a classic example of a sequential compound option, where the value of a predecessor option depends on the value of the successor option.

Learning option — In the parallel compound option example above, the final phase of human testing is a learning option, because it helps resolve the uncertainty related to the effectiveness of the test drug through active learning. (There are no learning options in the sequential compound example above, because there is no active learning associated with the options.)

Rainbow option — In the sequential compound option example above for the manufacture of creatin, the payoff is subject to two different sources of uncertainty: one related to the chemical's future sales and the other to the price of its primary ingredient. Because of more than one source of uncertainty, it is a rainbow option.

The next two chapters focus on the option valuation models and the process; Chapters 7 and 8 present the step-by-step options calculations for the different types of options introduced in this chapter.

PROBLEM

4-1. A major business unit of a global corporation is evaluating a portfolio of projects for next year's investments. Preliminary analysis of the projects provided the following information. What projects would you strongly recommend for further analysis using ROA?

Project No.	Investment Cost (Millions)	DCF-Based Payoff (Millions)	Payoff Uncertainty	Flexibility with Contingent Decisions
1	$10	$2	High	High
2	$18	$20	High	Moderate
3	$26	$62	High	High
4	$55	$53	Low	High
5	$15	$14	High	None
6	$45	$44	High	High
7	$38	$39	Moderate	High
8	$22	$22	Low	Low

5

REAL OPTIONS
ANALYSIS
CALCULATIONS

Discounted cash flows (DCFs), simulations, and decision trees are relatively easy methods to understand, because the theoretical framework behind these methods is rather simple and requires no more than freshman college mathematics. DCF and decision tree analyses are also relatively easy from a computational standpoint; a handheld calculator will suffice. Simulations, however, will take enormous time with a handheld calculator and require special software because of the hundreds of simulations involved. Real options analysis (ROA) is far more complex compared to these traditional tools and requires a higher degree of mathematical understanding. The theoretical framework of real options solutions is complex, whereas the calculations involved are relatively simple. Once the equations for the options solution are formulated, the computations can be done easily with a handheld calculator.

In this chapter, commonly used methods to solve real options valuation problems are introduced. We do not delve into the theoretical basis and the derivation of the solutions; focus is on the application. There are several books that you can refer to for a better understanding of the concepts and mathematics behind the theory. Since the objective of this book is to help the practitioner, we have excluded detailed theoretical discussions.

There seems to be a false notion within the practicing community that real options valuation is a substitute for the DCF method. This is far from the truth. It is paramount that the practitioner first understand that ROA is not a substitute for but a supplement to DCF — for that matter, decision trees and simulations as well. In fact, as you will see before finishing this book, DCF forms the foundation for ROA, and decision trees and simulations can be integrated into the valuation process depending upon the application and the method used to solve the options problem.

Calculation of the real options value of a project basically starts with the computation of the underlying asset value by the traditional DCF method using a risk-adjusted discount rate. Next it incorporates the investment cost (strike price) and the value created by the uncertainty of the asset value and flexibility due to the contingent decision. If there is no uncertainty, management can make a decision today and there is no option value. Uncertainty creates future management decision opportunities that are reflected in the value of the option. The higher the uncertainty is, the higher the option value.

Real options solutions are based on models developed for pricing financial options. The Nobel Prize–winning breakthrough by three MIT economists — Fischer Black, Robert Merton, and Myron Scholes — paved the way to simple and elegant solution of financial option problems, which in turn became the foundation for real options applications. Several methods are available to calculate option values, and within each method there are many alternative computational techniques to deal with the mathematics. The choice depends on simplicity desired, available input data, and the validity of the method for a given application. Some methods include complex mathematics, which may be difficult to explain to senior management, while other methods are more intuitive and can be illustrated easily. The solution methods and computational techniques are summarized in Table 5-1. The following sections illustrate the principles and framework behind each method.

Table 5-1. Real Options Analysis Solution Methods

Option Valuation Technique	Specific Method
Partial differential equations	■ Closed form solutions using Black-Scholes and other similar equations ■ Analytical approximations ■ Numerical methods (e.g., finite difference method)
Simulations	Monte Carlo
Lattices	■ Binomial ■ Trinomial ■ Quadrinomial ■ Multinomial

PARTIAL DIFFERENTIAL EQUATIONS

The partial differential equations method involves solving a partial differential equation with specified boundary conditions (i.e., type of option, option values at known points and extremes, etc.) that describes the change in option value with respect to measurable changes of certain variables in the market. In a closed form analytical solution to the partial differential equation, the option value is given by one equation. The most famous such equation to calculate the value of a European call option is Black-Scholes, named after the authors of the publication wherein they presented their breakthrough in 1973. (Merton's contribution, an integral part of the Black-Scholes solution, was published in a separate paper around the same time. In 1997, Merton and Scholes received the Nobel Prize in Economics; Black had died in 1995.)

In cases where completely closed form solutions are not possible, approximations may be made to arrive at analytical solutions. Such approximations are computationally complex and difficult to explain. If analytical solutions or approximations are not at all possible, numerical solutions can be used to solve the partial differential equation. Finite difference is one of the most widely used numerical methods, where a set of simultaneous equations that hold over short time increments is solved to compute the option value. The disadvantage with this method is the computational complexity and its inability to deal with multiple sources of uncertainty related to the underlying asset value.

Black-Scholes Equation

The famous Black-Scholes equation is:

$$C = N(d_1)S_o - N(d_2)X \exp(-rT) \tag{5-1}$$

where C = value of the call option, S_o = current value of the underlying asset, X = cost of investment or strike price, r = risk-free rate of return, T = time to expiration, $d_1 = [\ln (S_o/X) + (r + 0.5\sigma^2)T]/\sigma\sqrt{T}$, $d_2 = d_1 - \sigma\sqrt{T}$, σ = annual volatility of future cash flows of the underlying asset, and $N(d_1)$ and $N(d_2)$ are the values of the standard normal distribution at d_1 and d_2 (available in Microsoft Excel® as a function).

The Black-Scholes equation is the easiest way to calculate the option value, if applicable to your options problem. The input parameters, S_o, X, T, and r, are easy to identify. $N(d_1)$ and $N(d_2)$ can be obtained from a Microsoft Excel® spreadsheet. The volatility factor, σ, which represents the uncertainty of the underlying asset value, is probably the most difficult to obtain, compared to all the other input parameters. (A detailed discussion of the input parameters and the estimation methods to calculate the volatility factor is presented in the next chapter.) Once the input data are identified, solving the Black-Scholes equation is rather simple.

SIMULATIONS

The simulation method for solving real options problems is similar to the Monte Carlo technique for DCF analysis discussed in Chapter 2. It involves simulation of thousands of paths the underlying asset value may take during the option life given the boundaries of the cone of uncertainty (Figure 5-1) as defined by the volatility of the asset value. First, the input parameters required to conduct the simulations are defined:

- Current value of the underlying asset (S_o)
- Volatility of the asset value (σ)
- Strike price (X)
- Option life (T)
- Risk-free rate corresponding to the option life (r)
- Incremental time step to be considered over the option life (δt)

The current value of the underlying asset value is calculated using the DCF method with a risk-adjusted discount rate. Volatility refers to the variability of the asset value, as in the Black-Scholes model.

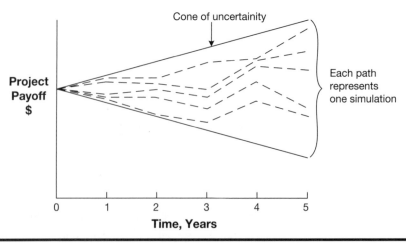

Figure 5-1.   Monte Carlo Simulations and Cone of Uncertainty

In the simulation method, the option life is divided into a selected number of time steps, and thousands of simulations are made to identify the asset value at each step of each simulation. At time = 0, for every simulation, you start with the expected underlying asset value (S_o). In the next step, the asset value, which may go up or down, is calculated by using the following equation with a random variable function:

$$S_t = S_{t-1} + S_{t-1}(r * \delta t + \sigma \varepsilon \sqrt{\delta t}) \qquad (5\text{-}2)$$

where S_t and S_{t-1} are the underlying asset values at time t and time $t-1$, respectively; σ is the volatility of the underlying asset value; and ε is the simulated value from a standard normal distribution with mean zero and a variance of 1.0 (Mun, 2002). The underlying asset value is again calculated for the next time increment using the same equation. In this fashion, asset values for each time step are calculated until the end of the option life. The decision rule is then applied by comparing the end asset value with the strike price; that is, for example, project investment for a call option and project abandonment value for a put option.

In the case of a simple call option, if the exercise price is lower than the end asset value, the option to invest is presumably exercised and the project value would be equal to the difference between the asset value and the exercise price. On the other hand, if the exercise price is higher, the project asset value would be zero because the option would not be exercised. For a put option, it would be vice versa. Each resulting project value is then discounted back to today using a risk-free rate. The average of these values from all the simulations is the option value for the project.

Simulations easily can be used for European options, where there is a fixed option exercise date. The option life can be divided into a selected number of time steps and the evolution of the asset price simulated from one time step to the next for the total option life. The higher the number of time steps and the higher the number of simulations, the more accurate the results.

With an American option, since it can be exercised anytime during its life, the simulations have to be conducted by setting the option life to correspond to every possible exercise day, which would be an enormous task. It becomes particularly challenging to apply simulations to staged (sequential) options, because each possible decision leads to a new path, and simulations would have to be conducted for every path. For example, a project with two sequential binary decision points will have four paths (three decision points will have eight paths, four decision points will have sixteen paths, and so on.) To create thousands of simulations for each path for every day of the life of an American option would be a daunting task even with a fast computer.

LATTICES

Lattices look like decision trees and basically lay out, in the form of a branching tree, the evolution of possible values of the underlying asset during the life of the option. An optimal solution to the entire problem is obtained by optimizing the future decisions at various decision points and folding them back in a backward recursive fashion into the current decision.

Binomial Lattice

The most commonly used lattices are binomial trees. The binomial model can be represented by the binomial tree shown in Figure 5-2. S_o is the initial value of the asset. In the first time increment, it either goes up or down and from there continues to go either up or down in the following time increments. The up and down movements are represented by u and d factors, where u is >1 and d is <1 and we assume $u = 1/d$. The magnitude of these factors depends on the volatility of the underlying asset.

The first time step of the binomial tree has two nodes, showing the possible asset values ($S_o u$, $S_o d$) at the end of that time period. The second time step results in three nodes and asset values ($S_o u^2$, $S_o ud$, $S_o d^2$), the third time step in four ($S_o u^3$, $S_o u^2 d$, $S_o ud^2$, $S_o d^3$), and so on.

The last nodes at the end of the binomial tree represent the range of possible asset values at the end of the option life. These asset values can be represented

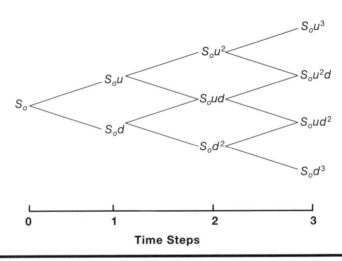

Figure 5-2. A Generic Recombining Binomial Tree

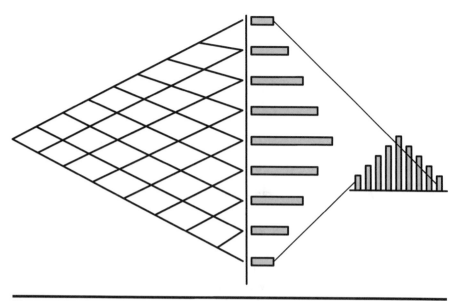

Figure 5-3. Distribution of Outcomes

in the form of a frequency histogram. Each histogram signifies a single asset value outcome, and the height of the histogram is a function of the number of times that outcome will result through all possible paths on the binomial tree (Figure 5-3).

The total time length of the lattice is the option life and can be represented by as many time steps as you want. While the range (minimum and maximum) of outcomes at the end of the lattice may not change significantly with an increase in the number of time steps, the number of possible outcomes increases exponentially and their frequency distribution curve will become smoother. The higher the number of time steps, the higher the level of granularity and therefore the higher the level of accuracy of option valuation.

Other Lattices

In the so-called "recombining" lattice, a center node (e.g., S_oud of time step 2 in Figure 5-2) is the same for its upper predecessor's (S_ou) downward movement and its lower predecessor's (S_od) upward movement. Recombining binomial lattice is the most commonly used model and the focus of this book. In a nonrecombining lattice, the center nodes are different (S_oud^*, S_odu^*) for the predecessor nodes' downward (S_ou) and upward (S_od) movements, as shown in Figure 5-4.

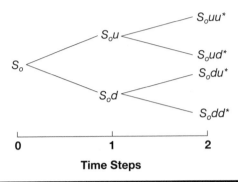

Figure 5-4.   A Generic Nonrecombining Binomial Lattice

Trinomial and quadrinomial lattices also can be used to solve real options problems. They are fairly similar in concept to binomials but are more computationally complex. An example of a quadrinomial lattice is provided in Figure 5-5, where two sets of upward and downward factors are applied to the asset values as you move through the lattice.

Binomial Method: Solution

Binomial lattices can be solved to calculate option values using two different approaches:

■   Risk-neutral probabilities
■   Market-replicating portfolios

The first approach is discussed in the following pages and used throughout this book. The second method is presented in detail and used by Copeland and Antikarov (2001). A brief summary of this method is provided in Appendix A. The theoretical framework for both approaches is the same, yielding identical answers, while the mathematics involved are slightly different.

The basic methodology of the risk-neutral probabilities approach involves risk adjusting the cash flows throughout the lattice with risk-neutral probabilities and discounting them at the risk-free rate. Irrespective of the option to be valued, the binomial lattice representing the underlying asset value has the same properties and can be described by the equations presented below. The up and down factors, u and d, are a function of the volatility of the underlying asset and can be described as follows:

$$u = \exp(\sigma \sqrt{\delta t}) \qquad (5\text{-}3)$$

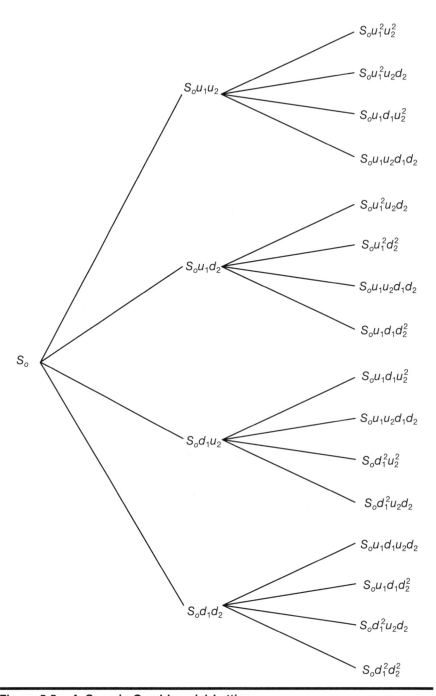

Figure 5-5. A Generic Quadrinomial Lattice

$$d = \exp(-\sigma \sqrt{\delta t}) \qquad (5\text{-}4)$$

where σ is the volatility (%) represented by the standard deviation of the natural logarithm of the underlying free cash flow returns, and δt is the time associated with each time step of the binomial tree. (σ and δt units should be consistent.) Equation 5-4 can be rewritten as follows, which is mathematically the same:

$$d = 1/u \qquad (5\text{-}5)$$

The risk-neutral probability, p, is defined as follows:

$$p = \frac{\exp(r\delta t) - d}{u - d} \qquad (5\text{-}6)$$

where r is the risk-free interest rate or rate of return on a riskless asset during the life of the option. The risk-neutral probabilities are not the same as objective probabilities. (The latter is used, for example, to describe the probability that a certain event will occur, as in decision tree analysis.) The risk-neutral probability is just a mathematical intermediate that will enable you to discount the cash flows using a risk-free interest rate.

The inputs required to build the binomial trees and calculate the option value are: σ, r, S_o, X, T, and δt, where σ is the volatility factor, r the risk-free rate, S_o the present value of the underlying asset value, X the cost of exercising the option, T the life of the option, and δt the time step chosen for the calculations.

REAL OPTIONS ANALYSIS EXAMPLE

An options example is presented in this section, with step-by-step calculations to solve the options problem and an analysis of the results.

Problem

Erp Corporation, a leading enterprise resource planning software company with an established market share, is contemplating development of a software product that would complement its existing products. Based on its experience with existing similar products, it can wait for a maximum of five years before releasing the new product without experiencing any substantial loss of revenues. The DCF estimate using an appropriate risk-adjusted discount rate shows that the present value of the expected future cash flows for the new product will be $160 million, while the investment to develop and market it is $200 million.

The annual volatility of the logarithmic returns of the future cash flows is estimated to be 30% and the continuous annual risk-free rate over the option's life of five years is 5%. What is the value of the option to wait?

Solution

Step-by-step calculations of the real options value (ROV) for the sample problem are presented using the three major methods: Black-Scholes, Monte Carlo simulation, and binomial.

Black-Scholes Equation

1. Identify the input parameters:
   S_o (current asset value) = $160 million
   X (strike price) = $200 million
   σ (volatility) = 30%
   r (risk free rate) = 5%
   T (time to expiration) = 5 years
2. Calculate the option parameters:
   $d_1 = [\ln (S_o/X) + (r + 0.5\sigma^2)T]/\sigma\sqrt{T}$
   $= [\ln(\$160 \text{ million}/\$200 \text{ million}) + (0.05 + 0.5 * 0.3^2)5]/(0.3 * \sqrt{5})$
   $= 0.375$
   $d_2 = d_1 - \sigma\sqrt{T}$
   $= 0.375 - 0.3 * \sqrt{5}$
   $= -0.295$
3. Find $N(d_1) = 0.646$ (from Microsoft Excel®)
4. Find $N(d_2) = 0.384$ (from Microsoft Excel®)
5. Solve the Black-Scholes equation for ROV:
   $C = N(d_1)S_o - N(d_2)X \exp(-rT)$
   $= 0.646 * \$160 \text{ million} - 0.384 * \$200 \text{ million} * \exp(-0.05 * 5)$
   $= \$44 \text{ million}$

Monte Carlo Simulation

1. Identify the input parameters:
   $S_o = \$160$ million
   $X = \$200$ million
   $\sigma = 30\%$
   $r = 5\%$
   $T = 5$ years
   δt (incremental time step) = 0.5 year

2. Conduct numerous simulations for asset values using Equation 5-2. You can utilize your own spreadsheet/software program or one that is commercially available (e.g., @Risk® or Crystal Ball®) and calculate the option value.
3. The simulation results from a custom-made spreadsheet show an average ROV of $43 million. Table 5-2 shows the results of one particular simulation with the first 10 out of 1,000 trials as a sample.

Equation 5-2 is applied to calculate the asset value for every time increment. The asset value at the end of year 5 is compared to the strike price of $200 million. If it is above the strike price, the call option is in the money and is exercised, and the option value for that simulation would be the difference between the asset value and $200 million. Otherwise, the option is not exercised and becomes worthless, resulting in an option value of $0 for that simulation. The option value for each trial is discounted back to today using a risk-free rate. The average of these values is considered the ROV of the project.

Binomial Method

1. Identify the input parameters:
   S_o = $160 million
   X = $200 million
   T = 5 years
   σ = 30%
   r = 5%
   δt = 1 year
2. Calculate the option parameters, which are the up (u) and down (d) factors and the risk-neutral probability (p):
   u = exp($\sigma\sqrt{\delta t}$)
     = exp(0.30 * $\sqrt{1}$)
     = 1.350
   d = 1/u
     = 1/1.350
     = 0.741
   $$p = \frac{\exp(r\delta t) - d}{u - d}$$
     = [exp(0.05 * 1) – 0.741]/(1.350–0.741)
     = 0.510
3. Build the binomial tree and calculate the asset values at each node of the tree. Build the binomial tree, as shown in Figure 5-6, using one-year time

Table 5-2. Monte Carlo Simulation for Real Options Analysis: Erp Corporation

Input Parameters	
Present value of future cash flows	$160 million
Volatility	30%
Risk-free rate of return	5%
Time to expiration	5 years
Strike price	$200 million
Time step	0.5 year
Total no. of simulation trials	1,000

Results	
Net present value	–$40 million
Real options value	$43 million
Value added	$83 million
Probability that the option is exercised	42%

The First 10 Simulation Trials

Trial No.	Time Increment No.											Option Value at Year 5	Present Value of the Option
	0	1	2	3	4	5	6	7	8	9	10		
1	$160	$167	$148	$211	$249	$248	$262	$242	$195	$217	$190	$0	$0
2	$160	$146	$178	$139	$189	$220	$277	$272	$193	$170	$162	$0	$0
3	$160	$138	$107	$105	$109	$80	$57	$85	$59	$44	$35	$0	$0
4	$160	$202	$241	$315	$335	$311	$346	$299	$251	$259	$363	$163	$127
5	$160	$202	$279	$306	$270	$263	$284	$281	$292	$373	$316	$116	$90
6	$160	$165	$200	$237	$276	$374	$380	$413	$236	$314	$234	$34	$27
7	$160	$145	$177	$184	$215	$170	$197	$235	$247	$206	$172	$0	$0
8	$160	$182	$180	$209	$190	$224	$256	$229	$288	$295	$372	$172	$134
9	$160	$146	$163	$179	$121	$105	$91	$111	$127	$100	$89	$0	$0
10	$160	$145	$130	$113	$124	$105	$115	$121	$131	$146	$134	$0	$0

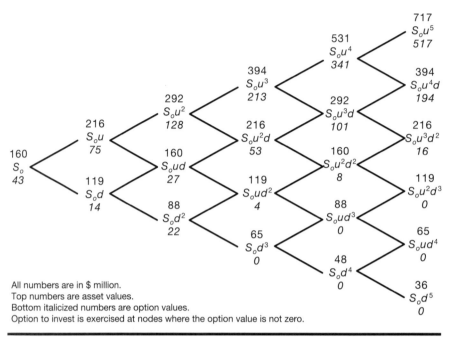

All numbers are in $ million.
Top numbers are asset values.
Bottom italicized numbers are option values.
Option to invest is exercised at nodes where the option value is not zero.

Figure 5-6.   Option Valuation Binomial Tree for Erp's Software Product

intervals for five years, and calculate the asset values over the life of the option. Start with S_o and multiply it by the up factor and the down factor to obtain $S_o u$ and $S_o d$, respectively, for the first time step, and continue in a similar manner for every node of the binomial tree until the last step. For example, $S_o u$ = $160 million ∗ 1.350 = $216 million; $S_o d$ = $160 million ∗ 0.741 = $119 million. Moving to the right, continue in a similar fashion for every node of the binomial tree until the last time step. In Figure 5-6, the upper value at each node represents the asset value at that node.

4. Calculate the option values at each node of the binomial tree using what is known as backward induction. This is represented by the bottom italicized numbers in Figure 5-6. Each node represents the value maximization of investing at that point or waiting until the next time period. At every node, you have the option to either invest in product development or the option to wait until the next time period before the option expires.

   A. Start with the terminal nodes representing the last time step first. At node $S_o u^5$, the expected asset value is $717 million if you invested $200 million for the new product; therefore, the net asset value is:

$$\$717 \text{ million} - \$200 \text{ million} = \$517 \text{ million}$$

But if you waited until the next time period, the revenues will be zero for this time period. The reason is that, by definition of the problem, the option expires at the end of the fifth year and becomes worthless if it is not exercised. Therefore, the rational decision at node $S_o u^5$ will be to invest — but not to wait — and the option value at this node will be $517 million.

B. At node $S_o u^2 d^3$, the expected asset value is $119 million if an investment of $200 million is made, resulting in a net loss of $81 million. Therefore, the decision at this node will be not to invest in product development, which means the option value at this node will be $0.

C. Next, move on to the intermediate nodes, one step away from the last time step. Starting at the top, at node $S_o u^4$, calculate the expected asset value for keeping the option open. This is simply the discounted (at the risk-free rate) weighted average of potential future option values using the risk-neutral probability. That value at node $S_o u^4$ is:

$$[p(S_o u^5) + (1 - p)(S_o u^4 d)] * \exp(-r\delta t)$$

$$= [0.510(\$517 \text{ million}) + (1 - 0.510)(\$194 \text{ million})]$$
$$* \exp(-0.05)(1)$$

$$= \$341 \text{ million}$$

If the option is exercised at this node by investing $200 million, the payoff would be $531 million (the asset value at $S_o u^4$), resulting in a net asset value of $331 million. Since keeping the option open shows a higher asset value ($341 million), you would not exercise the option but instead continue to wait; the option value at this node becomes $341 million.

D. Similarly, at node $S_o u d^3$, the expected asset value for keeping the option open, taking into account the downstream optimal decisions, is:

$$[0.510(\$0 \text{ million}) + (1 - 0.510)(\$0 \text{ million})] \exp(-0.05)(1)$$

$$= \$0 \text{ million}$$

If the option is exercised by investing $200 million, the payoff at this node is $88 million (the asset value at $S_o u d^3$), showing a net loss of $112 million. Therefore, the decision would be to keep the option open.

E. Complete the option valuation binomial tree all the way to time = 0.

Analysis

The ROVs for the Erp project based on the three methods used are:

- Black-Scholes = $44 million
- Simulations = $43 million
- Binomial = $43 million

Given the margins of error for the estimated input parameters, the above values can be considered to be virtually the same.

As the calculations show, the Black-Scholes solution simply involves inserting the numbers into the equation and solving it, which makes it the easiest model of the three. However, there is no transparency with this model in the sense that the logic behind the solution is not clear.

With simulations, you can see that, using the volatility factor, a path is created for the underlying asset value starting at time zero. At the end of the option life, the value maximization rule is applied. If the value of the call option is greater than the strike price, the option is in the money and therefore exercised; otherwise, the option expires worthless. The average of the option values from 1,000 trials in this example is the value of the option at the end of five years. In the simulation from which the first 10 trials are presented in Table 5-2 as a sample, the option was exercised 42% of the time. (Note that the results will be different every time you run the simulation but approximately the same.) The solution presented in Table 5-2 is for a European option, where the option can be exercised only on a fixed date, that is, at the end of the option life. However, for an American option, you need to run simulations for every day of the life of the option, which, as was pointed out earlier, can be a daunting task.

Let us now analyze the binomial method in view of the solution to the Erp problem. The upper numbers on the binomial tree in Figure 5-6 present the expected future values of the underlying asset over the option life as it evolves according to its cone of uncertainty. For example, at the end of year 2, Erp's new software product is expected to generate a total payoff of anywhere between $88 million and $292 million and at the end of year 5 between $36 million and $717 million (all in today's dollars). The bottom italicized numbers on the binomial tree represent the option values based on maximization of investing at that point or waiting until the next time period. At the end of year 5, however, you cannot wait any longer to invest because the option expires after that point. This means either you exercise the option by investing $200 million (strike price) because it is in the money (that is, the expected asset value is more than $200 million) or you let it expire because it is out of the money (the expected asset value is less than $200 million). The reason the option expires at the end of year 5 is because that is how the option is framed, presumably considering competitive forces and other such factors in the marketplace.

The option values at the end nodes of the binomial tree in Figure 5-6 show the value of the Erp project at the end of five years, corresponding to each asset value shown. For example, if the uncertainty has cleared in five years and the expected payoff from the project is $216 million (node $S_o u^3 d^2$), the value of the project is $16 million.

We will now evaluate what the value-maximizing decisions would be at the nodes representing the earlier years. For instance, at node $S_o u^4$ of year 4, you may either exercise the option by investing $200 million for an expected payoff of $531 million, resulting in a net present value (NPV) of $331 million, or keep the option open until the next year, when the option value is expected to be $341 million based on the expected future decision the following year. Therefore, as a rational decision maker, you would keep the option open. At node $S_o u d^3$ of year 4, if you invest $200 million, the expected payoff is only $88 million, resulting in a net loss of –$112 million. But if you keep the option open and continue to wait, the expected option value is $0. To maximize your value, you would not invest at this point. It turns out that the option has the highest value at year 5, which means that you would only exercise your option to invest at that time — but not earlier.

The binomial method offers transparency by showing the project values in the future for given expected payoffs and the rational decisions one would make. The idea is that as the uncertainty clears in the future, management can make appropriate decisions at that time by comparing the expected payoff with the investment cost. The binomial method provides a strategic map to facilitate that process.

Let us now compare the decisions you would make strictly based on DCF results versus ROV results. The DCF method, using a risk-adjusted discount rate, shows a payoff of $160 million for the new product, which is expected to cost $200 million for development and marketing. This means the NPV of the project is –$40 million ($160 million – $200 million), which does not favor the investment. Strictly based on the NPV alone, your decision may be not to invest in this project. However, the project has an ROV of approximately $43 million created by the option characteristics of the project related to the high uncertainty. The additional value created by the option is the difference between the ROV of $43 million and the DCF-based NPV of –$40 million, which equals $83 million.

With such substantial additional value created by the option, Erp may want to explore alternatives other than abandonment of the project at this time. For example, it may simply wait until the market uncertainty clears by itself (passive learning), at which time it would re-estimate the project payoff. If the payoff is unfavorable, it may still continue to wait or abandon the project idea altogether. If, on the other hand, the conditions are favorable with high expected payoff, it may invest in the project. Alternatively, Erp may decide to conduct a small market survey to test the demand for the proposed product to clear the uncertainty (active learning) — instead of waiting for the uncertainty to resolve itself. As the uncertainty is resolved, Erp may introduce the product anytime during the option life. The life of the new product is assumed to be fixed irrespective of when it is introduced within the option lifetime of five years. Therefore, the payoff does not vary based on when the investment is made. In other words, there is no "leakage" in the asset value because of waiting. (How to address leakage will be discussed in the next chapter.)

Although ROA does not alter Erp's DCF-based decision not to invest in the project at the proposed scale at this time, it quantifies the value of waiting and provides a strategic road map for future contingent decisions. This offers managers a choice of decisions and helps them to be more proactive and rational.

It should be evident from the foregoing calculations and discussion that ROA is a supplement to rather than an alternative to the DCF-based NPV. If Erp's candidate project has either an extremely high positive or extremely high negative NPV, the project may be accepted or rejected for investment, respectively, irrespective of the option value. Since the NPV is not highly negative and the project has a high option value, management may want to consider alternative decisions related to passive or active learning and keep the project "alive."

The Erp example involves an option to wait, a simple option that is embedded in virtually every project with high payoff uncertainty. Chapter 7 presents step-by-step binomial calculations for valuation of projects with characteristics of other types of simple options. Chapter 8 does the same for compound options.

PROBLEM

5-1. Splice & Sequence developed a new tool that accelerates the DNA sequencing of genomes. This advanced technology has great market potential while exhibiting high market uncertainty at the same time. The project launch cost is expected to be $300 million, with the same estimated DCF-based payoff. The annual volatility factor is 30%, and the continuous annual risk-free rate for the next five years is 5%. If the company can wait for five years before introducing the product into the market, what is the real options value of this project? Calculate the ROV based on the Black-Scholes, binomial, and Monte Carlo simulation methods for comparison purpose.

6

REAL OPTIONS ANALYSIS APPLICATION

The Nobel Prize–winning work by Fischer Black, Myron Scholes, and Robert Merton in 1973 helped solve a complex financial options pricing problem that had perplexed economists since the early 1900s. Although the theory behind the solution is mathematically complex, the now famous Black-Scholes equation is so simple that you need no more than high school math to use it in pricing financial options, once the input parameters are known. Whereas the Nobel Prize–winning breakthrough laid the groundwork for financial options, it is not widely used to value real options because of its limited applicability and inherent complexity. Over the years, other solutions, including the binomial method, have evolved that offer more universal application and relative ease of use.

In this chapter, we first present the theoretical limitations of applying financial option valuation models to real options and then discuss practical challenges in solving the real options models. Finally, we also offer a six-step process for real options analysis of projects using what we believe is the most effective solution method that is theoretically sound, valid for a wide variety of applications, and easily understood with no need for high-level math.

LIMITATIONS TO APPLYING FINANCIAL OPTION MODELS TO REAL OPTIONS ANALYSIS

Although financial and real options have similar characteristics, as discussed in Chapter 1, application of financial option pricing models to real options warrants extreme caution because of the limited validity of the underlying framework of the financial models when applied to real options. Therefore, it is important that the real options practitioners clearly understand the framework and the assumptions, so proper adjustments can be made to ensure validity of the application. There are two related concepts that form the foundation of the Black-Scholes formula and other option valuation models: arbitrage and replicating portfolios. Let us now examine briefly the role of these concepts in real options solutions.

One important assumption behind the options pricing models is that no "arbitrage" opportunity exists. This means that in efficient financial markets, you cannot buy an asset at one price and simultaneously sell it at a higher price. Professional investors supposedly will buy and sell assets quickly, closing any price gaps, thereby making arbitrage opportunities rare. Critics argue that a "no arbitrage" condition is impossible with real assets because they are not as liquid as financial assets, and therefore option pricing models are inappropriate for real options valuation. We believe that a categorical denial of the validity of the models to real option problems is inappropriate and that a "no arbitrage" condition is only a limitation of the model and can be overcome easily by proper adjustments. Practitioners have used three different types of adjustment:

1. Use an interest rate that is slightly higher than the riskless rate in the option pricing model.
2. Use a higher discount rate in calculating the discounted cash flow (DCF) value of the underlying asset.
3. Apply an "illiquidity" discount factor to the final option value.

Basically, the objective of these adjustments is to account for any overvaluation caused by not meeting the "no arbitrage" condition. All three methods, therefore, decrease the option value, making it more conservative.

A replicating portfolio consists of a certain number of shares of the underlying financial asset and riskless bonds which has the same payoff as the option. Assuming a no arbitrage condition, the option valuation model ensures that the option value equals the value of the portfolio as the price of the portfolio components evolves. The value of the option is calculated as the current value of the replicating portfolio, since these two values correlate with each other. (The calculations are provided in Appendix A.) The replicating portfolio approach is valid when the underlying asset is a traded security, because the risk related to the underlying asset value is strictly market risk and is captured in the traded security. Since most real options are not traded assets, application of financial option models to real options is questioned by some critics. The real options proponents, however, argue that you can create a replicating portfolio for a real option on paper, which should suffice (Damodaran, 2002). Some (Amram and Kulatilaka, 2000) suggest that instead of simply assuming private risk, the practitioners should look hard to correlate the risk — even partially — with a portfolio of traded securities.

We believe that it is no longer a question of whether options pricing models can be applied to real options problems. It is a matter of the practitioner understanding clearly the assumptions and limitations behind the application, using the right tools to solve the problem, and exercising caution in interpreting the results.

Apart from the "validity challenges" mentioned above, real options practitioners are frequently faced with difficulties in estimating the input parameters of the valuation models.

ESTIMATION OF INPUT VARIABLES

The major challenge a practitioner faces in calculating the option values is estimating the input parameters. The following sections define the input parameters and present best practices and limitations in estimating them.

Underlying Asset Value (S_o)

The value of the underlying security at time zero represents the underlying asset value and is easily known for a financial option, because it is a traded security. With real options, however, the asset value is estimated from the cash flows the asset is expected to generate over the production phase of the project life cycle. The present value of the expected free cash flows based on the DCF calculation is considered the value of the underlying asset. As part of this standard calculation, you will forecast the revenues based on assumed market share, number of units expected to be sold, price per unit, the cost associated with these sales, and so on. Most likely, there will be great uncertainty associated with these estimates, and therefore you will use an appropriate risk-adjusted discount rate in the DCF calculation.

There are specific challenges an analyst faces in estimating the underlying asset value:

1. In deriving the option pricing models, the value of the underlying asset is assumed to change in a continuous process without any sharp up and down turns, generally referred to as "jumps." The assumption typically

holds up well for short-term options, but with long-term options, which many real options are, jumps are not uncommon. A sharp decline in the asset value is typical when, for example, a patent expires, a competitor suddenly enters the market, an unexpected turn of events totally out of your control takes place, etc. While it is difficult to account for such jumps with the Black-Scholes method, the binomial method allows easy corrections, as we will demonstrate with the option-to-wait example in Chapter 7.

2. The basic Black-Scholes model assumes that there are no dividends (negative cash flows) given out during the option life, and the underlying asset value changes as dictated by the volatility factor only. With real options, both dividend equivalent negative cash flows as well as positive cash flows can affect the underlying asset value, and these "leaks" must be adjusted for accordingly. These changes are not related to the volatility of the asset value dictated by the market conditions or to the jump processes mentioned above. Examples of positive cash flow leaks include royalty income and interest, and cash outflows can be royalty fees, storage costs, etc. The leakage can be constant or varied during the option's life. Adjustments for leakage can be incorporated into either the Black-Scholes or the binomial model, although the latter offers more flexibility and makes the results more transparent. An example using the binomial model is provided in Chapter 7 for an option to wait that demonstrates the real options valuation for an asset with constant leakage.

Volatility of the Underlying Asset Value

Volatility is an important input variable that can have a significant impact on the option value and is probably the most difficult variable to estimate for real options problems. The following sections provide a detailed discussion on volatility.

What Is Volatility?

Volatility is a measure of the variability of the total value of the underlying asset over its lifetime. It signifies the uncertainty associated with the cash flows that comprise the underlying asset value. The volatility factor (σ) used in the options models, however, is the volatility of the *rates of return*, which is measured as the standard deviation of the natural logarithm of cash flow *returns* — not the actual cash flows. The return for a given time period is the ratio of the current time period cash flow to the preceding one. For example, if the cash flows for years 1 and 2 are $1 million and $1.2 million, respectively, the return for year 2 will be 1.2. Methods of estimating the volatility factor (σ) are presented later in this chapter.

In any options model, the volatility factor used should be consistent with the time step used in the corresponding equations. For instance, if the time steps are annual, the volatility factor should be annualized. The volatility factor based on one time frame can be converted to another using the following equation:

$$\sigma(T_2) = \sigma(T_1) * \sqrt{(T_2 / T_1)} \tag{6-1}$$

where $\sigma(T_2)$ and $\sigma(T_1)$ are the volatility factors based on time steps T_2 and T_1, respectively. For example, if $\sigma(T_1)$ is 20% based on annual cash flow data, $\sigma(T_2)$ for a half-year time step will be: $20\% * \sqrt{(0.5/1)} = 14.14\%$. If $\sigma(T_1)$ is 10% based on quarterly cash flow data, the annual volatility, $\sigma(T_2)$, will be: $10\% * \sqrt{(1/0.25)} = 20\%$.

Sources of Volatility

Although a single "aggregate" volatility factor is used in the options models, it is important to recognize that it is a function of uncertainties related to several variables, such as unit price, quantity expected to be sold, margins, etc., that control the project cash flows, as illustrated in Table 2-4. Furthermore, the volatility factor can be different for the revenue versus the cost component of the present value representing the underlying asset value. You have two choices in addressing different sources of volatility:

1. You can keep the variances separate, if you believe the controlling variables are independent of each other, evolve differently over time, and impact the asset value in different directions. For instance, suppose you develop a new chemical product for which the market uncertainty is significant. If the price of one of the ingredients of this chemical is also highly vulnerable to market forces, you now have two sources of uncertainty. If these two sources of uncertainty are uncorrelated, keeping the variances separate in calculating the real options value makes it a better estimate and gives you more useful insight into the problem. When there are more than two such independent sources of uncertainty, you can conduct a preliminary analysis to determine which two of the variables have the greatest impact on the asset value and focus on them. If you decide to keep the variances separate, you will need to use a special options framework known as "rainbow" options (defined in Chapter 5) because they explicitly allow for project valuation where multiple sources

of uncertainty exist. An example of a rainbow option is included in Chapter 8.

2. You can combine all the uncertainties into one aggregate value and use it in solving the options model. In this case, you can directly start with an estimate of the aggregate volatility factor independent of the controlling variables, or you can start with estimating the uncertainty related to each one of these variables and calculate the resulting aggregate volatility factor. Irrespective of the approach used, the estimation methods are basically the same, as discussed below.

Methods to Estimate Volatility

Estimation of the volatility factor is perhaps the greatest challenge a practitioner faces in using real options models. The volatility of financial options (for example, a stock) is easily estimated because historical information on the value of that stock is readily available. Such information is lacking with real options, and this is where the difficulty with estimation lies. Some of the commonly used methods are discussed below.

Logarithmic Cash Flow Returns Method

This method provides a volatility factor that is based on the variability of the same cash flow estimates that are used in calculating the underlying asset value itself; therefore, it is most representative of the volatility of the asset value. The steps involved are as follows:

- Forecast project cash flows during the production phase of the project at regular time intervals (for example, years).
- Calculate the relative returns for each time interval, starting with the second time interval, by dividing the current cash flow value by the preceding one.
- Take the natural logarithm of each relative return.
- Calculate the standard deviation of the natural logarithms of the relative returns from the previous step, which becomes the volatility factor (σ) for the underlying asset value. This factor is commonly expressed as a percentage and is specific to the time period.

Table 6-1 presents a sample calculation where the monthly volatility factor is 6% because its computation is based on monthly cash flows, which translates to an annual volatility factor of 21% (6% * $\sqrt{12}$) using Equation 6-1.

Table 6-1. **Volatility Factor Estimation: Logarithmic Cash Flow Returns Approach**[a]

Date	Cash Flow (S_t)	Return (R_t)[b]	In R_t	Deviation (In R_t – Average In R)	Square of Deviation (In R_t – Average In R)²
Dec-05	300	1.042	0.041	–0.031	0.001
Nov-05	288	1.108	0.102	0.030	0.001
Oct-05	260	1.044	0.043	–0.029	0.001
Sep-05	249	1.078	0.075	0.003	0.000
Aug-05	231	1.027	0.026	–0.046	0.002
Jul-05	225	1.066	0.064	–0.008	0.000
Jun-05	211	1.060	0.059	–0.014	0.000
May-05	199	1.053	0.052	–0.021	0.000
Apr-05	189	1.056	0.054	–0.018	0.000
Mar-05	179	0.952	–0.049	–0.121	0.015
Feb-05	188	1.056	0.055	–0.018	0.000
Jan-05	178	1.148	0.138	0.066	0.004
Dec-04	155	1.033	0.033	–0.039	0.002
Nov-04	150	1.145	0.135	0.063	0.004
Oct-04	131	1.048	0.047	–0.025	0.001
Sep-04	125	1.136	0.128	0.056	0.003
Aug-04	110	1.048	0.047	–0.026	0.001
Jul-04	105	1.105	0.100	0.028	0.001
Jun-04	95	1.234	0.210	0.138	0.019
May-04	77	0.963	–0.038	–0.110	0.012
Apr-04	80	1.176	0.163	0.090	0.008
Mar-04	68	1.046	0.045	–0.027	0.001
Feb-04	65	1.140	0.131	0.059	0.003
Jan-04	57	—	—	—	—
Average In R			0.072		
Total of squares of deviation					0.080

[a] Volatility factor is the square root of (total of squares of deviation/n – 1), where n is the number of values included = square root [0.080/(23 – 1)] = 0.060.
[b] $R_t = S_t/S_{t-1}$.

There are advantages to the logarithmic cash flow returns method: It is simple to use, mathematically valid, and consistent with the assumed variability of the very cash flows that are used to calculate the asset value. The major disadvantage is that when a cash flow is negative, the return associated with it will also be a negative number, for which a natural logarithm does not exist. This may produce erroneous results. Furthermore, some of the mathematical models (e.g., time series, constant growth rate) used to forecast the cash flows may also result in erroneous data for volatility estimation. Therefore, caution should be exercised in using this method.

Monte Carlo Simulation

In a Monte Carlo simulation, numerous cash flow profiles are simulated over the project life, and a volatility factor is computed for each profile using the logarithmic cash flow returns method presented in the preceding section. This method thus produces as many volatility factors as the number of simulations, thereby providing a distribution of these factors rather than just one.

There are multiple variables, such as the revenues, costs, and discount factor, that contribute to the present values of the project cash flows that comprise the underlying asset value. As discussed in Chapter 2, in a Monte Carlo simulation, you provide the input data (including the expected average and variance of the input variables that represent their respective distributions), conduct numerous simulations, and calculate the volatility factor associated with each simulation. The input data can be generated based on historical information or management estimates. Although many input variables contribute to the asset value, usually only a few have the most impact. Practitioners typically identify such variables by performing an initial sensitivity analysis and focus on them in simulations to calculate the volatility factor.

An example of a Monte Carlo simulation to calculate the volatility factor is shown in Table 6-2. As in the example presented in Table 2-5, 1,000 simulations are conducted using a custom-made spreadsheet to calculate 1,000 DCF-based net present values for the given input data. The simulation results show

Table 6-2. Volatility Factor Estimation: Monte Carlo Simulation

	Input Data[a]										
	Year										
	0	**1**	**2**	**3**	**4**	**5**	**6**	**7**	**8**	**9**	**10**
Investment cost	$10										
Base case annual cost		$3	$3	$3	$3	$3	$3	$2	$2	$2	$2
Base case annual revenue		$5	$6	$7	$8	$9	$10	$10	$9	$8	$7
Standard deviation of annual costs	5%										
Standard deviation of annual revenues	30%										
Risk-adjusted discount factor	25%										
Number of simulations	1,000										
	Results										
Annual volatility (σ) of asset value	65%										
Standard deviation of σ	38%										

[a] Cost and revenue data in million dollars.

an average annual volatility of 65% for the underlying asset value with a standard deviation of 38.

Although simulations involve a significant effort, the Monte Carlo method offers the most insightful information on the volatility of the underlying asset value. One advantage of this method is that it offers the distribution of the volatility factor, which can be used in evaluating the sensitivity of the real options value of the project under scrutiny to the volatility factor.

Project Proxy Approach

This is an indirect approach to estimate the volatility factor of the underlying asset. It uses as a proxy the data from a historical project which is assumed to have market performance and a cash flow profile similar to the project being considered. This translates to using the volatility factor of a previous project that has real world market information. This method is simple and easy and in some way accounts for the market reality. For example, if you are valuing a development project for a new version of an existing software product, you can use the cash flow data from the previous versions of the product as a proxy to determine the volatility of the new project. This would be tantamount to using the historic project information to estimate the new project cash flows in the first place and then estimating the volatility factor by the direct methods discussed in the preceding sections.

Market Proxy Approach

This is similar to the project proxy approach except that instead of using cash flow information from a similar historic project, the closing stock price of a publicly traded company that has a cash flow profile and risks comparable to the project under consideration is used. This method is simple and easy to use if you can find a comparable company. However, there are two main factors which should be properly accounted for in applying this method: First, a company's equity price is based on a multitude of its products/services, market psychology, and many other factors that may be immaterial to the project under consideration. Second, public companies usually are leveraged, but individual projects are not; therefore, a leveraged company's price does not accurately represent the value of a specific project.

Management Assumption Approach

In this approach, management estimates optimistic (S_{opt}), pessimistic (S_{pes}), and average (S_o) expected payoffs for a given project lifetime (t). An optimistic estimate of $100 million means that there is a 98% probability that the payoff will not exceed $100 million. Similarly, a pessimistic estimate of $20 million means that there is only a 2% probability that the payoff will be less than $20 million. The average estimate corresponds to 50% probability. Assuming that the payoff follows lognormal distribution, by knowing any two of the three estimates mentioned above, you can calculate the volatility of the underlying asset value using one of the following equations:

$$\sigma = \frac{\ln\left(\dfrac{S_{opt}}{S_o}\right)}{2\sqrt{t}} \tag{6-2}$$

$$\sigma = \frac{\ln\left(\dfrac{S_o}{S_{pes}}\right)}{2\sqrt{t}} \tag{6-3}$$

$$\sigma = \frac{\ln\left(\dfrac{S_{opt}}{S_{pes}}\right)}{4\sqrt{t}} \tag{6-4}$$

Change in Volatility Over the Option Life

Option pricing theory assumes that the volatility of the underlying asset value remains constant over the option life, which is reasonable for short-term options on traded stocks. Real options, however, typically have longer lives, and the volatility can change over time. The change may be due to a shift in general economic conditions, sudden market fluctuations, unexpected global events, and so on. Although many such events are unpredictable, you may want to assume more probable changes in estimating volatility variations. Both the Black-Scholes and binomial models allow you to incorporate volatility changes, although the latter offers more flexibility and transparency. (An example in Chapter 8 illustrates how this can be done with the binomial method.)

Exercise or Strike Price

Exercise is instantaneous with financial options. In the real options world, exercising an option typically involves development of a product, construction of a new facility, launching a large marketing campaign, etc., which does not happen in an instant but in fact takes a long time. This shortens the true life of the option compared to the stated life. For example, the true life of an option to turn a patent into a marketable product is less than the stated life because of the long product development and commercialization time.

The strike price or the investment cost directly impacts the option value, the sensitivity of which must be evaluated to gain better insight into the option value. It is possible that the strike price may change during the option life, and therefore, the option valuation equations must be adjusted accordingly. (An example in Chapter 7 shows how the binomial method allows such adjustment.)

Option Life

The time to maturity is clearly known (written in the contract) for a financial option, but, in most cases, that is not true for a real option. Often, you do not know exactly how long the opportunity will exist to exercise the option, and usually there is no deadline by which the decision must be made. For example, it may be difficult to know how long it will take to develop a product before it can be launched commercially. The option life has to be long enough for the uncertainty to clear, but not so long that the option value becomes meaningless because of entry of competitors in the meantime. In the case of a financial option, the value of the option increases with time to maturity, because the range of possible payoff values increases with long time frames, thereby boosting the upside potential. With real options, this relationship is not so direct, except when dealing with proprietary or patented assets. Issues related to loss of market share due to late market entry, loss of first mover advantage, competitive threats, and so on can reduce the option value even when the time to maturity increases.

Time Increments in the Model Framework

The Black-Scholes model offers a closed form analytical solution that does not require the life of the option to be split into time increments, as the binomial or any lattice-based method does. The binomial solution will approach Black-Scholes results as the time increments in the equation are increased. We believe that five or six time increments will suffice, and the final option value will not be significantly different from the Black-Scholes solution. In comparison to the errors involved in estimating many of the input parameters, the impact of the time increments in the model framework on the final option value may be insignificant.

Risk-Free Interest Rate

The risk-free annual interest rate used in real options models is usually determined on the basis of the U.S. Treasury spot rate of return, with its maturity equivalent to the option's time to maturity. The Black-Scholes and binomial models use continuously compounded discount rates as opposed to discretely compounded rates. The continuous rate can be calculated from the discretely compounded rate as follows:

$$r_f = \ln(1 + r_d) \qquad (6\text{-}5)$$

where r_f and r_d are the continuously and discretely compounded risk-free rates, respectively.

WHAT IS THE RIGHT MODEL?

In view of the foregoing discussion on the validity of the financial models for real options applications and the issues related to the input parameters, an obvious question for a practitioner to ask is: What is the best model to use to solve a given options problem?

Although several models are available to solve options problems, as discussed in Chapter 5, the Black-Scholes and binomial methods are by far the most commonly used, followed by simulations. The former two methods are able to address most of the issues presented in the preceding discussion on the input variables. The difference, however, basically lies in how easily you can adjust the model to account for those issues and how effectively you can explain the results to your audience. The following section presents a brief discussion on the real world applicability of the models to real option problems.

Black-Scholes Equation

The Black-Scholes equation may seem to be the right method for real options analysis (ROA) because it is so widely employed in financial options valuation and easy to use. But its application in real options is limited for many reasons:

■   It is difficult to explain the derivation of the equation because of its mathematical complexity. This promotes a "black box" approach, where the intuition behind the application is lost, thereby making it difficult to get management buy-in.

■ Black and Scholes developed their model for European financial options, which means that the option is exercised only on a fixed date and no dividends are paid during the option life. Real options can be exercised at any time during their life and, as discussed earlier in this chapter, there can be leakages, which are equivalent to the dividends of a financial security. The Black-Scholes equation can be adjusted for leakages as follows when the leakage is at a constant rate (Damodaran, 2002):

$$C = N(d_1)S_o \exp(-yT) - N(d_2)X \exp(-rT) \qquad (6\text{-}6)$$

$$d_1 = [\ln(S_o/X) + (r - y + 0.5\sigma^2)T]/\sigma\sqrt{T} \qquad (6\text{-}7)$$

where y is the dividend yield (dividend/current asset value) and the rest of the terms are as defined in Chapter 5. If the leakage is nonuniform, it will be difficult to adjust the model.

■ Black-Scholes assumes a lognormal distribution of the underlying asset value, which may not be true with the cash flows related to real assets.

■ Black-Scholes also assumes that the increase in the underlying asset value is continuous as dictated by its volatility and does not account for any drastic ups and downs (jumps).

■ Black-Scholes allows only one strike price for the option, which can change for a real option during its life.

While some of these limitations can be overcome by making adjustments to the Black-Scholes approach, the already complex model becomes even more complex.

Simulations

Simulations are more easily applicable to European options, where there is a fixed exercise date. The computations, however, become tedious when simulating all the possible option exercise dates for an American option. For example, you may run 1,000 simulations to value a one-year European option. However, for an American option, in order to consider any exercise date during the year, you would have to run 1,000 simulations, 365 times each. It becomes an even bigger challenge when dealing with sequential options, because each decision leads to a new path. For example, a project with one binary decision will involve twice as many simulations, two sequential binary decision points will have four paths and therefore four times as many simulations, three decision points will have eight paths, four decision points will have sixteen paths, and so on. This can involve millions of simulations, which can be an enormous computational task even with today's fast computers.

Binomial Method

The binomial method offers the most flexibility compared to Black-Scholes and the simulation approach. Input parameters such as the strike price and volatility can be changed easily over the option life. Jumps and leakage also can be accommodated without any complex changes.

The key advantage the binomial method offers to a practitioner is that it is transparent in its underlying framework, making the results easy to explain to upper management for buy-in and approval.

While Black-Scholes gives you the most accurate option value, the binomial method is a close approximation to it. Because of the underlying mathematical framework of the binomial method, it will always be an approximation of the Black-Scholes equation. The higher the time increments used in the binomial method, the closer you will get to this value. However, with only four to six time steps, a relatively good approximation can be obtained. This is adequate for practical purposes, especially considering the errors involved in the input parameter estimates.

Binomial is the preferred method for most practitioners because its advantages far outweigh the drawbacks. We recommend that you employ both the binomial and Black-Scholes methods, because the latter can verify the results and give you more insight. When dealing with upper management, however, we suggest that you present and explain the results using the binomial framework for easier understanding of and buy-in to the valuation analysis. Binomial is our method of choice for solving the options examples presented in the rest of the book, because it is the most effective for communication and illustrative purposes. However, for comparison, we also briefly present Black-Scholes solutions wherever appropriate.

REAL WORLD APPLICATION OF REAL OPTIONS SOLUTIONS

Any real options valuation starts with framing the application. Options are available in every major project investment decision but often are not easily recognized or considered. For example, the abandonment option exists for every project investment, but for emotional reasons many decision makers do not like to think about project termination when they are initiating a new project. Some projects involve more than one option and perhaps one option that leads to other options. Identification and framing of such options may even be more difficult. The practitioner should take the time to map out the structure and sequence of options for easier understanding and easier valuation. Use of graphical images may help you as well as your target audience understand and appreciate the option better.

After framing the option application, the first question to ask is whether there is even a need for real options valuation in the first place. Perhaps DCF alone will suffice in providing the right information to make the investment decision. As discussed in Chapter 4, when the net present value is close to zero and the uncertainty and flexibility with contingent decisions are low, ROA may not provide much benefit. Even with high uncertainty, if it is only related to private risk with insignificant market risk, options valuation may not even be the right application to begin with.

If ROA is indeed the right tool, the next question is what options solution method would be appropriate. As suggested earlier, practitioners may want to use both the binomial and Black-Scholes methods, the former for flexibility, transparency, and easy communication and the latter to verify and gain better insight into the binomial results. In Chapters 7 and 8, we use the binomial method for detailed illustration of different option examples and compare the results with those of Black-Scholes wherever applicable. A six-step process basically similar to the solution provided in Chapter 5 is used for the binomial method outlined below.

A SIX-STEP PROCESS

Once the practitioner decides that ROA is the right tool for the project under consideration, a six-step process can be used to calculate and analyze the option value for the project using the binomial method.

1. Frame the application

Framing a real option is more difficult than framing a financial option. It involves describing the problem in simple words and pictures, identifying the option, and stating clearly the contingent decision and the decision rule. Some applications involve more than one decision or option. For example, chooser options may include abandon, defer, expand, contract, and other options. Compound options involve options on options, which may be parallel or sequential. You must identify these dependencies very clearly. Keeping the problem simple and making it more intuitive will help you communicate the results more effectively to get upper management's buy-in.

2. Identify the input parameters

The basic input parameters for the binomial method to value any type of option include the underlying asset value, strike price, option life, volatility factor, risk-free interest rate, and time increments to be used in the binomial tree. These parameters can be calculated using the approaches suggested earlier in this chapter. Additional information is required for some of the options, such as expansion and contraction options.

3. Calculate the option parameters

The option parameters are intermediates to the final option value calculations and are calculated from the input variables. These are the up (u) and down (d) factors and the risk-neutral probability (p) required for the binomial solution.

4. Build the binomial tree and calculate the asset values at each node of the tree

The binomial tree is built based on the number of time increments selected. The underlying asset value at each node of the tree is calculated starting with S_o at time zero at the left end of the tree and moving toward the right by using the up and down factors.

5. Calculate the option values at each node of the tree by backward induction

Starting at the far right side of the binomial tree, the decision rule is applied at each node and the optimum decision selected. The option value is identified as the asset value that reflects the optimum decision. Moving toward the left of the tree, the option values at each node are calculated by folding back the option values from the successor nodes by discounting them by a risk-free rate and using the risk-neutral probability factor. This process is continued until you reach the far left end of the tree, which reflects the option value of the project. Whereas asset valuation (step 4) shows the value of the underlying asset at each node without accounting for management decision, the option valuation step identifies the asset value that reflects management's optimal decision at that node.

6. Analyze the results

After the option value has been calculated, the appropriate first step is to compare the net present value derived from the DCF method versus ROA and evaluate the value added as a result of the flexibility created by the option(s). In order to get a better perspective on the option solution, several analyses can be performed by asking the following questions, among many others:

- What would be the critical investment cost (strike price) that drives the option at the money? If the critical cost is exceeded, a call option moves out of the money.
- What is the sensitivity of the option value to the uncertainty represented by the volatility factor, investment cost, discount rate, time to expiration, etc.?
- What is the probability that an option may have to be abandoned versus continued, expanded, or contracted?
- What is the option "space" which shows when to abandon, contract, expand, continue, or modify the investment?
- How would the option value change if there are jumps or leaks associated with it?
- How do the option values based on the binomial method versus Black-Scholes compare?
- Is the asset value influenced by market uncertainty only? If private uncertainty also exists, does it precede or co-exist with market uncertainty?
- Are there multiple sources of uncertainty, and if so, what is their individual impact on the real options value?
- Does the exercise of the current option create one or more additional options?
- How does the real options value change if a compound option problem is reframed as an equivalent simple option?
- What if the framing of the option is changed?

These and other similar questions help you in gauging the validity and reliability of the option results and give you better insight into the option characteristics of the project, so that you can ultimately make better investment decisions. The next two chapters demonstrate how to calculate the option values for different types of options using examples similar to real world projects.

PROBLEMS

6-1. For the following cash flow data (in million dollars), calculate the quarterly volatility factor using the logarithmic cash flow returns method.

Date	Cash Flow
12/31/04	$243
9/30/04	$220
6/30/04	$181
3/31/04	$182

12/31/03	$176
9/30/03	$162
6/30/03	$149
3/31/03	$152
12/31/02	$144
9/30/02	$132
6/30/02	$125
3/31/02	$100

6-2. What is the annual volatility factor for the above problem?

6-3. For the data given in the following table (in million dollars), calculate the annual volatility of the asset value and the standard deviation of the volatility using the Monte Carlo simulation method.

					Year						
	0	1	2	3	4	5	6	7	8	9	10
Investment cost	$25										
Base case annual cost		$6	$6	$7	$7	$9	$10	$11	$9	$8	$7
Base case annual revenue		$10	$12	$15	$16	$18	$22	$23	$20	$18	$15
Standard deviation of annual costs	4%										
Standard deviation of annual revenues	35%										
Risk-adjusted discount rate	20%										
No. of simulations	1,000										

6-4. Senior management estimates the optimistic and pessimistic payoffs over the next five years of a project under scrutiny to be $300 million and $55 million, respectively. What is the annual volatility of the payoff?

SIMPLE OPTIONS

In the last three chapters, the real options analysis (ROA) tool was introduced, along with discussion of how it can be applied for project valuation using different options models. In this chapter, several real world examples are presented to illustrate how ROA can be applied for project valuation. The following simple options are the focus of this chapter:

- Option to abandon
- Option to expand
- Option to contract
- Option to choose
- Option to wait
- Barrier options

For each option example, the six-step process presented in the previous chapter is applied. First, the problem is framed, then the solution is shown in an easily understood step-by-step process, and finally the results are analyzed and the options application discussed. For every option, the discussion focuses on one or two aspects (such as practical issues, input parameter variability, etc.) that are most relevant to that option type. For instance, the option to abandon discussion involves how to solve the options problem for various strike prices. How to calculate the probability of exercising the option, that is, abandoning the project, is also illustrated. In the case of the option to expand, the effect of option life on the option value is shown. Using the option to contract example, the impact of the volatility factor on the option value is highlighted. The discussion on the chooser option, where the best of the available options, including the option to abandon, contract, and expand, is chosen, presents the differences in the option value between the combined chooser option versus the individual options of abandonment, expansion, and contraction for a given project investment. Finally, the analysis of the option to wait discusses how leakage of asset value can be accounted for in the options calculation. The binomial model is our choice for all the examples because of its benefits as discussed in the previous chapter. For comparison, however, options results based on the Black-Scholes model are also presented wherever applicable.

OPTION TO ABANDON

The option to abandon is embedded in virtually every project. This option is especially valuable where the net present value (NPV) is marginal but there is a great potential for losses. As the uncertainty surrounding the payoff clears and if the payoff is not attractive, you can abandon the project early on without incurring significant losses. The losses can be minimized by selling off the project assets either on the spot or preferably by prearranged contracts. The contingent decision in this option is to abandon the project if the expected payoff (the underlying asset value) falls below the project salvage value, the strike price. This option therefore has the characteristics of a put option.

Example

1. Frame the application
Bio Pharma is a drug-related-products company with a number of initiatives in its R&D pipeline. One of the new patented product ideas from its R&D lab has become a lead candidate for a development effort because of its potential market demand. The total estimated cost to launch the product, including its development, is estimated to be $95 million. Code-named Bluneon, it faces stiff competition, however, from other major projects in the pipeline. The vice president of the division concerned decides to create a strategic abandonment option.

The discounted cash flow (DCF) analysis on Bluneon's market potential shows that the present value of the payoff discounted at an appropriate market risk-adjusted discount rate would be $100 million. At any time during the next five years of development, based on the results, Bio Pharma can either continue with the development effort or sell off its intellectual property for $65 million (considered the salvage value) to a strategic partner. This technology is of importance to the partner, because it can upsell it to its existing customer base. The annual volatility of the logarithmic returns of the future cash flows is calculated to be 35%, and the continuous annual riskless interest rate over the next five years is 5%. What is the value of the abandonment option?

2. Identify the input parameters

S_o = \$100 million
X = \$65 million
T = 5 years
σ = 35%
r = 5%
δt = 1 year

3. Calculate the option parameters

u = $\exp(\sigma\sqrt{\delta t})$
   = $\exp(0.35 * \sqrt{1})$
   = 1.419

d = $1/u$
   = 1/1.419
   = 0.705

p = $\dfrac{\exp(r\delta t) - d}{u - d}$

p = $[\exp(0.05 * 1) - 0.705]/(1.419 - 0.705)$
   = 0.485

4. Build the binomial tree and calculate the asset values at each node of the tree

Build a binomial tree, as shown in Figure 7-1, using one-year time intervals for five years and calculate the asset values over the life of the option. Start with S_o at the very first node on the left and multiply it by the up factor and down factor to obtain $S_o u$ (\$100 million $*$ 1.419 = \$142 million) and $S_o d$ (\$100 million $*$ 0.705 = \$70 million), respectively, for the first time step. Moving to the right, continue in a similar fashion for every node of the binomial tree until the last time step. In Figure 7-1, the top value at each node represents the asset value at that node.

5. Calculate the option values at each node of the tree by backward induction

Figure 7-1 shows the option values (bottom italicized numbers) at each node of the binomial tree by backward induction. Each node represents the value maximization of abandonment versus continuation. At every node, you have an option to either abandon the project for a salvage value of \$65 million or continue keeping the option open until it expires.

   A. Start with the terminal nodes that represent the last time step. At node $S_o u^5$, the expected asset value is \$575 million, compared to the salvage value of \$65 million. Since you want to maximize your return, you

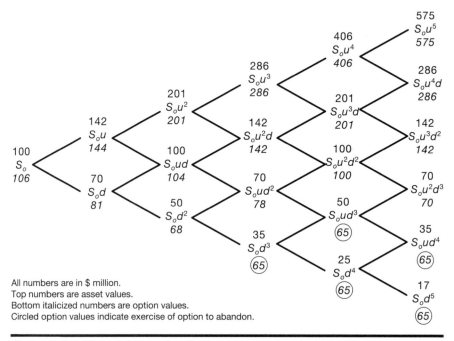

All numbers are in $ million.
Top numbers are asset values.
Bottom italicized numbers are option values.
Circled option values indicate exercise of option to abandon.

Figure 7-1.   Binomial Tree for Option to Abandon for Bio Pharma

would continue rather than abandon the project. Thus the option value
at this node is $575 million.

B.   At node $S_o ud^4$, the expected asset value is $35 million, compared to the
salvage value of $65 million; therefore, it makes sense to sell off the
asset and abandon the project, which makes the option value at this node
$65 million.

C.   Next, move on to the intermediate nodes, one step away from the last
time step. Starting at the top, at node $S_o u^4$, calculate the expected asset
value for keeping the option open. This is simply the discounted (at the
risk-free rate) weighted average of potential future option values using
the risk-neutral probability as weights:

$$[p(S_o u^5) + (1 - p)(S_o u^4 d)] * \exp(-r\delta t)$$

$$= [0.485(\$575 \text{ million}) + (1 - 0.485)(\$286 \text{ million})]$$
$$* \exp(-0.05)(1)$$

$$= \$406 \text{ million}$$

Since this value is larger than the salvage value of $65 million, you would keep the option open and continue; therefore, the option value at $S_o u^4$ is $406 million.

D. Similarly, at node $S_o u d^3$, the expected asset value for keeping the option open, taking into account the downstream optimal decisions, is:

$$[0.485(\$70 \text{ million}) + (1 - 0.485)(\$65 \text{ million})] * \exp(-0.05)(1)$$

$$= \$64 \text{ million}$$

Since this value is smaller than the salvage value of $65 million, you would sell the assets for the salvage value and abandon the project.

E. Complete the option valuation binomial tree all the way to time = 0 using the approach outlined above.

6. Analyze the results

The payoff of the project based on the DCF method without flexibility is $100 million, but the cost to develop and launch the product is $95 million, leaving a relatively small project NPV of $5 million. ROA, however, shows a total project value of $106 million, yielding an additional $6 million ($106 million – $100 million) due to the abandonment option. This is exactly the same value obtained by using the Black-Scholes equation for this put option. Thus, the project NPV more than doubled ($5 million + $6 million = $11 million) because of the abandonment option. This can make an important difference to the survival of the Bluneon product in Bio Pharma's R&D portfolio.

Additional information on the probability of the survival of Bluneon also can be of use to the portfolio manager in making the investment decision. That information can be obtained easily from the binomial lattice used in solving the options problem. An examination of Figure 7-1 (or any five-year recombining lattice with one-year time increments) reveals six possible asset values at the end nodes of the five-time-step binomial lattice. Of the six, two nodes are below the strike price and hence will trigger the option exercise. At the surface, it may seem, therefore, that the probability of exercising the option — that is, abandoning the project — at the end of the option life is 2/6 or 0.33. This in fact is wrong.

Since the binomial tree in this example is recombining, there are many different paths leading to each node. The number of paths contributing to each node must be calculated first before estimating the probability of exercising the option at the end of the option life. This can be done using Pascal's triangle (named after the discoverer), as shown in Figure 7-2. If the triangle is rotated 90 degrees counterclockwise, it will represent a binomial lattice showing the

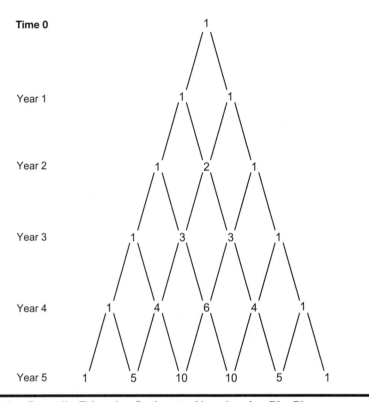

Figure 7-2. Pascal's Triangle: Option to Abandon for Bio Pharma

number of paths each node represents. Each node's value in this triangle is the sum of the values of the two nodes that lead up to that node. This shows the total number of paths for all the end nodes combined in a five-step binomial lattice to be 32 (1 + 5 + 10 + 10 + 5 + 1). The total number of paths corresponding to the two bottom end nodes where the abandonment option will be exercised in our example is 6 (5 + 1 = 6). Therefore, the probability that the project will be abandoned at the end of the option life is 6/32 = 19%. Conversely, the probability that the project will succeed is 81%. This information can be helpful in making decisions in a project portfolio context when projects with similar NPVs and even similar option values are compared.

The option to abandon is a put option where the option has value if the underlying asset value falls below the strike price and its value increases as the strike price increases. In comparison, a call option has no value if the asset value is below the strike price and its value increases as the strike price decreases. Using sensitivity analysis, you can calculate the "critical" strike price below which the put option has no value. Such analysis can help you define and

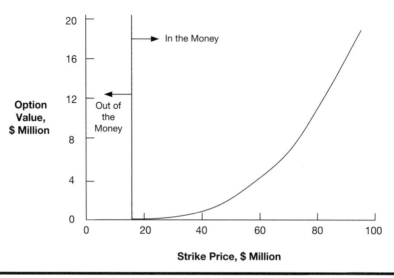

Figure 7-3. Critical Strike Price for Bio Pharma to Sell Bluneon

negotiate abandonment alternatives such as asset sell-off price, insurance contracts, and so on.

In the case of Bluneon, if the uncertainty clears and the payoff (that is, the asset value) is expected to be less than $65 million, Bio Pharma will sell off the intellectual property for $65 million, thus limiting its downside. If the payoff is expected to be more than $65 million, Bio Pharma will continue with its development effort. Figure 7-3 exhibits the relationship between the strike price and the option value, indicating a critical (that is, minimum) strike price for Bluneon to be approximately $17 million. This means that the abandonment option has no value if Bio Pharma sells Bluneon's intellectual assets for less than $17 million. In this example, the strike price is built into the contract between Bio Pharma and its strategic partner and remains the same for the entire life of the option. In many cases, this is not true. Some common issues related to the strike price of an abandonment option are:

1. The salvage value cannot be determined with complete certainty.
2. The strike price can change from year to year during the life of the option. Changing strike prices is a common problem in the high-tech industry, where assets can lose considerable value each passing year due to short product shelf life.
3. The abandonment of the project can even cost a company— instead of providing positive salvage value — due to environmental cleanup, severance wages, or some such factor.

If there is uncertainty related to the salvage value, you can use the sensitivity analysis, as we did for the Bluneon example. If the strike price changes over the life of the option, the changes easily can be incorporated into the value maximization rule used in calculating the option values during the backward induction process, as illustrated in the next example. If abandonment costs are too high, perhaps an option to contract may be a better alternative, which is discussed later in this chapter.

Option to Abandon with Varying Strike Price

Immaculate Identifiers plans to enter the radio frequency identification (RFID) market by developing software that would support the entire RFID supply chain. This requires a substantial investment including the hardware (RFID readers, tags, servers, etc.). The expected payoff from this project is estimated to be $500 million with an annual volatility factor of 50%. If the market conditions turn sour anytime during the next five years, the company is willing to abandon the project and recoup some of the investment by salvaging the hardware. Immaculate Identifiers expects the salvage value of the assets to decrease by 30% annually, starting at $300 million for the first year. The company is interested in calculating the value of the abandonment option given a continuous annual risk-free interest rate of 5% over the next five years.

The input parameters and the values of u, d, and p for this problem are summarized in Table 7-1. In solving this problem, the binomial tree is first built showing the asset values. The top values at each node of the tree shown in Figure 7-4 represent the asset values. However, in calculating the option values during backward induction, instead of applying the same strike price at every node of the binomial lattice to determine the contingent decision, you apply the strike price of $72 million for year 5 at the end nodes, $103 million at the nodes for year 4, $147 million at the nodes for year 3, and so on. For example, at node $S_o d^5$, the expected asset value is $41 million, which is compared to the salvage value of $72 million for year 5. Since the salvage value is greater, the decision will be to abandon the project. At node $S_o d^4$ for year 4, the salvage value is $103 million, which is compared to the expected asset value for keeping the option open, taking into account the downstream optimal decisions:

$$[0.427(\$112 \text{ million}) + (1 - 0.427)(\$72 \text{ million})] * \exp(-0.05)(1) = \$85 \text{ million}$$

Since the salvage value is higher, the decision at $S_o d^4$ will be to abandon the project. By completing the option value calculations using varying strike prices across the entire binomial tree, the option value for the RFID project is

Table 7-1. Option to Abandon with Varying Strike Prices

Input Parameters	
S_o	$500 million
T	5 years
X	
Year 1	$300 million
Year 2	$210 million
Year 3	$147 million
Year 4	$103 million
Year 5	$72 million
σ	50%
r	5%
δt	1 year
Calculated Parameters	
u	1.649
d	0.607
p	0.427

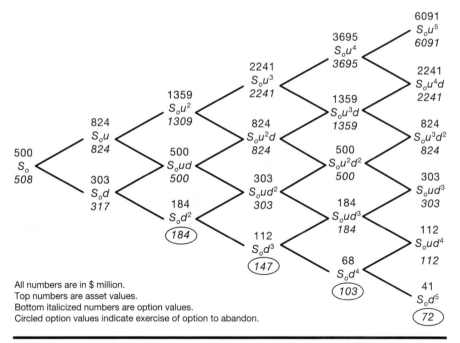

All numbers are in $ million.
Top numbers are asset values.
Bottom italicized numbers are option values.
Circled option values indicate exercise of option to abandon.

Figure 7-4. Binomial Tree for Option to Abandon with Changing Strike Price for Immaculate Identifiers

estimated to be $8 million. If the strike price were to be $300 million across the entire lattice, the option would be incorrectly overvalued at $53 million. Similarly, even with an average strike price ($166 million) for the entire life of the option, the option would be incorrectly overvalued at $17 million. The binomial method not only provides the flexibility to incorporate changing strike prices into the option solution but also makes it transparent, which the other methods fail to do.

OPTION TO EXPAND

The option to expand is common in high-growth companies, especially during economic booms. For some projects, the initial NPV can be marginal or even negative, but when growth opportunities with high uncertainty exist, the option to expand can provide significant value. You may accept a negative or low NPV in the short term because of the high potential for growth in the future. Without considering an expansion option, great opportunities may be ignored due to a short-term outlook. Investment for expansion is the strike price that will be incurred as a result of exercising the option. The option would be exercised if the expected payoff is greater than the strike price, thereby making it a call option.

Example

1. Frame the application
Voodoo Video Vision has just introduced video-on-demand services in two major metropolitan areas in the United States. The initial market response has been lukewarm but not totally disappointing. The DCF valuation of the project free cash flows using a risk-adjusted discount rate currently indicates a present value of $80 million over the project life. Using the project proxy approach, the annual volatility of the logarithmic returns on these cash flows is calculated to be 30%. The company believes there is great potential for its services in seven other metropolitan areas and decides to explore the option to expand. This move is expected to result in a threefold expansion of current operations, at a cost of expansion of $200 million. What is the value of the expansion option over the next four years, if the continuous annual riskless interest rate for that time period is 5%?

2. Identify the input parameters
S_o = $80 million
T = 4 years

$\sigma = 30\%$
$r = 5\%$
Expansion factor $= 3.0$
Cost of expansion $= \$200$ million
$\delta t = 1$ year

3. Calculate the option parameters
$u = \exp(\sigma\sqrt{\delta t})$
$ = \exp(0.30 * \sqrt{1})$
$ = 1.350$
$d = 1/u$
$ = 1/1.350 = 0.741$
$p = \dfrac{\exp(r\delta t) - d}{u - d}$
$ = [\exp(0.05 * 1) - 0.741]/(1.350 - 0.741)$
$ = 0.510$

4. Build the binomial tree and calculate the asset values at each node of the tree

Build a binomial tree, as shown in Figure 7-5, using one-year time intervals for four years and calculate the asset values over the life of the option. Start with S_o at the very first node on the left and multiply it by the up factor and down

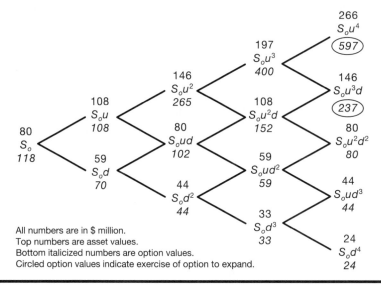

All numbers are in $ million.
Top numbers are asset values.
Bottom italicized numbers are option values.
Circled option values indicate exercise of option to expand.

Figure 7-5. Binomial Tree for Option to Expand for Voodoo Video Vision

factor to obtain $S_o u$ ($80 million * 1.350 = $108 million) and $S_o d$ ($80 million * 0.741 = $59 million), respectively, for the first time step. Moving to the right, continue in a similar fashion for every node of the binomial tree until the last time step. In Figure 7-5, the top value at each node represents the asset value at that node.

5. Calculate the option values at each node of the tree by backward induction
Figure 7-5 shows the option values (bottom italicized numbers) at each node of the binomial tree calculated by backward induction. Each node represents the value maximization of continuation versus expansion by threefold at a cost of $200 million. At every node, you have an option to either continue the operation and keep the option open for the future or expand it by three times by committing the investment for expansion.

A. Start with the terminal nodes that represent the last time step. At node $S_o u^4$, the expected asset value is $266 million. However, if you invest $200 million and expand the operation by threefold, the asset value would be: (3 * $266 million) – $200 million = $597 million. Since you want to maximize your return, you would expand rather than continue, because expansion results in an asset value of $597 million, whereas continuation of the status quo would yield a value of only $266 million. Thus the option value at this node would become $597 million.

B. At node $S_o u^2 d^2$, the expected asset value with no expansion is $80 million. However, if you invest $200 million and grow the operation by threefold, the asset value would be: (3 * $80 million) – $200 million = $40 million. To maximize your return, you would continue your operations without expansion, because that gives you an asset value of $80 million, whereas expansion would result in only $40 million.

C. Next, move on to the intermediate nodes, one step away from the last time step. Starting at the top, at node $S_o u^3$, calculate the expected asset value for keeping the option open and accounting for the downstream optimal decisions. This is simply the discounted (at the risk-free rate) weighted average of potential future option values using the risk-neutral probability. That value, for example, at node $S_o u^3$, is:

$$[p(S_o u^4) + (1 - p)(S_o u^3 d)] * \exp(-r\delta t)$$

$$= [0.510(\$597 \text{ million}) + (1 - 0.510)(\$237 \text{ million})] * \exp(-0.05)(1)$$

$$= \$400 \text{ million}$$

If the option is exercised to expand the operation by three times by spending $200 million, the expected asset value would be:

$$(3.0 * \$197 \text{ million}) - \$200 \text{ million} = \$391 \text{ million}$$

Since this value is less than the $400 million that corresponds to the alternative to continue, you would not exercise the expand option, and the option value at this node would be $400 million.

D. Similarly, at node $S_o ud^2$, the expected asset value for keeping the option open, taking into account the downstream optimal decision, is:

$$[0.510(\$80 \text{ million}) + (1 - 0.510)(\$44 \text{ million})] * \exp(-0.05)(1)$$

$$= \$59 \text{ million}$$

If, on the other hand, you exercise the option to expand the operation by three times at a cost of $200 million, the expected asset value would be:

$$(3.0 * \$59 \text{ million}) - \$200 \text{ million} = -\$23 \text{ million}$$

Maximizing $59 million versus –$23 million, you would not exercise the expand option. Therefore, the option value at node $S_o ud^3$ would be $59 million.

E. Complete the option valuation binomial tree all the way to time = 0.

6. Analyze the results

Let us first compare the value of the expansion option based on DCF versus ROA. The present value of the cash flows for the current operations based on the risk-adjusted DCF method is $80 million. If the operation were to be expanded today, the additional value created would be:

$$3.0(\$80 \text{ million}) - \$80 \text{ million} = \$160 \text{ million}$$

Since the investment is $200 million, the NPV of the expansion project would be:

$$\$160 \text{ million} - \$200 \text{ million} = -\$40 \text{ million}$$

This means that your decision would be not to expand. However, ROA suggests that the expanded project's worth (taking into account the investment cost of

$200 million) is $118 million. This means that the NPV of the expansion project is $38 million after subtracting the present value of the cash flows associated with the current operations ($118 million – $80 million). The expansion option value calculated using the Black-Scholes equation for a call option is $36 million, which is fairly close to the value ($38 million) obtained through binomial lattice calculations. Comparing this with the baseline NPV of –$40 million for the project, the additional value provided by the expansion option, therefore, is:

$$\$38 \text{ million} - (-\$40 \text{ million}) = \$78 \text{ million}$$

The difference is substantial and is the value added to the project because of the real options approach which management can take into consideration in decision making. Management may decide to keep the option of expansion open at this time and exercise it when the uncertainty clears and conditions become favorable.

Some of the practical considerations with this option relate to the expansion factor, volatility of the underlying asset value, cost of expansion (strike price), and time until the option expires.

The expansion factor is based on the underlying asset value, because it represents the cash flows from not only the current operation but also the expansion. It is estimated through correlations between the current operation and future expansion. The volatility of the asset value is kept constant due to the implicit assumption that it is the same for the current as well as the expanded operation. This is an important consideration because the framework of the option used in this example will not be applicable if the cash flow structure (asset value and its volatility) is significantly different for the expansion operation. For example, if Voodoo Video Vision is considering expanding its operations into China, the underlying asset value and its volatility would be expected to follow a different profile due to the difference in demographics compared to the current operation in the United States.

Voodoo Video Vision's estimated cost of expansion ($200 million) and the expansion factor (3.0) may change over time for the same demographics even within the United States. You can easily incorporate these changes into the binomial lattice and recalculate the results because of the flexibility it provides. In this example, however, considering that the company has already launched the project in two markets, it presumably has relatively good estimates for these factors. It is also implicitly assumed in this analysis that Voodoo Video Vision has access to capital and the other resources needed for expansion; otherwise the option valuation calculation may be meaningless after all. The framing of a real option problem should be rooted in reality.

Although the option to expand is implicit in most operations, the ROA calculation helps to quantify the value of the option. If the expansion option is indeed valuable, then management can take the necessary steps to keep the option alive. To clear the uncertainty, management can have a process in place to periodically gather information on market demand or arrange for a market study to proactively gather information on the asset value for better decision making.

In framing an expansion option, as is the case for many other options, a practitioner most likely is challenged with what value should be used for the option's time to expire, one of the inputs to the options model. You may not want to choose a long time frame because competitors can enter the market and change the cash flow profile. Competition can be a big factor if your technology is not protected by patents or the barriers to entry are low. Another factor that works against long option time frames is the ever-decreasing product life in today's marketplace — especially for technology products. By using longer option lifetimes, you may end up overvaluing the option. On the other hand, a shorter time to expiration may not be desirable either, as there may not be enough time for the uncertainty surrounding the cash flows to clear, which would make the option valuation exercise meaningless. It is therefore important to think through the time implications and use the appropriate value for the option's time to expire.

In the Voodoo Video Vision example, a four-year time frame is used because it is assumed that competition will not have a significant impact on cash flows if the company expands within four years. A sensitivity analysis as a function of the option's time to expire would reveal that the option value will change as follows:

2 years	$62 million
3 years	$67 million
4 years	**$78 million**
5 years	$83 million

In the Voodoo Video Vision example, the option is framed as an expansion option. However, the expansion can be valued as a separate project by itself instead of as an expansion of the current operation. In that case, it can be considered an option to wait, where the underlying asset would be valued at $160 million (3.0 ∗ $80 million − $80 million) and the other input parameters kept the same. (An example of an option to wait is presented in Chapter 5 and another example is discussed in detail toward the end of this chapter.) The solution of this option yields exactly the same results as the option to expand. You may want to treat the expansion of current operations as an option to wait if the underlying asset value and its volatility have a different structure compared to the current operation, a scenario mentioned earlier in this section.

Growth companies and novel products are good candidates to be considered for expansion options. Such assets have very high market uncertainty and hence start out on a small scale, but as uncertainty clears, they can be expanded if conditions are favorable.

OPTION TO CONTRACT

The option to contract is significant in today's competitive marketplace, where companies need to downsize or outsource swiftly as external conditions change. Organizations can hedge themselves through strategically created options to contract. The option to contract has the same characteristics as a put option, because the option value increases as the value of the underlying asset decreases.

Example

1. Frame the application
Contracting Cars recently introduced a new product line and built two assembly plants in the United States. Now it appears that a Chinese automaker is going to introduce a similar line of cars in the U.S. market at a 30% cheaper cost. Contracting Cars is contemplating scaling down its operations by either selling or outsourcing one of the two plants to gain efficiencies through consolidation within the next five years. It frames an option to contract the size of its current operation by a factor of two and gain $250 million in savings because of lower general overhead expenses. Using the traditional DCF analysis and appropriate risk-adjusted discount rate, the present value of the future free cash flows of both plants is $600 million. The annual volatility of the logarithmic returns on the future cash flows is estimated to be 35%, and the continuous annual risk-free interest rate is 5% over the option life. What would be the value of the option to contract?

2. Identify the input parameters
S_o = $600 million
T = 5 years
σ = 35%
r = 5%
Contraction factor = 0.5
Savings of contraction = $250 million
δt = 1 year

3. Calculate the option parameters

u = $\exp(\sigma\sqrt{\delta t})$
    = $\exp(0.35 * \sqrt{1})$
    = 1.419

d = $1/u$
    = $1/1.419$ = 0.705

p = $\dfrac{\exp(r\delta t) - d}{u - d}$
    = $[\exp(0.05 * 1) - 0.705]/(1.419 - 0.705)$
    = 0.485

4. Build the binomial tree and calculate the asset values at each node of the tree

Build a binomial tree, as shown in Figure 7-6, using one-year time intervals for five years and calculate the asset values over the life of the option. Start with S_o at the very first node on the left and multiply it by the up factor and down factor to obtain S_ou ($600 million * 1.419 = $851 million) and S_od ($600 million * 0.705 = $423 million), respectively, for the first time step. Moving to the right,

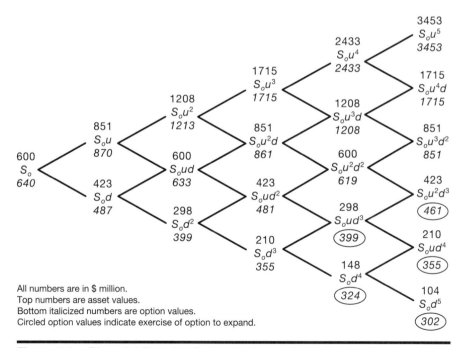

All numbers are in $ million.
Top numbers are asset values.
Bottom italicized numbers are option values.
Circled option values indicate exercise of option to expand.

Figure 7-6. Binomial Tree for Option to Contract for Contracting Cars

continue in a similar fashion for every node of the binomial tree until the last time step. In Figure 7-6, the top value at each node represents the asset value at that node.

5. Calculate the option values at each node of the tree by backward induction
Figure 7-6 shows the option values (bottom italicized numbers) at each node of the binomial tree calculated by backward induction. Each node represents the value maximization of continuation versus contraction by 50% with savings of $250 million. At every node, you have an option to either continue the operation and keep the option open or contract it by half.

A. Start with the terminal nodes that represent the last time step. At node $S_o u^5$, the expected asset value is $3,453 million. However, if you shrink the operation by half and save $250 million, the asset value would be: (0.5 * $3,453 million) + $250 million = $1,977 million. Since your objective is to maximize your return ($3,453 million versus $1,977 million), you would continue rather than contract. Thus the option value at this node becomes $3,453 million.

B. At node $S_o u^2 d^3$, the expected asset value without contraction is $423 million. However, if you shrink the operation by half and save $250 million, the asset value would be: (0.5 * $423 million) + $250 million = $461 million. Since you want to maximize your return ($423 million versus $461 million), you would contract rather than continue. Your option value at $S_o u^2 d^3$ would, therefore, be $461 million.

C. Next, move on to the intermediate nodes, one step away from the last time step. Starting at the top, at node $S_o u^4$, calculate the expected asset value for keeping the option open and accounting for the downstream optimal decisions. This is simply the discounted (at the risk-free rate) weighted average of potential future option values using the risk-neutral probability. That value at node $S_o u^4$ is:

$$[p(S_o u^5) + (1 - p)(S_o u^4 d)] * \exp(-r\delta t)$$
$$= [0.485(\$3,453 \text{ million}) + (1 - 0.485)(\$1,715 \text{ million})]$$
$$* \exp(-0.05)(1)$$
$$= \$2,433 \text{ million}$$

If the option is exercised to shrink the operation by half to gain a savings of $250 million, the expected asset value would be:

(0.5 * $2,433 million) + $250 million = $1,467 million

Since this value is less than the $2,433 million corresponding to the alternative to continue, you would not exercise the contract option, and the option value at this node would be $2,433 million.

D. Similarly, at node $S_o ud^3$, the expected asset value for keeping the option open, taking into account the downstream optimal decisions, is:

$$[0.485(\$461 \text{ million}) + (1 - 0.485)(\$355 \text{ million})] * \exp(-0.05)(1)$$

$$= \$387 \text{ million}$$

If, on the other hand, you exercise the contract option to shrink the operation by half to gain a savings of $250 million, the expected asset value would be:

$$(0.5 * \$298 \text{ million}) + \$250 \text{ million} = \$399 \text{ million}$$

Maximizing $387 million versus $399 million, you would exercise the contract option. Therefore, the option value at node $S_o ud^3$ would be $399 million.

E. Complete the option valuation binomial tree all the way to time = 0.

6. Analyze the results

Let us first compare the NPV of the asset based on DCF versus ROA. The present value of the project based on the risk-adjusted DCF method is $600 million, compared to the real options value (ROV) of $640 million. The difference of $40 million is the value added to the project from the ROA which management can take into consideration in making its decision today on contraction. The Black-Scholes equation provides a value of $33 million for this put option, which is relatively close to the binomial lattice option value. If Contracting Cars wanted to contract its operations today, the present value of the contracted project would be:

$$(0.5 * \$600 \text{ million}) + \$250 \text{ million} = \$550 \text{ million}$$

Since this is less than the expected present value of $600 million for the current operation, Contracting Cars would not contract. However, the looming competition from China may have a significant impact on this expected payoff. Because of this uncertainty, it is possible that one of the plants would have to be shut down. How do you calculate the impact of that uncertainty on the value of the operation? This is where ROA gives us the answers. You can capture the value and impact of the uncertainty through ROA. In the foregoing example,

Table 7-2. Option to Contract: Option Values Versus Volatility

Volatility	Option Value
0%	$0
10%	$0.7
15%	$5
25%	$21
35%	$40
45%	$59
55%	$78
100%	$148

we used a volatility factor of 35%, but you can easily calculate the option values for various volatility factors using the same approach as illustrated above. The option values from such calculations are shown in Table 7-2. The option value increases by almost 50% as the volatility increases 10% (from 35% to 45%) and decreases by the same factor as the volatility decreases 10% (from 35% to 25%).

Volatility of the asset value has a significant impact on the value of any option. The higher the volatility of the underlying asset value, the higher the range of asset values at any given time frame on the binomial tree. More important, as the volatility increases, the option value also increases, as pointed out in Chapter 6. On the contrary, as the volatility factor approaches zero, the *u* and *d* factors will approach 1.0 and the binomial tree collapses into a straight line (Figure 7-7). At zero volatility, for the example above, the ROV will be $600 million, which is the same as the baseline payoff. This means that when the uncertainty is zero, real options do not add any value. If Contracting Cars is absolutely certain about its future payoff of $600 million, there is no real option value. Thus, DCF can be considered a special case of ROA where the uncertainty is zero. This also shows that ROA is not a substitute for but a logical extension of the DCF that takes project valuation to the next level of sophistication.

One of the other inputs in the Contracting Cars example is the contraction factor. As in the case of an expansion option, it is important for the practitioner to choose the contraction factor that accurately reflects the cash flow stream of the contracted operation. Contracting Cars has two assembly plants, and management wants to consider selling one of them as part of the contraction. The contraction factor of 0.5 is appropriate only if the two plants are contributing equally to the cash flow streams. If the cash flows of the two plants are different, the contraction factor needs to be adjusted accordingly.

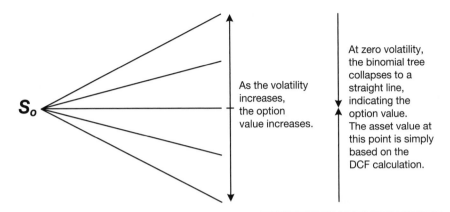

As the volatility increases, the option value increases.

At zero volatility, the binomial tree collapses to a straight line, indicating the option value. The asset value at this point is simply based on the DCF calculation.

Figure 7-7.   Binomial Tree: Same as Discounted Cash Flow at Zero Volatility

All real options have real value only if management will make the value-maximizing decision when faced with choices analyzed by ROA. In the real world, however, decisions are made based not just on quantitative data that can be obtained through an ROA calculation but on political and emotional considerations. The option to contract is especially sensitive to these issues, as it may involve loss of jobs and selling of assets. Therefore, caution should be exercised in framing and valuing an option to contract.

OPTION TO CHOOSE

The option to choose consists of multiple options combined as a single option. The multiple options are abandonment, expansion, and contraction. The reason it is called a chooser option is that you can choose to keep the option open and continue with the project or choose to exercise any one of the options to expand, contract, or abandon. The main advantage with this option is the choice. This is a unique option in the sense that, depending upon the choice to be made, it can be considered a put (abandonment or contraction) or call (expansion) option.

Example

1. Frame the application

Multiple Choice Drugs is faced with the dilemma of choosing among four strategies (continuation, expansion, contraction, or total abandonment) for one of its manufacturing operations. The present value of the projected future free cash flows for this operation using DCF analysis with the appropriate risk-adjusted discount rate is $200 million. The volatility of the logarithmic returns on the projected future cash flows is 25%, and the risk-free rate is 5% over the next five years. At any time during this time period, the company can expand by 30% by investing $50 million, contract one-quarter of its current operations to save $40 million, or abandon the operation altogether by selling the property for a salvage value of $100 million. What is the value of the chooser option for Multiple Choice Drugs?

2. Identify the input parameters
S_o = $200 million
T = 5 years
σ = 25%
r = 5%
Expansion factor = 1.3
Cost of expansion = $50 million
Contraction factor = 0.75
Savings of contraction = $40 million
Salvage value = $100 million
δt = 1 year

3. Calculate the option parameters
u = $\exp(\sigma\sqrt{\delta t})$
  = $\exp(0.25 * \sqrt{1})$
  = 1.284
d = $1/u$
  = $1/1.284$
  = 0.779
p = $\dfrac{\exp(r\delta t) - d}{u - d}$
  = $[\exp(0.05 * 1) - 0.779]/(1.284 - 0.779)$
  = 0.539

4. Build the binomial tree and calculate the asset values at each node of the tree
Build a binomial tree, as shown in Figure 7-8, using one-year time intervals for five years and calculate the asset values over the life of the option. Start with S_o at the very first node on the left and multiply it by the up factor and down factor to obtain $S_o u$ ($200 million * 1.284 = $257 million) and $S_o d$ ($200 million * 0.779 = $156 million), respectively, for the first time step. Moving to the right,

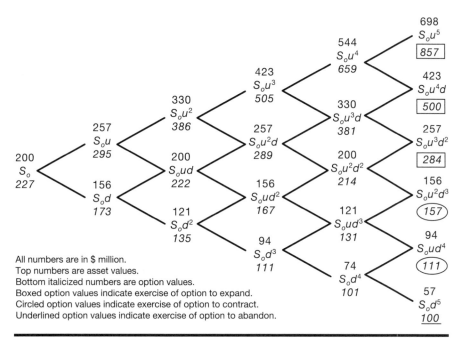

Figure 7-8. Binomial Tree for Option to Choose for Multiple Choice Drugs

continue in a similar fashion for every node of the binomial tree until the last time step. In Figure 7-8, the top value at each node represents the asset value at that node.

5. Calculate the option values at each node of the tree by backward induction
Figure 7-8 shows the option values (bottom italicized numbers) at each node of the binomial tree calculated by backward induction. Each node represents the value maximization of different mutually exclusive options available. At every node, you have the option to either continue the operation and keep the option open for the future or:

- Abandon for a salvage value of $100 million
- Expand 30% with an investment cost of $50 million
- Contract 25% to save $40 million

This means you need to calculate the asset values for each of the above options at each node and compare them against the continuation alternative. If continuation turns out to provide the maximum return, you would keep the option open for the future. Otherwise, you would exercise the option that provides you the maximum return.

A. Start with the terminal nodes that represent the last time step. At node $S_o u^5$, the expected asset value is $698 million. Now calculate the asset values for exercising each of the available options:
- Abandon: $100 million
- Expand: (1.3 * $698 million) – $50 million = $857 million
- Contract: (0.75 * $698 million) + $40 million = $564 million
Maximization shows that the option to expand would be exercised at this node, so the option value here becomes $857 million. It turns out that you also would exercise the option to expand at nodes $S_o u^4 d$ and $S_o u^3 d^2$.

B. At nodes $S_o u^2 d^3$ and $S_o u d^4$, you would exercise the contract option, and at node $S_o d^5$ you would exercise the abandon option, because those actions provide the maximum value, which now become the option values at those nodes.

C. Next, move on to the intermediate nodes, one step away from the last time step. Starting at the top, at node $S_o u^4$, calculate the expected asset value for keeping the option open and accounting for the downstream optimal decisions. This is simply the discounted (at the risk-free rate) weighted average of potential future option values using the risk-neutral probability. That value, for example, at node $S_o u^4$, is:

$$[p(S_o u^5) + (1 - p)(S_o u^4 d)] * \exp(-r\delta t)$$

$$= [0.539(\$857 \text{ million}) + (1 - 0.539)(\$500 \text{ million})]$$
$$* \exp(-0.05)(1)$$

$$= \$659 \text{ million}$$

Now calculate the asset value for exercising each of the available options:
- Abandon: $100 million
- Expand: (1.3 * $544 million) – $50 million = $657 million
- Contract: (0.75 * $544 million) + $40 million = $448 million
Maximization shows that you would keep the option open at this node. Therefore, the option value at this point becomes $659 million.

D. Similarly, at node $S_o u d^3$, calculate the expected asset value for keeping the option open and accounting for the downstream optimal decisions:

$$[0.539(\$157 \text{ million}) + (1 - 0.539)(\$111 \text{ million})] * \exp(-0.05)(1)$$
$$= \$131 \text{ million}$$

Now calculate the asset value for exercising each of the available options:

- Abandon: $100 million
- Expand: (1.3 * $121 million) − $50 million = $107 million
- Contract: (0.75 * $121 million) + $40 million = $131 million

Maximization shows that you would contract the project or keep the option open (both have equal values). Therefore, the option value at this node becomes $131 million.

E. Complete the option valuation binomial tree all the way to time = 0.

6. Analyze the results

The NPV of the project based on the risk-adjusted DCF method is $200 million, compared to the ROV of $227 million. The difference of $27 million is substantial and is the value added to the project by real options which management can take into consideration in making the project decisions. Figure 7-8 shows the strategic choices you would make at different points during the option life. It appears that you would either continue the project keeping the options open, abandon, contract, or expand depending on the expected asset values. Using Pascal's triangle (Figure 7-2), at the end of five years, the probability of expanding the project is even at 50/50.

If Multiple Choice Drugs considers the individual options separately, rather than a combined chooser option, the ROV can be calculated as follows:

- Abandonment: $1 million
- Expansion: $24 million
- Contraction: $3 million

As you might expect, the combined option ($27 million) has more value than any one of the individual options. Summation of the individual options ($28 million) may not necessarily be the same as the combined chooser option. This is because the individual options are mutually exclusive and independent of each other. For example, you cannot abandon and expand the project at the same time. The value of a chooser option will always be less than or equal to the summation of the individual options that make up the chooser option. At each node of the binomial lattice, among the choices to abandon, expand, or contract versus continue the project, you choose whichever provides the maximum value; you do not add up the individual option values.

As with other options discussed earlier, you can change the salvage value, analyze the impact of volatility, calculate the probability of exercising a given option at a given time, and so on with the chooser option also. The binomial method gives you the flexibility and makes the calculations visible, so the results can be easily understood and communicated to management. A chooser option need not include all three choices (abandonment, expansion, and contraction). You can have an option that only has two of these choices and still value it in the same manner.

OPTION TO WAIT

The option to wait, also called the option to defer, is embedded in virtually every project. An organization may want to wait to invest in a project because it currently shows either negative or marginal NPV but has high uncertainty, which when cleared may tip the project into the high-NPV territory. High NPVs are a result of payoffs that exceed the project investment, which corresponds to the strike price in ROA. If and when the payoff is expected to be greater than the investment, the decision would be to make the investment at that time or else no investment would be made. These characteristics make the option to wait a call option. Deferral options are most valuable on assets where the owners have proprietary technology or exclusive ownership rights and the barriers to entry are high, so that the owners are not losing revenues to the competition by waiting.

A patent owner may not want to develop and market the product immediately because the payoff is not attractive at the time. Whereas the option to wait has the utmost benefit in such situations, there are potential losses of revenue every year the project is delayed because of the finite life of a patent, making the total asset value smaller. This is called leakage, as mentioned in Chapter 6, and is equivalent to the dividends on financial assets, which decrease the overall asset value.

In Chapter 5, the binomial method of option valuation using an option to wait example was illustrated. Erp Corporation had to decide when to develop and introduce a proprietary product that is complementary to its existing enterprise resource planning software. In this case, leakage is presumably nonexistent, and the total asset value is the same whether the project is executed today or in the near future because:

1. The barriers to entry are high. This is a proprietary product and would be an "add-on" to the existing product, which has an established customer base. The probability that customers will switch to an entirely new product is small due to the enormous costs.
2. The life of the add-on product is approximately five years irrespective of when it is introduced; therefore, the asset value remains the same throughout the option life.

Whereas leakage may be nonexistent in such scenarios as mentioned above, it is common in valuation of patents, oil leases, properties with exclusive rights, etc. Depending upon the project, the leakage can be at a constant rate or varying rates, a single cash payment, or variable with time or the asset values. It is important to adjust the option model to account for these leakages, so that the option value is realistic. The following example illustrates how the constant leakage rate scenario can be solved through such an adjustment, and the accompanying analysis discusses briefly how the other scenarios may be addressed.

Example

Tailored Tomatoes is an emerging biotech company that specializes in genetically modified foods. It has a patent for growing tomatoes in same-size cuboid shapes, which is expected to save enormous shipping costs. There is payoff uncertainty with the project because of the public perception of genetically modified foods and the odd-shaped tomatoes. Tailored Tomatoes wants to evaluate the value of the option to wait before investing in development and marketing efforts. The DCF-based payoff based on the risk-adjusted discount rate is $200 million. The annual volatility of the logarithmic returns for the projected future cash flows is 30% with a continuous annual risk-free interest rate of 5% over the 15-year option life. The investment cost required to commercialize and market this product is estimated to be $220 million. What is the value of the option to wait assuming an annual 10% leakage of value?

Solution

The input parameters for this problem are:

S_o = $200 million
T = 15 years
σ = 30%
r = 5%
X = $220 million
l (leakage rate) = 10% (annual rate)
δt = 3 years

The calculations to solve this problem are exactly the same as illustrated in Chapter 5 for the Erp Corporation example, except for calculation of the risk-neutral probability and the δt value used. A time step of three years will be used instead of one year to simplify the spreadsheet calculations. This will result in an asset valuation tree with five total steps. The calculation process is not affected by the choice of this time step. The risk-free rate in the risk-neutral probability equation is replaced by the difference between the risk-free rate and the leakage rate:

$$\frac{\exp[(r - l)\delta t] - d}{u - d}$$

where *l* is the annual leakage rate or revenues lost due to the delayed investment. The risk-neutral probability for Tailored Tomatoes is:

$$\{\exp[(0.05 - 0.1) * 3] - 0.595\}/(1.681 - 0.595) = 0.245$$

The binomial tree (Figure 7-9) shows the asset and option values for this example. The ROV is $29 million for an annual leakage of 10% asset value. If there is no leakage of the asset value, a recalculation of the binomial tree would show an ROV of $124 million, more than a fourfold increase compared to the option value corresponding to an annual leakage of 10%.

Analysis

A DCF-based payoff of $200 million for an investment of $220 million shows an NPV of –$20 million for Tailored Tomatoes; therefore, the project would

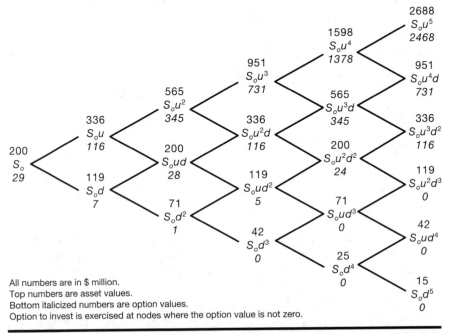

All numbers are in $ million.
Top numbers are asset values.
Bottom italicized numbers are option values.
Option to invest is exercised at nodes where the option value is not zero.

Figure 7-9.   Binomial Tree for Option to Wait with Constant Leakage for Tailored Tomatoes

be rejected. The option valuation, however, shows an ROV of $29 million for an option to wait. Since the option value is relatively high, management may want to create a deferral option for this project. Although the option valuation does not alter the DCF-based decision not to invest at this time, it does help management with strategies for further decisions on the project:

1. If the cuboid tomatoes project is part of a portfolio, which many product development projects are, its ROV can be taken into consideration to compare this project with the other projects. If there is another project with a similar NPV based on the DCF alone but a lower option value, this project would receive higher prioritization.

2. Instead of completely abandoning the project, management may decide to provide minimum funding to keep the project alive until the payoff uncertainty clears and a categorical invest/terminate decision can be made.

3. Option valuation gives some idea of when it might be a good time to invest in the future, so management can plan for the investment while observing the market closely for the right timing.

4. Management can actively seek to clear the uncertainty by conducting focused market surveys.

5. A sensitivity analysis showing the impact of the leakage rate on the option's value (Figure 7-10) provides additional information for decision making. For example, if the leakage represents a royalty fee that Tailored Tomatoes has to pay its licensor, it can determine the fee "cap" above which the option has little value.

Let us now consider how other types of leakage can be addressed using the binomial method. If the leakage is at varying rates throughout the life of the option, you will need to calculate separate values of p for each node of the binomial tree where the leakage value changes. This differs from the constant leakage scenario in that the solution there involved one-time adjustment of "standard" p for the entire tree by subtracting the leakage rate (l) from the risk-free rate (r) in solving the equation for p, whereas with varying leakage, p is adjusted at every node where the leakage rate changes.

If the leakage changes with respect to time or the asset value, the probability (p) will have to be adjusted at every single node accordingly. If there is one-time leakage of the underlying asset value (say, for example, due to a single cash payment), the corresponding asset value at the appropriate time has to be decreased in accordance with the leakage amount. From that point on, the binomial tree becomes nonrecombining (Figure 7-11) because of the shift in the asset value. A sample solution to an options problem involving a nonrecombining

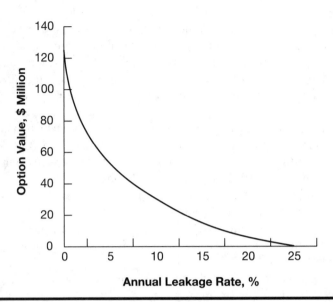

Figure 7-10. Effect of Leakage Rate on the Option Value for Tailored Tomatoes

binomial lattice is presented in Chapter 8. Although the binomial tree in this case becomes nonrecombining due to volatility changes during the life of the option, the principle of the solution is the same for the one-time leakage also.

BARRIER OPTIONS

A barrier option is an option where your decision to exercise it depends not only on the strike and asset prices but also on a predefined "barrier" price. This type of option can be either a call or a put option, such as an option to wait or an option to abandon, respectively. A traditional call option (Figure 7-12A) is in the money when the asset value is above the strike price, whereas a barrier call option (Figure 7-12B) is in the money when the asset value is above the barrier price, which is predefined at a value higher than the strike price. As a rational investor, you exercise the barrier call only when the asset value is above the barrier price, irrespective of the strike price. Similarly, you exercise a barrier put when the asset value is *below* the barrier price, which is set at a value lower than the strike price. Figure 7-13 presents the option payoff diagrams for simple put and barrier put options. In the following sections, two examples are presented, one for a barrier put (option to abandon) and one for a barrier call (option to wait).

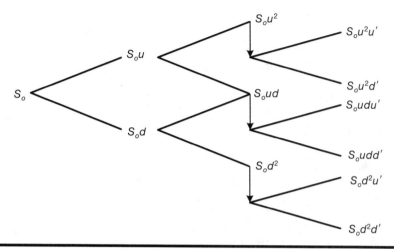

Figure 7-11. Schematic Representation of a Binomial Tree Where the Asset Value is Adjusted for a One-Time Leakage

Barrier Put Option

Often in practice, stakeholders are reluctant to make the decision to abandon a project if the expected project value falls just below the salvage value. Many factors (for example, the stakeholders' psychological attachment to the project and political issues involved with closing down a project) contribute to this so-called "project stickiness." The traditional abandonment option problem is framed with the assumption that the abandonment decision will be completely rational; that is, once the expected asset value falls below the salvage value, the decision will be made to abandon the project. The option value calculated under this assumption does not account for scenarios where other factors such as project stickiness may affect the abandonment decision, thereby not representing the true project value. One way to account for these factors is to treat the option as a barrier option. The stakeholders of the project can agree on a barrier value (lower than the salvage value) below which the project will definitely be abandoned. The option value calculated using the barrier value presumably represents the true value of the project.

Example

1. Frame the application

Fibroptics owns a manufacturing facility that produces fiber optic cables for the telecommunications industry. Due to competition from Asia, there is great

A. Simple Call Option

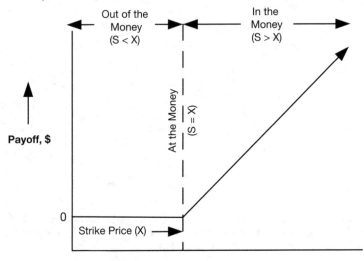

B. Barrier Call Option

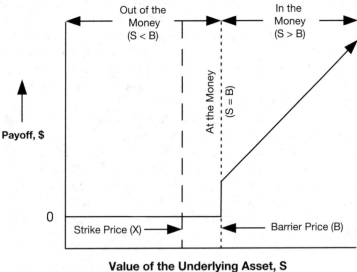

Figure 7-12. Payoff Diagrams for a Barrier Call Option

A. Simple Put Option

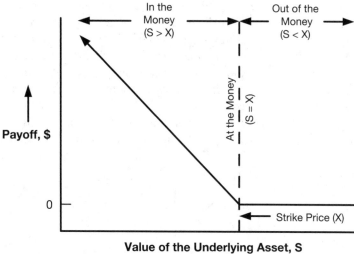

Value of the Underlying Asset, S

B. Barrier Put Option

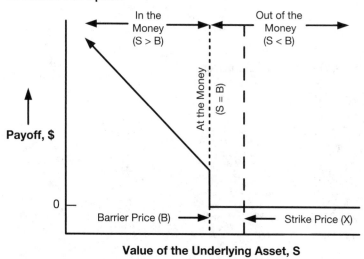

Value of the Underlying Asset, S

Figure 7-13. Payoff Diagrams for a Barrier Put Option

uncertainty about future cash flows, and the company is considering a strategic abandonment option. The DCF analysis of the current operation shows that the present value of the payoff discounted at an appropriate market risk-adjusted discount rate would be $200 million. At any time during the next five years, Fibroptics can either continue with the operation or shut down the facility and sell off the assets to a strategic partner for a salvage value of $70 million. The annual volatility of the logarithmic returns for future cash flows is calculated to be 45%, and the continuous annual riskless interest rate over the next five years is 5%. Given the political and emotional implications related to closing down the manufacturing facility, Fibroptics is considering a barrier value (B) of $50 million, below which it will exercise the abandonment option. What is the value of this barrier option?

2. Identify the input parameters
S_o = $200 million
X = $70 million
B = $50 million
T = 5 years
σ = 45%
r = 5%
δt = 1 year

3. Calculate the option parameters
u = $\exp(\sigma\sqrt{\delta t})$
  = $\exp(0.45 * \sqrt{1})$
  = 1.568
d = $1/u$
  = $1/1.568$
  = 0.638
$$p = \frac{\exp(r\delta t) - d}{u - d}$$
p = $[\exp(0.05 * 1) - 0.638]/(1.568 - 0.638)$
  = 0.444

4. Build the binomial tree and calculate the asset values at each node of the tree
Build a binomial tree, as shown in Figure 7-14, using one-year time intervals for five years and calculate the asset values over the life of the option. Start with S_o at the very first node on the left and multiply it by the up factor and down factor to obtain $S_o u$ ($200 million * 1.568 = $314 million) and $S_o d$ ($200 million * 0.638 = $128 million), respectively, for the first time step. Moving

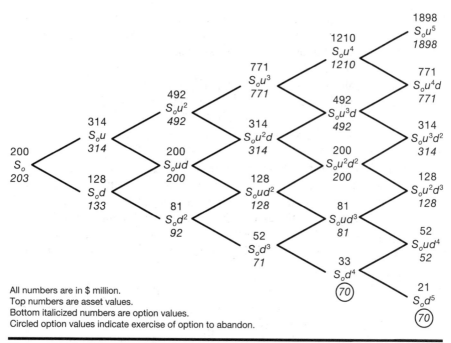

All numbers are in $ million.
Top numbers are asset values.
Bottom italicized numbers are option values.
Circled option values indicate exercise of option to abandon.

Figure 7-14. Binomial Tree for Barrier Put Option for Fibroptics

to the right, continue in a similar fashion for every node of the binomial tree until the last time step. In Figure 7-14, the top value at each node represents the asset value at that node.

5. Calculate the option values at each node of the tree by backward induction
Figure 7-14 shows the option values (bottom italicized numbers) at each node of the binomial tree by backward induction. Each node represents the option value after exercise of the barrier option. At every node, you have the option to either abandon the project for a salvage value of $70 million, if the asset value goes below the barrier value of $50 million, or continue to keep the option open until it expires.

A. Start with the terminal nodes that represents the last time step. At node $S_o u^5$, the expected asset value is $1,898 million, compared to the barrier value of $50 million. Since this is greater than the barrier value, you would continue rather than abandon the project. Thus the option value at this node is $1,898 million.

B. At node $S_o u d^4$, the expected asset value is $52 million, compared to the barrier value of $50 million; since this is greater than the barrier value, you would continue rather than abandon, which makes the option value at this node $52 million. Note that you do not abandon the project here even though the asset value is less than the salvage value.

C. At node $S_o d^5$, the expected asset value is $21 million, compared to the barrier value of $50 million; since this is less than the barrier value, you would abandon the project for the salvage value of $70 million, which makes the option value at this node $70 million. Note that even though the decision to abandon depends on the barrier value, the option value is still equal to the salvage value.

D. Next, move on to the intermediate nodes, one step away from the last time step. Again, at each intermediate node, you have the option to continue or the option to abandon. Starting at the top, at node $S_o u^4$, calculate the expected asset value for keeping the option open. This is simply the discounted (at the risk-free rate) weighted average of potential future option values using the risk-neutral probability as weights:

$$[p(S_o u^5) + (1 - p)(S_o u^4 d)] * \exp(-r\delta t)$$

$$= [0.444(\$1,898 \text{ million}) + (1 - 0.444)(\$771 \text{ million})] * \exp(-0.05)(1)$$

$$= \$1,210 \text{ million}$$

Since the asset value at this node is larger than the barrier value of $50 million, you do not want to abandon the project. You want to keep the option open and continue; therefore, the option value at $S_o u^4$ is $1,210 million.

E. Similarly, at node $S_o d^4$, the expected asset value for keeping the option open, taking into account the downstream optimal decisions, is:

$$[0.444(\$52 \text{ million}) + (1 - 0.444)(\$70 \text{ million})] * \exp(-0.05)(1)$$

$$= \$59 \text{ million}$$

The asset value at this node is $33 million, which is less than the barrier value of $50 million; therefore, you have the option to abandon, the value of which would be equal to the salvage value of $70 million. Since this value is greater than the option to continue ($59 million), you would abandon at this node, and hence the option value here becomes $70 million.

F. Complete the option valuation binomial tree all the way to time = 0 using the approach outlined above.

6. Analyze the results

The project payoff based on the DCF method without flexibility is $200 million. ROA, however, shows a project value of $203 million, yielding an additional value of $3 million ($203 million – $200 million) due to the barrier option. This provides the true value of the abandonment option in light of management's unwillingness to abandon the project as soon as the asset value falls just below the salvage value. Treating this as a traditional abandonment option without considering a barrier, the additional option value would be $5.3 million. The difference between the abandonment and barrier options then would be $2.3 million ($5.3 million – $3 million), and this is the price you pay to account for the emotional and political factors before making your abandonment decision. A key question in framing the barrier option is what the barrier value should be. While there are no quantitative methods to estimate this value, a practitioner can arbitrarily define it based on project stakeholder input.

At first thought, to account for the project stickiness factor, a practitioner may be inclined to lower the strike price itself and keep the option as a simple abandonment option rather than treating it as a more complex barrier option. This translates to lowering the salvage value, which would be an inaccurate representation of the project conditions. As a result, the option value will be lower than the true value of the project based on a barrier, because the project salvage value used in the options calculations would be lower than the true salvage value. Therefore, lowering the salvage value would not be a correct approach. In the Fibrotics example above, if the salvage value is set at $50 million, the option value would only be $1 million, which is less than the option value corresponding to the $50 million barrier price.

Barrier Call Option

Project executives do not necessarily want to invest in a project when the expected asset value is above the strike price but by only a small margin. They may want higher levels of confidence that the asset value will stay higher than the strike price. One way to increase that confidence is to treat this as a barrier option, where the option will be exercised if the asset value goes above a predefined barrier price.

Example

1. Frame the application

International Ventures is considering investing in a project in an Asian country. Due to the uncertainty related to both the project payoff and the exchange rate, the company wants to consider an option to invest in the next five years instead of investing right away. It wants to evaluate the value of this option to wait before investing in keeping the opportunity alive. The project payoff based on DCF using the appropriate risk-adjusted discount rate is estimated to be $100 million. The annual volatility of the logarithmic returns for the projected future cash flows is 35% with a continuous annual risk-free interest rate of 5% over the five-year option life. The investment cost required for this project is estimated to be $130 million. Since this will be the first project for International Ventures in this country, the stakeholders want to be especially cautious in view of the currency exchange rate uncertainty and invest only if the asset value goes above a barrier value of $150 million. What is the value of this barrier option?

2. Identify the input parameters

S_o = $100 million
X = $130 million
B = $150 million
T = 5 years
σ = 35%
r = 5%
δt = 1 year

3. Calculate the option parameters

u = $\exp(\sigma\sqrt{\delta t})$
  = $\exp(0.35 * \sqrt{1})$
  = 1.419
d = $1/u$
  = $1/1.419$
  = 0.705
p = $\dfrac{\exp(r\delta t) - d}{u - d}$
  = $[\exp(0.05 * 1) - 0.705]/(1.419 - 0.705)$
  = 0.485

4. Build the binomial tree and calculate the asset values at each node of the tree

Build a binomial tree, as shown in Figure 7-15, using one-year time intervals for five years and calculate the asset values over the life of the option. Start with S_o and multiply it by the up factor and the down factor to obtain $S_o u$ and $S_o d$, respectively, for the first time step, and continue in a similar manner for every node of the binomial tree until the last step. For example, $S_o u$ = $100 million * 1.419 = $142 million; $S_o d$ = $100 million * 0.705 = $70 million. Moving to the right, continue in a similar fashion for every node of the binomial

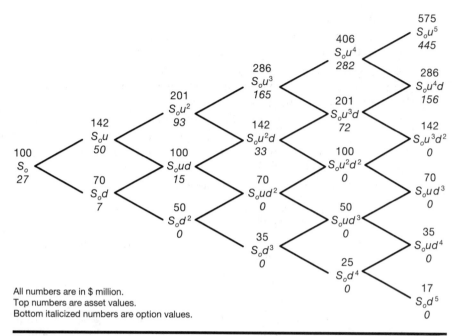

All numbers are in $ million.
Top numbers are asset values.
Bottom italicized numbers are option values.

Figure 7-15.   Binomial Tree for Barrier Call Option for International Ventures

tree until the last time step. In Figure 7-15, the top value at each node represents the asset value at that node.

5. Calculate the option values at each node of the binomial tree using backward induction

Figure 7-15 shows the option values (bottom italicized numbers) at each node of the binomial tree calculated by backward induction. Each node represents the value maximization of investing at that point or waiting until the next time period. At every node, you have the option to either invest in the project or wait until the next time period before the option expires.

A. Start with the terminal nodes that represent the last time step. At node $S_o u^5$, the expected asset value is $575 million. Since this is greater than the barrier value of $150 million, you will invest $130 million in the project; therefore, the net asset value is:

$$\$575 \text{ million} - \$130 \text{ million} = \$445 \text{ million}$$

Therefore, the option value at this node is $445 million.

B. At node $S_o u^3 d^2$, the expected asset value is \$142 million, which is less than the barrier value of \$150 million. Therefore, the decision at this node will be not to invest in the project, which means the option value at this node will be \$0. Note that the decision at this node is not to invest even though the asset value is greater than the strike price. This is because of the constraint imposed by the barrier condition.

C. Next, move on to the intermediate nodes, one step away from the last time step. Starting at the top, at node $S_o u^4$, calculate the expected asset value for keeping the option open. This is simply the discounted (at the risk-free rate) weighted average of potential future option values using the risk-neutral probability. That value at node $S_o u^4$ is:

$$[p(S_o u^5) + (1 - p)(S_o u^4 d)] * \exp(-r\delta t)$$

$$= [0.485(\$445 \text{ million}) + (1 - 0.485)(\$156 \text{ million})]$$
$$* \exp(-0.05)(1)$$

$$= \$282 \text{ million}$$

Since the asset value of \$406 million at this node is greater than the barrier value, you have the option to invest. If the option is exercised at this node by investing \$130 million, the net asset value will be \$276 million (\$406 million − \$130 million). Since keeping the option open shows a higher asset value (\$282 million), you would not exercise the option and continue to wait; the option value at this node becomes \$282 million.

D. Similarly, at node $S_o u^2 d^2$, the expected asset value for keeping the option open, taking into account the downstream optimal decisions, is:

$$[0.485(\$0) + (1 - 0.485)(\$0)] * \exp(-0.05)(1) = \$0$$

The asset value at this node is \$100 million. Since this is less than the barrier value of \$150 million, you would not want to invest. Therefore, the decision would be to keep the option open with an option value of \$0.

E. Complete the option valuation binomial tree all the way to time = 0.

Analysis

The DCF method using an appropriate risk-adjusted discount rate shows a payoff of \$100 million with an investment cost of \$130 million for the International Ventures project. A call option on this project with a barrier price of $50 million has an ROV of $27 million. This means that the NPV of the project is –$30 million ($100 million – $130 million), with an additional $57 million in value [$27 million – (–$30 million)] due to the barrier option to wait. By ignoring the barrier value and treating it as a traditional option to wait, the project ROV would be $29 million. This is $2 million more than the ROV of the barrier option to wait, which translates to the price the company would pay for the cautious barrier option approach it wants to follow in making the investment decision.

As discussed earlier for the barrier abandonment option, in order to keep the option as a simple call, a practitioner may be inclined to increase the strike price to match the barrier price. This means that the strike price — the investment cost — is represented inaccurately in the options calculation. As a result, it will yield a higher ROV compared to the barrier option and does not represent the true value of the project as conceived by the project stakeholders. In the case of the International Ventures project, a strike price of $150 million will result in an NPV of –$50 million and an ROV of $58 million, compared to –$30 million and $27 million, respectively, for the equivalent barrier call. Strike and barrier prices are different and should be treated accordingly to represent the true conditions of the project decision framework.

PROBLEMS

7-1. NanoNano specializes in the development of new products using nanotechnology. It holds the patent for a novel catalyst, NanoCat, that can tremendously increase the output of ethylene in its manufacturing. The company wants to manufacture and market NanoCat and is considering an investment in a new plant. The total cost to build the factory is estimated to be $200 million. The DCF analysis of NanoCat's market potential shows that the present value of the payoff discounted at an appropriate market risk-adjusted discount rate would also be $200 million. The annual volatility of the logarithmic returns for the future cash flows is calculated to be 45%, and the continuous annual riskless interest rate over the next five years is 5%. There is considerable uncertainty in the expected payoff; therefore, NanoNano is considering an abandonment option. It has entered into an agreement with an equipment supplier to sell back the equipment anytime during the next five years for a total sum of $120 million. If the market turns out to be good, NanoNano would continue with its operations; otherwise, it would abandon its operations and salvage the equipment for $120 million. What is the value of the abandonment option?

7-2. Calculate the value of the abandonment option in Problem 7-1 for the following cases:

A. Salvage value = $100 million
B. Salvage value = $80 million
C. Salvage value = $140 million
D. Salvage value = $160 million

Plot the abandonment option value versus salvage value to show the sensitivity of the option value to the strike price. Using the plot, determine the critical salvage value below which the abandonment option has no value.

7-3. Calculate the value of NanoNano's abandonment option assuming that the salvage value is $120 million in the first year and it decreases by $10 million each following year, ending with $80 million in the fifth and final year. How does this option value compare with that for the base case where the salvage value ($120 million) is static throughout the option life?

7-4. NanoNano's management does not want to shut down the plant and salvage the equipment as soon as the expected payoff falls below the salvage value. Management wants to take a cautious and conservative approach by exercising its abandonment option only if the expected payoff falls below a barrier value of $100 million. Calculate the value of this barrier abandonment option assuming the salvage value remains constant at $120 million over the option life. How does this compare with the value calculated for the regular abandonment option?

7-5. HiWiFi has just introduced broadband wireless service in the Chicago metropolitan area. It is still too early to say whether this service will be a success. The DCF valuation of the project free cash flows using a risk-adjusted discount rate indicates a present value of $100 million over the project life. Using the project proxy approach, the annual volatility of the logarithmic returns on these cash flows is calculated to be 40%. The company believes there is great potential for its services in other metropolitan areas and decides to explore the option to expand. This move is expected to result in a fivefold expansion of the current operation, at a cost of expansion of $500 million. What is the value of the expansion option over the next three years if the continuous annual riskless interest rate for the same period is 5%? How does the DCF-based project expansion value (that is, the NPV) compare with the ROV?

7-6. Recalculate the expansion option value in Problem 7-5 for option lives of:

A. 2 years

B. 4 years

C. 5 years

What is the effect of the option life on the option value? What is the reason for this effect?

7-7. VCR International owns four plants that manufacture VCRs. Since the advent of DVDs, the demand for VCRs has been on the decline and hence the company is considering an option to shut down three of its four plants if the current trend continues. This option to contract its operations by a factor of four will result in a savings of $200 million. Using the traditional DCF analysis and appropriate risk-adjusted discount rate, the present value of the future free cash flows for the current operation has been valued at $400 million. The annual volatility of the logarithmic returns on the future cash flows is estimated to be 30%, and the continuous annual risk-free interest rate is 5% over the option life. What would be the value of the option to contract?

7-8. Recalculate the option to contract for VCR International using annual volatility factors of 40%, 50%, 20%, and 10%.

7-9. Flash Memory International is in the business of manufacturing flash memory sticks. The present value of the projected future free cash flows for this operation using DCF analysis with the appropriate risk-adjusted discount rate is $400 million. The volatility of the logarithmic returns on the projected future cash flows is 30%, and the risk-free rate is 5% over the next five years. Considering the uncertainty in the market conditions, the company is considering a chooser option where it could either abandon, contract, expand, or continue its operations in their current state depending on how the market conditions play out. At any time during this time period, the company can contract half of its current operations to save $150 million, expand by 40% by investing $150 million, or abandon the operation altogether by selling the property for a salvage value of $200 million. What is value of the chooser option for Flash Memory International?

7-10. For Problem 7-9, calculate the ROV of the:

A. Abandonment option alone

B. Expansion option alone

C. Contraction option alone

How does the sum of these individual option values compare with the value of the chooser option? How would you explain the difference in these two values?

7-11. DermaDrug has a patent for a biomaterial that can be used to deliver drugs gradually throughout the day through the skin and is considering commercialization. There is payoff uncertainty with the project because of the novel nature of the drug delivery mechanism. DermaDrug wants to evaluate the value of the option to wait before investing in development and marketing efforts. The DCF-based payoff based on the risk-adjusted discount rate is $100 million. The annual volatility of the logarithmic returns on the projected future cash flows is 25%, with a continuous annual risk-free interest rate of 5% over the five-year option life. The investment cost required to commercialize and market this product is estimated to be $100 million. What is the value of the option to wait assuming an annual 10% leakage of the asset value?

7-12. Calculate the ROV of the option to wait in Problem 7-11 for the following scenarios:

A. Annual leakage = 5%
B. Annual leakage = 15%
C. Annual leakage = 20%

What is the effect of leakage on the option value? Why?

ADVANCED OPTIONS

A real option in its simplest form is a right — with no obligation — to invest in a project at a later time. A deferral option is an American call option with a right to delay the start of a project. An expansion option is also an American call that gives the owner the right to scale up a project. Abandonment and contraction options are American puts where the owner holds the right to terminate or scale down a project by selling all or some of its assets, respectively. An option has value because there is market uncertainty related to the underlying asset. The idea is that once the uncertainty clears, the option may be exercised and the project initiated, expanded, scaled down, or abandoned accordingly. The option lets you take advantage of the upside while avoiding the downside.

In the previous chapter, we illustrated how to use the binomial technique to value projects embedded with the aforementioned simple options. In this chapter, real options solution methods are presented for more complex project scenarios dealing with compound and rainbow options and options where volatility of the asset value changes during the option life. Also illustrated in this chapter is how real options analysis can be integrated with decision tree analysis in order to account for both market and private risks in the overall project valuation. As in the previous chapter, first the options example problem is framed, then a step-by-step method is presented to calculate the real options value using the binomial or a similar lattice model (integrated with decision tree analysis where applicable), and finally the results are analyzed. Whereas many of the principles discussed in the analysis step of the simple options solutions in Chapter 7 are also applicable to the options in this chapter, the focus here is on characteristics specific to the options considered in this chapter.

COMPOUND OPTIONS (OPTION TO STAGE)

Many project initiatives (research and development, capacity expansion, launching of new services, etc.) are multistage project investments where management can decide to expand, scale back, maintain the status quo, or abandon the project after gaining new information to resolve uncertainty. For example, a capital investment project divided into multiple phases, including permitting, design, engineering, and construction, can either be terminated or continued into the next phase depending upon the market conditions at the end of each phase. These are compound options where exercising one option generates another, thereby making the value of one option contingent upon the value of another option. A compound option derives its value from another option — not from the underlying asset. The first investment creates the right but not the obligation to make a second investment, which in turn gives you the option to make a third investment, and so on. You have the option to abandon, contract, or scale up the project at any time during its life.

A compound option can either be sequential or parallel, also known as simultaneous. If you must exercise an option in order to create another one, it is considered a sequential option. For example, you must complete the design phase of a factory before you can start building it. In a parallel option, however, both options are available at the same time. The life of the independent option is longer than or equal to the dependent option. A television broadcaster may be building the infrastructure for digital transmission and acquiring the required broadcast spectrum at the same time, but cannot complete testing of the infrastructure without the spectrum license. Acquiring the spectrum — an option itself — gives the broadcaster the option to complete the infrastructure and launch the digital broadcast service. For both sequential and compound options, valuation calculations are essentially the same except for minor differences. Examples of each option are presented in the following sections.

Sequential Option

This section includes a sequential compound option example, a binomial solution, and analysis of the results. The same six-step process introduced in Chapter 6 and used in solving simple options examples in Chapter 7 is also applied here with a few modifications in step 5.

1. Frame the application

Sweet 'n Sour Cola is considering investment in a bottling plant for HyperCola, its new beverage that recently came off its R&D pipeline. Despite sales in test markets for a short period of time, there still is some market uncertainty regarding future sales; therefore, the company wants to use the options approach to value the project for a go/no-go investment decision. The project is divided into three sequential phases: land acquisition and permitting (simply referred to as permitting hereafter), design and engineering (referred to as design hereafter), and construction. Each phase has to be completed before the next phase can begin. Sweet 'n Sour Cola wants to bring HyperCola to market in no more than seven years. The construction will take two years to complete, and hence the company has a maximum of five years to decide whether to invest in the construction. The design phase will take two years to complete, and since design is a prerequisite to construction, the company has a maximum of three years to decide whether to invest in the design and engineering phase. The permitting process will take two years to complete, and since it must be completed before the design phase can begin, the company has a maximum of one year from today to decide on permitting. Permitting is expected to cost $30 million, design $90 million, and construction another $210 million. Discounted cash flow analysis using an appropriate risk-adjusted discount rate values the plant, if it existed today, at $250 million. The annual volatility of the logarithmic returns for the future cash flows for the plant is estimated to be 30%, and the continuous annual risk-free interest rate over the next five years is 6%.

2. Identify the input parameters
S_o = $250 million
X_1, X_2, and X_3 = $30, $90, and $210 million, respectively
T_1, T_2, and T_3 = 1, 3, and 5 years, respectively (cumulative option life for each
          stage)
σ = 30%
r = 6%
δt = 1 year

3. Calculate the option parameters
u = $\exp(\sigma\sqrt{\delta t})$
   = $\exp(0.30 * \sqrt{1})$
   = 1.350
d = 1/u
   = 1/1.350
   = 0.741
$$p = \frac{\exp(r\delta t) - d}{u - d}$$
p = [exp(0.06 * 1) − 0.741]/(1.350 − 0.741)]
   = 0.527

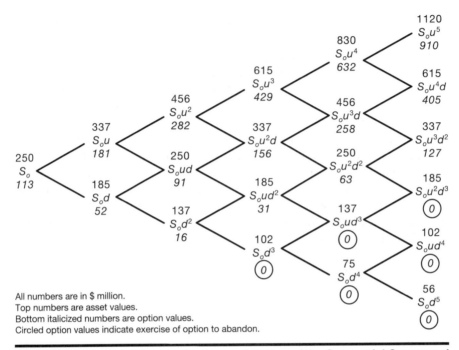

All numbers are in $ million.
Top numbers are asset values.
Bottom italicized numbers are option values.
Circled option values indicate exercise of option to abandon.

Figure 8-1.   Binomial Tree for the Longest Option of the Sequential Compound Option

4. Build the binomial tree and calculate the asset values at each node of the tree

Build a binomial tree, as shown in Figure 8-1, using one-year time intervals for five years and calculate the asset values over the life of the option. Start with S_o and multiply it by the up factor and the down factor to obtain S_ou and S_od, respectively. For the first time step: S_ou = $250 million * 1.350 = $337 million; S_od = $250 million * 0.741 = $185 million. Moving to the right, continue in a similar fashion for every node of the binomial tree until the last time step. In Figure 8-1, the top value at each node represents the asset value at that node.

5. Calculate the option values for each of the three sequential options

There are three sequential options available on this project. Construction is dependent on design, which in turn is dependent on permitting. The option value calculations are done in sequence, starting with the longest option. First, you calculate the option values for the construction option using the binomial tree, as discussed in the previous chapter. The option values of the longest option (construction) then become the underlying asset values for the preceding option (design), for which you calculate the option values using backward induction. These option values become the underlying asset values for the next preceding option (permitting), for which you employ backward induction to calculate its option values.

5.1. Calculate the option values for the longest option at each node of the tree by backward induction

Figure 8-1 shows the option values (bottom italicized numbers) for the longest dependent option (that is, plant construction) at each node of the binomial tree calculated by backward induction. Each terminal node represents the value maximization of exercising the option by investing $210 million versus letting the option expire. Each intermediate node represents the value maximization of continuation versus exercising the option.

A.   Start with the terminal nodes that represent the last time step. At node $S_o u^5$, the expected asset value is $1,120 million. If you invest $210 million to build the plant, the net payoff will be $1,120 million – $210 million = $910 million. Since your objective is to maximize your return, you would exercise your option by investing. Thus the option value at this node becomes $910 million.

B.   At node $S_o d^5$, the expected asset value is $56 million. Since this is less than the investment cost of $210 million, you would not invest and would let the option expire. Your option value would, therefore, be $0.

C.   Next, move on to the intermediate nodes, one step away from the last time step. Starting at the top, at node $S_o u^4$, calculate the expected asset value for keeping the option open and accounting for the downstream optimal decisions. This is simply the discounted (at the risk-free rate) weighted average of potential future option values using the risk-neutral probabilities. That value at node $S_o u^4$ is:

$$[p(S_o u^5) + (1 - p)(S_o u^4 d)] * \exp(-r\delta t)$$
$$= [0.527(\$910 \text{ million}) + (1 - 0.527)(\$405 \text{ million})]$$
$$* \exp(-0.06)(1)$$
$$= \$632 \text{ million}$$

If, on the other hand, the option is exercised by investing $210 million, the expected asset value would be:

$$\$830 \text{ million} - \$210 \text{ million} = \$620 \text{ million}$$

Since this value is less than the $632 million corresponding to the alternative to continue, you would not exercise the option, and the option value at this node would be $632 million.

D. Similarly, at node $S_o u^3 d$, the expected asset value for keeping the option open, taking into account the downstream optimal decisions, is:

$$[0.527(\$405 \text{ million}) + (1 - 0.527)(\$127 \text{ million})] * \exp(-0.06)(1)$$

$$= \$258 \text{ million}$$

If, on the other hand, you exercise the option to invest, the expected asset value would be:

$$\$456 \text{ million} - \$210 \text{ million} = \$246 \text{ million}$$

Maximizing $258 million versus $246 million, you would keep the option open. Therefore, the option valuation at node $S_o u^3 d$ would be $258 million.

E. Complete the option valuation binomial tree all the way to time = 0 using the approach outlined above.

5.2. Calculate the option values for the preceding option at each node of the tree by backward induction

Calculate the option values for the predecessor option (design) for its three-year life using the option values of the successor option (construction) as the underlying asset values. Exercising the option to design creates the option to construct the plant; hence the construction option values are treated as the underlying asset values for this calculation. Figure 8-2 shows the underlying asset values (top numbers) for the first three years, which are the same as the option values (bottom italicized numbers in Figure 8-1) for the construction option. Calculate the option values (bottom italicized numbers in Figure 8-2) at each node of the binomial tree by backward induction. Each node represents the value maximization of investing versus continuation, where you have the option to either invest $90 million in the project and benefit from the payoff or continue to keep the option open until it expires. At the terminal nodes, you would invest if the payoff is greater than the investment of $90 million; otherwise, you would let the option expire worthless.

A. Start with the terminal nodes that represent the last time step. At node $S_o u^3$, the expected asset value is $429 million. If you invest $90 million to design the plant, the net payoff will be $429 million – $90 million

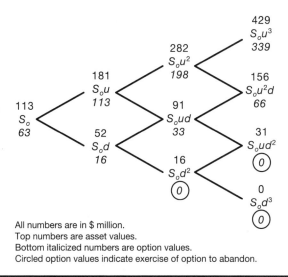

All numbers are in $ million.
Top numbers are asset values.
Bottom italicized numbers are option values.
Circled option values indicate exercise of option to abandon.

Figure 8-2. Binomial Tree for the Predecessor Option of the Sequential Compound Option

= $339 million. Since your objective is to maximize your return, you would exercise your option by investing. Thus the option value at this node becomes $339 million.

B. At node $S_o u d^2$, the expected asset value is $31 million. Since this is less than the investment cost of $90 million, you would not invest and would let the option expire. Your option value would, therefore, be $0 million.

C. Next, move on to the intermediate nodes, one step away from the last time step. Starting at the top, at node $S_o u^2$, calculate the expected asset value for keeping the option open and accounting for the downstream optimal decisions. This is simply the discounted (at the risk-free rate) weighted average of potential future option values using the risk-neutral probabilities:

$$[p(S_o u^3) + (1 - p)(S_o u^2 d)] * \exp(-r\delta t)$$

$$= [0.527(\$339 \text{ million}) + (1 - 0.527)(\$66 \text{ million})]$$
$$* \exp(-0.06)(1)$$

$$= \$198 \text{ million}$$

If, on the other hand, the option is exercised by investing $90 million, the expected asset value would be:

$282 million − $90 million = $192 million

Since this value is less than the $198 million corresponding to the alternative to continue, you would not exercise the option, and the option value at this node would be $198 million.

D. Similarly, at node $S_o ud$, the expected asset value for keeping the option open, taking into account the downstream optimal decisions, is:

[0.527($66 million) + (1 − 0.527)($0 million)] * exp(−0.06)(1)

= $33 million

If, on the other hand, you exercise the option to invest, the expected asset value would be:

$91 million − $90 million = $1 million

Maximizing $33 million versus $1 million, you would keep the option open. Therefore, the option value at node $S_o ud$ would be $33 million.

E. Complete the option valuation binomial tree all the way to time = 0 using the approach outlined above.

5.3. Calculate the option values for the next predecessor option at each node of the tree by backward induction

Calculate the option values for the next predecessor option (permitting), which happens to be the shortest option in this example. The life of this option is one year, and the underlying asset values of this option are the same as the option values for the successor option (design). Exercising the option to apply for a permit creates the option to design the plant, and so the design option values are treated as the underlying asset values for this calculation. Figure 8-3 shows the underlying asset values (top numbers) for the first year, which are the same as the option values (bottom italicized numbers in Figure 8-2) from the design option. Calculate the option values (bottom italicized numbers in Figure 8-3) at each node of the binomial tree by backward induction. Each node represents the value maximization of investing versus continuation, where you have the option to either invest $30 million to obtain the permit and benefit from the payoff or continue to keep the option open until it expires. At the terminal nodes, you would invest if the payoff is greater than the investment of $30 million; otherwise, you would let the option expire worthless.

A. Start with the terminal nodes that represent the last time step. At node $S_o u$, the expected asset value is $113 million. If you invest $30 million

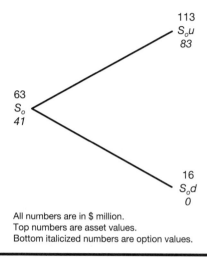

113
$S_o u$
83

63
S_o
41

16
$S_o d$
0

All numbers are in $ million.
Top numbers are asset values.
Bottom italicized numbers are option values.

Figure 8-3. Binomial Tree for the Shortest Option of the Sequential Compound Option

to apply for permits, the net payoff will be $113 million – $30 million = $83 million. Since your objective is to maximize your return, you would exercise your option by investing. Thus the option value at this node becomes $83 million.

B. At node $S_o d$, the expected asset value is $16 million. If you invest $30 million to apply for permits, the net payoff will be $16 million – $30 million = –$14 million. Since your objective is to maximize your return, you would not exercise your option. Thus the option value at this node becomes $0 million.

C. Next, move on to the root node, one step away from the last time step. At node S_o, calculate the expected asset value for keeping the option open and accounting for the downstream optimal decisions. This is simply the discounted (at the risk-free rate) weighted average of potential future option values using the risk-neutral probabilities:

$$[p(S_o u) + (1 - p)(S_o d)] * \exp(-r\delta t)$$

$$= [0.527(\$113 \text{ million}) + (1 - 0.527)(\$0 \text{ million})]$$
$$* \exp(-0.06)(1)$$

$$= \$41 \text{ million}$$

If, on the other hand, the option is exercised by investing $30 million, the expected asset value would be:

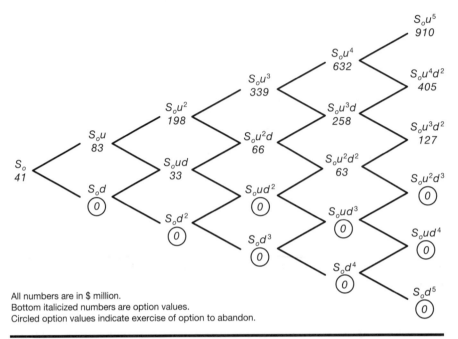

All numbers are in $ million.
Bottom italicized numbers are option values.
Circled option values indicate exercise of option to abandon.

Figure 8-4.   Binomial Tree for the Combined Sequential Compound Option

$$\$63 \text{ million} - \$30 \text{ million} = \$33 \text{ million}$$

Since this value is less than the $41 million corresponding to the alternative to continue, you would not exercise the option, and the option value at this node would be $41 million.

A combined lattice integrating the option values from the three options over the entire option life is presented in Figure 8-4.

6. Analyze the results

Let us first calculate the net present value (NPV) of the project by taking the difference between the expected payoff ($250 million) and the investment costs. Assuming Phase I investment ($30 million) is incurred at time = 0, the present values of the costs of the two subsequent phases can be calculated using a slightly higher rate (9%) than the risk-free rate. (The reason for using this rate is discussed under question 3 in the section on the discount rate dilemma in Chapter 3.) Thus, the present values of Phase II and Phase III costs are $75 million and $147 million, respectively. The project NPV, therefore, is:

$250 million – ($30 million + $75 million + $147 million) = –$2 million

By strictly considering the NPV alone, this project would be rejected for investment. The real options value (ROV), however, shows a total project value of $41 million, yielding an additional value of $43 million [$41 million – (–$2 million)] due to the compound option. Thus, consideration of the flexibility embedded in the project makes it attractive and more likely to be accepted. If the market uncertainty clears by the end of the design phase and the project payoff is expected to be significantly higher than the $210 million required for construction, Sweet 'n Sour Cola can move forward with the project; otherwise, it may abandon it or shelve it for later consideration. (Note that the prior investment of $120 million becomes a sunk cost and would not be considered in valuation of the project at that point.) Multiphase projects have a particular advantage in an options framework, when competitors face significant barriers to entry and there is a great deal of uncertainty about the market demand. The disadvantages include higher costs due to loss of economies of scale and loss of market to a competitor that may have entered the market full scale.

A closer examination of the HyperCola options results indicates that the ROVs for the options to permit, design, and construct are $41 million, $63 million, and $113 million, respectively. The value of the options increases simply because of the increase in uncertainty as a function of time, as discussed in Chapter 6. The option value can also increase due to resolution of technical uncertainty, as you exercise options in sequence and move toward project completion. For example, as mentioned before, the option value of launching a new technology increases after a pilot test. Another classic example of sequential options where technical uncertainty is resolved is drug development, where FDA approval follows successful clinical trials. However, in the HyperCola example, no efforts are made during the option life to resolve any technical uncertainty. In fact, presumably no technical uncertainty exists, because the company has already developed the formula for the cola and has the know-how to build the plant.

In this example, option lives of one, three, and five years are used for permitting, design, and construction, respectively. The individual option lives represent the amount of time the company has to make a go/no-go decision on the next phase and invest in it. For instance, Sweet 'n Sour Cola has a maximum of three years to decide to go forward with the design and invest in it. Then the company has an additional two years to decide on and start the construction. The total and individual option lives basically depend on the market competition and the amount of time it takes to complete each of the project phases.

For some projects, the option to stage may not be explicit or intuitive. However, when uncertainty is high, a project can be redesigned into appropriate phases based on real options analysis. You can also calculate the option values for multiple scenarios and choose the one that offers the highest value for project execution. As the number of phases increases, the options calculations become more complex. Any compound option obviously can be treated as a simple option, the value of which will be most conservative and can be treated as a floor for the option value. A key problem with that comparison is that for the simple options framework, you would have to assume that all the investment occurs at one time, which is not true for its parallel counterpart. Furthermore, in turning a compound option into a simple option for comparison purpose, you should be cautious about defining the option life. In the HyperCola example, if you assume that the entire investment is made at one time, then Sweet 'n Sour Cola has only one year to decide on that investment, so that the product can come to market in seven years (since it takes six years to complete the entire project). Thus, the appropriate option life for a simple option for HyperCola would be one year.

The Black-Scholes model can also be used to solve sequential options by solving for the options sequentially, starting with the longest option first. As in the binomial model, the option value of the successor option becomes the asset value for the predecessor option. The Black-Scholes-derived ROVs for the HyperCola project are computed to be $9, $37, and $107 million for permitting, design, and construction phases, respectively.

Breaking a project into phases offers advantages when you can afford to delay the project possibly due to competitors facing high barriers to entry, significant investment costs especially toward the front end of the project, and potential future opportunities for expansion. However, you may lose economies of scale, resulting in higher costs, and allow the competition to capture the market. Whereas the availability of the sequential compound options is obvious in multiphase projects, formal valuation of the options provides quantitative data to help management make rational decisions.

Parallel Option

This section presents a parallel compound option example, a binomial solution (essentially the same as used for the preceding sequential option), and analysis of the results. The six-step process introduced in Chapter 6 is used with a few modifications in step 5 as required to solve a parallel compound option.

1. Frame the application

KlearKom, a mid-size telecommunications company, is considering offering third-generation (3G) wireless services to its customers in a specific market. Upgrading the existing network to meet the 3G requirements will involve an investment of $500 million, and the license for the required radio spectrum is estimated to cost $100 million. Discounted cash flow analysis using an appropriate risk-adjusted discount rate places the NPV of the expected future cash flows at $600 million, and the annual volatility factor for this payoff is calculated to be 35%. Based on the competition, KlearKom estimates that it has three years to make a go/no-go decision on this project. The continuous annual risk-free interest rate over this period is 5%. KlearKom can start the infrastructure upgrade at any time, but the spectrum license must be obtained before the upgrade can be tested and the service launched. This creates a parallel option, which the company can take advantage of in valuation of the project to make a better investment decision that takes into account the payoff uncertainty. Since both options — the option to purchase the 3G license and the option to invest in the network upgrade — are alive during the same time frame, and the license purchase must be exercised before the network upgrade, this constitutes a parallel compound option. What is the value of this option?

2. Identify the input parameters
S_o = $600 million
X_1 and X_2 = $100 and $500 million, respectively
T_1 and T_2 = 3 years
σ = 35%
r = 5%
δt = 1 year

3. Calculate the option parameters
$$u = \exp(\sigma\sqrt{\delta t})$$
$$= \exp(0.35 * \sqrt{1})$$
$$= 1.419$$
$$d = 1/u$$
$$= 1/1.419$$
$$= 0.705$$
$$p = \frac{\exp(r\delta t) - d}{u - d}$$
$$= [\exp(0.05 * 1) - 0.705]/(1.419 - 0.705)$$
$$= 0.485$$

4. Build the binomial tree and calculate the asset values at each node of the tree
Build a binomial tree, as shown in Figure 8-5, using one-year time intervals for three years and calculate the asset values over the life of the option. Start with S_o and multiply it by the up factor and the down factor to obtain S_ou and S_od,

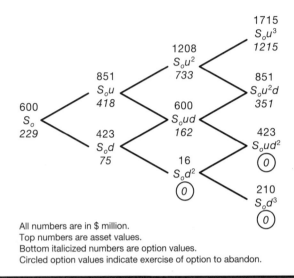

All numbers are in $ million.
Top numbers are asset values.
Bottom italicized numbers are option values.
Circled option values indicate exercise of option to abandon.

Figure 8-5. Binomial Tree for the Independent Option of the Parallel Compound Option

respectively. For the first time step: $S_o u$ = $600 million * 1.419 = $851 million; $S_o d$ = $600 million * 0.705 = $423 million. Moving to the right, continue in a similar fashion for every node of the binomial tree until the last time step. In Figure 8-5, the top value at each node represents the asset value at that node.

5. Calculate the option values for each of the two options

There are two parallel options for this project: the option to upgrade the network and the option to obtain a license. Both have the same lifetime, but the license must be obtained before the upgrade is completed for launch. The option calculations are basically the same as for the sequential option. The option values for the dependent option, the network upgrade, are calculated first, which then become the underlying asset values for the option to obtain the license.

5.1. Calculate the option values for the longest option at each node of the tree by backward induction

Figure 8-5 shows the option values (bottom italicized numbers) for the dependent option (network upgrade) at each node of the binomial tree by backward induction. At the terminal nodes, you would invest if the payoff is greater than the investment of $500 million; otherwise, you would let the option expire worthless. At each intermediate node, you have the option to either invest $500 million in the project and benefit from the payoff or continue to keep the option open until it expires.

A. Start with the terminal nodes that represent the last time step. At node $S_o u^3$, the expected asset value is $1,715 million, which is greater than $500 million. Therefore, you would invest and realize a net payoff of $1,215 million ($1,715 million – $500 million), thereby making the option value at this node $1,215 million.

B. At node $S_o d^3$, the expected asset value is $210 million, which is smaller than the investment value of $500 million; therefore, it does not make sense to invest in the project, which puts the option value at this node at $0 million.

C. Next, move on to the intermediate nodes, one step away from the last time step. Starting at the top, at node $S_o u^2$, calculate the expected asset value for keeping the option open. This is simply the discounted (at the risk-free rate) weighted average of potential future option values using the risk-neutral probabilities:

$$[p(S_o u^3) + (1 - p)(S_o u^2 d)] * \exp(-r\delta t)$$
$$= [0.485(\$1,215 \text{ million}) + (1 - 0.485)(\$351 \text{ million})] * \exp(-0.05)(1)$$
$$= \$733 \text{ million}$$

The expected asset value at this node is $1,208 million. Exercising the option at this node will provide an option value of $708 million ($1,208 million – $500 million). Since the value of keeping the option open is larger, you would keep the option open and continue; therefore, the option value at $S_o u^2$ is $733 million.

D. Similarly, at node $S_o d^2$, the expected asset value for keeping the option open, taking into account the downstream optimal decisions, is:

$$[0.485(\$351 \text{ million}) + (1 - 0.485)(\$0 \text{ million})] * \exp(-0.05)(1)$$
$$= \$162 \text{ million}$$

If, on the other hand, you exercise the option to invest, the expected asset value would be:

$600 million – $500 million = $100 million

Maximizing $162 million versus $100 million, you would keep the option open. Therefore, the option value at node $S_o d^2$ would be $162 million.

E. Complete the option valuation binomial tree all the way to time = 0 using the approach outlined above.

5.2. Calculate the option values for the preceding option at each node of the tree by backward induction

Calculate the option values for the independent option (purchase the 3G license) using the dependent option (network upgrade) values as the underlying asset values. The top numbers in Figure 8-6 show the underlying asset values, which are the same as the option values (bottom italicized numbers in Figure 8-5) from the network upgrade option. Calculate the option values (bottom italicized numbers in Figure 8-6) at each node of the binomial tree by backward induction. Each node represents the value maximization of investing versus continuation, where you have the option to either invest $100 million in the project or keep the option open. At the terminal nodes, you would invest if the payoff is greater than the investment of $100 million; otherwise, you would let the option expire worthless.

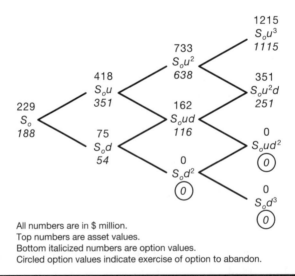

All numbers are in $ million.
Top numbers are asset values.
Bottom italicized numbers are option values.
Circled option values indicate exercise of option to abandon.

Figure 8-6. Binomial Tree for the Dependent Option of the Parallel Compound Option

A. Start with the terminal nodes that represent the last time step. At node $S_o u^3$, the expected asset value is $1,215 million. Since this is greater than $100 million, you would invest and realize a net payoff of $1,115 million ($1,215 million – $100 million). The option value at this node now would be $1,115 million.

B. At node $S_o u d^2$, the expected asset value is $0; therefore, no investment would be made, resulting in an option value of $0 at that node.

C. Next, move on to the intermediate nodes, one step away from the last time step. Starting at the top, at node $S_o u^2$, calculate the expected asset value for keeping the option open. This is simply the discounted (at the risk-free rate) weighted average of potential future option values using the risk-neutral probability as weights:

$$[p(S_o u^3) + (1 - p)(S_o u^2 d)] * \exp(-r\delta t)$$

$$= [0.485(\$1,115 \text{ million}) + (1 - 0.485)(\$251 \text{ million})]$$
$$* \exp(-0.05)(1)$$

$$= \$638 \text{ million}$$

The expected asset value at this node is $733 million. Exercising the option at this node will provide an option value of $633 million ($733 million – $100 million). Since the value of keeping the option open is larger than this, you would keep the option open and continue; therefore, the option value at $S_o u^2$ is $638 million.

D. Similarly, at node $S_o u d$, the expected asset value for keeping the option open, taking into account the downstream optimal decisions, is:

$$[0.485(\$251 \text{ million}) + (1 - 0.485)(\$0 \text{ million})] * \exp(-0.05)(1)$$

$$= \$116 \text{ million}$$

The expected asset value at this node is $162 million. Exercising the option at this node will provide an option value of $62 million ($162 million – $100 million). Since the value of keeping the option open is larger than this, you would keep the option open and continue; therefore, the option value at $S_o u d$ is $116 million.

E. Complete the option valuation binomial tree all the way to time = 0 using the approach outlined above.

6. Analyze the results
The project NPV is calculated to be $0 million for a payoff of $600 million, assuming the total investment of $600 million ($500 million + $100 million)

occurs at time = 0. This project would not be considered for investment because of this NPV. Real options analysis (ROA), however, shows an ROV of $188 million due to the compound option. Thus, consideration of the flexibility embedded in this project makes it more likely to be accepted for investment.

Although the option available in this example seems similar to the sequential compound option discussed in the previous section, there is a minor difference. In both cases, the predecessor option must be exercised to take advantage of the successor option. But for KlearKom, both the options — the option to invest in the network upgrade and the option to purchase the 3G license — are alive during the same time frame, and one must be exercised (purchase of the license) before the exercise of the other is completed, thereby creating a parallel compound option. The infrastructure construction can be started at any time, but the spectrum license must be obtained before the network upgrade can be tested and the service launched. This creates a parallel option, which the company can take advantage of in valuation of the project to make a better investment decision that takes into account the payoff uncertainty. The options solution method is essentially the same for sequential and compound options, yielding exactly the same ROV. The difference lies in framing the option.

RAINBOW OPTIONS

A key input parameter of any ROA problem is the volatility factor that represents the uncertainty associated with the underlying asset value. Typically, it is calculated as an aggregate factor built from many of the uncertainties that contribute to it. For example, the aggregate volatility used in the ROA of a product development project is representative of and a function of multiple uncertainties, including the unit price, number of units sold, unit variable cost, etc. If one of the sources of uncertainty has a significant impact on the options value compared to the others or if management decisions are to be tied to a particular source of uncertainty, you may want to keep the uncertainties separate in the options calculations. For instance, if you own a lease on an undeveloped oil reserve, you face two separate uncertainties: the price of oil and the quantity of oil in the reserve. You may want to treat them separately in evaluating the ROV.

When multiple sources of uncertainty are considered, the options are called rainbow options, and this warrants the use of different volatility factors — one for each source of uncertainty — in the options calculations. The options solution method is basically the same as for a single volatility factor except that it involves a quadrinomial tree instead of a binomial. This is because the asset can take one of four values as you move from one node to the nodes of the next time step in the lattice. The following illustration shows the solution to an options problem with two sources of uncertainty.

1. Frame the application

Schizo Petro Chemco is contemplating building a chemical plant to produce specialty polymers that can reduce construction costs. The raw materials for this plant are by-products of petroleum refining and are supplied by nearby refineries. The present value of the expected cash flows from future polymer sales is estimated to be $160 million. Plant construction is expected to cost $200 million. The project payoff is influenced by two types of uncertainty: market demand for the final product (specialty polymers), the annual volatility (σ_1) of which is estimated to be 30%, and the oil prices that dictate the cost of the raw materials, which are shown to exhibit an annual volatility (σ_2) of 20%. What is the value of the option to wait to invest given an option life of two years, over which the continuous annual risk-free rate is expected to be 5%?

2. Identify the input parameters

S_o = $160 million
X = $200 million
T = 2 years
σ_1 = 30%
σ_2 = 20%
r = 5%
δt = 1 year

3. Calculate the option parameters

$u_1 = \exp(\sigma_1 \sqrt{\delta t})$
    $= \exp(0.3 * \sqrt{1})$
    $= 1.350$
$d_1 = 1/u_1$
    $= 1/1.350 = 0.741$
$u_2 = \exp(\sigma_2 \sqrt{\delta t})$
    $= \exp(0.2 * \sqrt{1})$
    $= 1.221$
$d_2 = 1/u_2$
    $= 1/1.221 = 0.819$
$p_1 = \dfrac{\exp(r\delta t) - d_1}{u_1 - d_1}$
    $= [\exp(0.05 * 1) - 0.741]/(1.350 - 0.741)$

$$= 0.510$$

$$p_2 = \frac{\exp(r\delta t) - d_2}{u_2 - d_2}$$

$$= [\exp(0.05 * 1) - 0.819]/(1.221 - 0.819)$$

$$= 0.577$$

4. Build the quadrinomial tree and calculate the asset values at each node of the tree

Build a quadrinomial tree, as shown in Figure 8-7, using one-year time intervals for two years and calculate the asset values over the life of the option. The lattice in this example is a quadrinomial instead of a binomial, because the two volatility factors yield two up and down factors each. At any given node of the tree, therefore, there are four possible asset values in the next time period. The factors used to determine these values are: u_1u_2, u_1d_2, d_1u_2, d_1d_2. Start with S_o and multiply it separately by the four up/down factors to obtain $S_ou_1u_2$, $S_ou_1d_2$, $S_od_1u_2$, and $S_od_1d_2$ for the first time step. For example, $S_ou_1u_2 = \$160$ million $* 1.350 * 1.221 = \$264$ million; $S_od_1d_2 = \$160$ million $* 0.741 * 0.819 = \$97$ million. Continue in a similar fashion for every node of the quadrinomial tree for the next step, which is also the last step in this example, as shown in Figure 8-7, where the top value at each node represents the asset value.

5. Calculate the option values across the tree by backward induction

Figure 8-7 shows the option values (bottom italicized numbers) at each node of the quadrinomial tree calculated by backward induction. Each terminal node represents the value maximization of exercising the option by investing \$200 million versus letting the option expire. Each intermediate node represents the value maximization of continuation versus exercising the option.

A. Start with the terminal nodes that represent the last time step first. At node $S_ou_1u_2u_1u_2$, the expected asset value is \$435 million. If you invest \$200 million to build the plant, the net payoff will be \$435 million – \$200 million = \$235 million. Since your objective is to maximize your return, you would exercise the option by investing. Thus the option value at this node becomes \$235 million.

B. At node $S_od_1d_2d_1d_2$, the expected asset value is \$59 million. Since this is less than the investment cost of \$200 million, you would not invest and would let the option expire. The option value at this node would, therefore, be \$0.

C. Next, move on to the intermediate nodes, one step away from the last time step. Starting at the top, at node $S_ou_1u_2$, calculate the expected asset

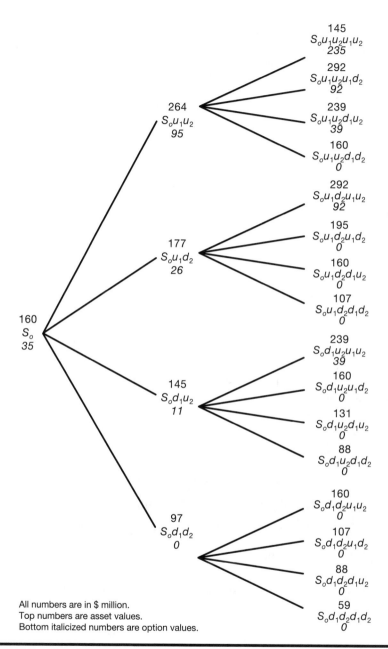

All numbers are in $ million.
Top numbers are asset values.
Bottom italicized numbers are option values.

Figure 8-7. Quadrinomial Tree for the Compound Rainbow Option

value for keeping the option open and accounting for the downstream optimal decisions. This is simply the discounted (at the risk-free rate) weighted average of potential future option values using the risk-neutral probabilities. That value at node $S_o u_1 u_2$ is:

$$[p_1 p_2 (S_o u_1 u_2 u_1 u_2) + p_1 (1 - p_2)(S_o u_1 u_2 u_1 d_2) + (1 - p_1) p_2 (S_o u_1 u_2 d_1 u_2)$$

$$+ (1 - p_1)(1 - p_2)(S_o u_1 u_2 d_1 d_2)] * \exp(-r\delta t)$$

$$= [0.510 * 0.577 * (\$235 \text{ million}) + 0.510 * (1 - 0.577)$$

$$* (\$92 \text{ million}) + (1 - 0.510) * 0.577$$

$$* (\$39 \text{ million}) + (1 - 0.510) * (1 - 0.577)$$

$$* (\$0 \text{ million})] * \exp(-0.05)(1)$$

$$= \$95 \text{ million}$$

If, on the other hand, the option is exercised by investing $200 million, the expected asset value would be:

$$\$264 \text{ million} - \$200 \text{ million} = \$64 \text{ million}$$

Since this value is less than the $95 million corresponding to the alternative to continue, you would not exercise the option, and the option value at this node would be $95 million.

D. Similarly at node $S_o d_1 u_2$, the expected asset value for keeping the option open, taking into account the downstream optimal decisions, is:

$$[0.510 * 0.577 * (\$39 \text{ million}) + 0.510 * (1 - 0.577) * (\$0 \text{ million})$$

$$+ (1 - 0.510) * 0.577 * (\$0 \text{ million}) + (1 - 0.510)$$

$$* (1 - 0.577) * (\$0 \text{ million})] * \exp(-0.05)(1)$$

$$= \$11 \text{ million}$$

If, on the other hand, you exercise the option to invest, the expected asset value would be:

$$\$145 \text{ million} - \$200 \text{ million} = -\$55 \text{ million}$$

Maximizing $11 million versus –$55 million, you would keep the option open. Therefore, the option value at node $S_o d_1 u_2$ would be $11 million.

E. Complete the option valuation quadrinomial tree to the next step on the left at time = 0.

6. Analyze the results

Let us first compare the NPV of the asset based on discounted cash flow (DCF) versus ROA. The project payoff value based on the DCF calculation is expected to be $160 million at an investment cost of $200 million, resulting in an NPV of –$40 million. The project value based on ROA, considering the two sources of uncertainty separately, is $35 million. The difference of $75 million [$35 million – (–$40 million)] is the value added to the project because of the ROV that management can take into consideration in making its investment decision. If the option value is calculated using only one aggregate volatility factor of 20% or 30%, the value of the option to wait for this example would be $10 or $19 million, respectively. This shows that unless the multiple sources of uncertainty are considered, the option value may not be completely realized.

The solution to a rainbow option problem requires a quadrinomial method because of multiple sources of uncertainty, and the calculations are cumbersome compared to a recombining binomial tree. In the Schizo Petro Chemco example, an option life of two years was used to keep the illustration simple. With longer lives, however, the calculations become even more complex due to the growing quadrinomial tree. Although the calculations are complex with this approach, the underlying theme in computing the option value remains the same as with the binomial method. The standard Black-Scholes equation cannot accommodate the multiple sources of uncertainty and is not useful for rainbow options.

For the sake of simplicity, practitioners typically combine all the known uncertainties that drive the asset value and estimate one aggregate volatility factor for the asset. As discussed in Chapter 6, Monte Carlo simulation is a commonly used method for this purpose. You may, however, want to treat the uncertainties separately, if the controlling variables are independent of each other, evolve differently over time, and especially impact the asset value in different directions. Separate treatment of the different sources of uncertainty gives you better insight into what variables have the highest impact on the option value. It also helps you to easily re-evaluate the project value when one of the two uncertainties clears. Most important, it will help you capture the true value of the option embedded in the project.

Strictly speaking, the quadrinomial lattice is appropriate when the sources of uncertainty are not related to each other. In the Schizo Petro Chemco example, the two sources of volatility (cost of the raw material and market demand for the final product) may be correlated, but we assumed the correlation to be insignificant for the purpose of illustration. In real world situations, the different sources of uncertainty, especially market uncertainty, may not be completely independent, but as long as the correlation is not significant, the quadrinomial method is expected to provide good approximation of the true option value. Private uncertainty related to the technical effectiveness of a project, on the other hand, is independent of market uncertainty and can be accounted for in options valuation as demonstrated with an example presented in a later section of this chapter. As you will see, decision tree analysis is used to address the private uncertainty, and either a binomial or quadrinomial approach is used to account for the market uncertainty, depending on whether it is a simple or rainbow option, respectively. The quadrinomial approach uses the nonrecombining lattice instead of the recombining lattice, which is a characteristic of the binomial approach. The nonrecombining lattice also is used when the volatility factor for the underlying asset value changes within the option life, as shown in the following example.

OPTIONS WITH CHANGING VOLATILITY

In most ROA calculations, the volatility of the project payoff is assumed to be relatively constant over the option life and is represented by a single aggregate factor. Therefore, a single volatility factor is used across the binomial tree to represent the option life. However, if the volatility is expected to change during the option life and is significant, it can be accounted for by modifying the binomial method. Start with the initial volatility factor, build the binomial tree, and calculate the asset values at each node of the tree using the corresponding up and down factors up to the point where the volatility changes. From that point on, calculate the asset values using the new up and down factors related to the new volatility factor, which will result in a nonrecombining lattice. The option value calculation method using backward induction will be the same for the entire tree. The following example for an option to wait demonstrates the calculations involved. (Although this is a simple option by definition, it requires an advanced form of the lattice method using the nonrecombining lattice and hence its inclusion in this chapter on advanced options.)

1. Frame the application
EnviroTechno, an environmental technology company, is considering an investment in a new patented product that can help industries comply with an environmental regulation that is under consideration by the U.S. Congress. Whereas the regulation is expected to be passed two years from now, many multinational companies based in the United States are beginning to comply because of

similar regulations already in place in Europe and many other countries. EnviroTechno forecasts the present value of the expected future cash flows and the investment (product development and launch) cost to be $400 million each. The annual volatility of the logarithmic returns for the future cash flows is estimated to be 30% for the next two years and is expected to decrease to 20% at the point when the regulations go into effect. The annual continuous risk-free rate for the next four years is 5%. What is the value of this project using ROA?

2. Identify the input parameters

S_o = $400 million
T = 4 years
σ = 30% (volatility during the first 2 years)
σ' = 20% (volatility after 2 years)
r = 5%
X = $400 million
δt = 1 year

3. Calculate the option parameters

Since the up and down factors depend on the volatility factor, which changes after two years, there will be two sets of up and down factors corresponding to the two volatility factors. They will be denoted by u, u', d, and d', respectively. There will also be two risk-neutral probability factors (p and p') corresponding to the two sets of up and down factors.

$$u = \exp(\sigma\sqrt{\delta t})$$
$$= \exp(0.30 * \sqrt{1})$$
$$= 1.350$$
$$d = 1/u$$
$$= 1/1.350 = 0.741$$
$$u' = \exp(\sigma'\sqrt{\delta t})$$
$$= \exp(0.20 * \sqrt{1})$$
$$= 1.221$$
$$d' = 1/u'$$
$$= 1/1.221 = 0.819$$
$$p = \frac{\exp(r\delta t) - d}{u - d}$$
$$= [\exp(0.05 * 1) - 0.741]/(1.350 - 0.741)$$
$$= 0.510$$
$$p' = \frac{\exp(r\delta t) - d'}{u' - d'}$$

= [exp(0.05 * 1) – 0.819]/(1.221 – 0.819)

= 0.577

4. Build the binomial tree and calculate the asset values at each node of the tree

Build a binomial tree, as shown in Figure 8-8, using one-year time intervals for four years to account for the change in the up and down factors after the first two years. Start with S_o and multiply it by the up factor and down factor to obtain $S_o u$ and $S_o d$, respectively. For example, $S_o u$ = $400 million * 1.350 = $540 million; $S_o d$ = $400 million * 0.741 = $296 million. Continue in a similar fashion for every node of the binomial tree for the next time step. After two years, the volatility changes, and so do the up and down factors. Therefore, from this point on, the asset values are calculated using u' and d'. Because of the change in these factors, the tree will no longer be recombining starting at the third year. For example, the value at node $S_o u^2$ is $729 million. There are two nodes in the third year that originate from this node. The upper node $S_o u^2 u'$ = $729 million * 1.221 = $890 million; the lower node $S_o u^2 d'$ = $729 million * 0.819 = $597 million. Continue in a similar fashion until the last time step, as shown in Figure 8-8, where the top values at each node represent the asset value.

5. Calculate the option values at each node of the tree by backward induction

Calculate the option values at each node of the binomial tree using backward induction. These are the bottom italicized numbers in Figure 8-8. Each terminal node represents the value maximization of investing at a cost of $400 million versus letting the option expire. At every node in the prior years, you have a choice to either keep the option open for the future or exercise it by committing the investment.

A. Start with the terminal nodes that represent the last time step. At node $S_o u^2 u'^2$, the expected asset value is $1,087 million. Since this is greater than the investment value of $400 million, you will exercise the option, and the option value would be $1,087 million – $400 million = $687 million.

B. At node $S_o d^2 d'^2$, the expected asset value is $147 million. Since this is less than the exercise cost of $400 million, you will let the option expire worthless. Thus the option value at this node is $0.

C. Next, move on to the intermediate nodes, one step away from the last time step. Starting at the top, at node $S_o u^2 u'$, calculate the expected value for keeping the option open and accounting for the downstream optimal decisions. This is simply the discounted (at the risk-free rate) weighted

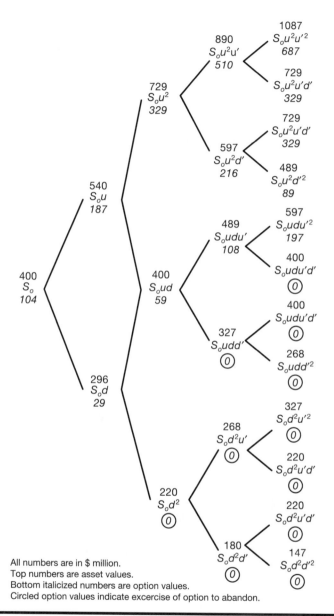

All numbers are in $ million.
Top numbers are asset values.
Bottom italicized numbers are option values.
Circled option values indicate excercise of option to abandon.

Figure 8-8.   Nonrecombining Binomial Tree for the Option to Wait with Changing Volatilities

average of potential future option values using the risk-neutral probability. That value, for example, at this node is:

$$[p'(S_ou^2u'^2) + (1 - p')(S_ou^2u'd')] * \exp(-r\delta t)$$

$$= [0.577(\$687 \text{ million}) + (1 - 0.577)(\$329 \text{ million})]$$
$$* \exp(-0.05)(1)$$

$$= \$510 \text{ million}$$

If the option is exercised to invest by spending $400 million, the expected option value would be:

$$(\$890 \text{ million}) - \$400 \text{ million} = \$490 \text{ million}$$

Since this value is less than the $510 million corresponding to the alternative to continue, you would not exercise the option, and the option value at this node would be $510 million.

D. Similarly at node S_ou^2d', the expected asset value for keeping the option open, taking into account the downstream optimal decisions, is:

$$[0.577(\$329 \text{ million}) + (1 - 0.577)(\$89 \text{ million})] * \exp(-0.05)(1)$$

$$= \$216 \text{ million}$$

If, on the other hand, you exercise the option to invest at a cost of $400 million, the expected asset value would be:

$$(\$597 \text{ million}) - \$400 \text{ million} = \$197 \text{ million}$$

Maximizing $216 million versus $197 million, you would not exercise the option. Therefore, the option value at node S_ou^2d' would be $216 million.

E. Complete the option valuation binomial tree all the way to time = 0. You should use the value of p' as the risk-neutral probability for nodes in year 3 and year 2. For the nodes in year 1 and year 0, however, you should use the value of p as the risk-neutral probability. For example, at node S_ou, the expected value of keeping the option open, taking into account the downstream optimal decisions, is:

$$[0.510(\$329 \text{ million}) + (1 - 0.510)(\$59 \text{ million})] * \exp(-0.05)(1)$$

$$= \$187 \text{ million}$$

If, on the other hand, you exercise the option to invest at a cost of $400 million, the expected asset value would be:

$$(\$540 \text{ million}) - \$400 \text{ million} = \$140 \text{ million}$$

Maximizing $187 million versus $140 million, you would not exercise the option. Therefore, the option valuation at node S_0u would be $187 million.

6. Analyze the results

Let us first compare the value of this project based on DCF versus ROA. The present value of the cash flows for the current operation based on the risk-adjusted DCF method is $400 million, and with the same amount of investment the NPV is:

$$\$400 \text{ million} - \$400 \text{ million} = \$0 \text{ million}$$

Based on the DCF analysis alone, EnviroTechno would decide not to proceed with this project. However, ROA suggests that the option to wait to undertake this project is worth $104 million. Comparing this with the baseline NPV of $0 million for the project, the additional value provided by the option, therefore, is:

$$\$104 \text{ million} - \$0 \text{ million} = \$104 \text{ million}$$

The value added to the project because of real options is substantial. Therefore, EnviroTechno may decide to keep the option to invest in this project open at this time and exercise it when the uncertainty clears and conditions become favorable.

The volatility of the underlying asset is expected to remain the same during the option lifetime in most cases but may change due to special circumstances, such as those encountered by EnviroTechno. When new regulations are established, the volatility is likely to decrease as the market tries to comply with them. If the volatility is assumed to be constant (30%) for the entire option life in the EnviroTechno example, the option value would be $112 million, whereas with 20% volatility after two years it decreases to $104 million. Further sensitivity analysis shows the following results:

25%	$108 million
15%	$100 million
10%	$97 million

The ROV in this example increases by about $8 million for a 10% increase in volatility. Consideration of volatility changes during the option life in the ROA calculations provides a more accurate estimate of the ROV of the project.

INTEGRATION OF DECISION TREES INTO REAL OPTIONS ANALYSIS

The real options examples presented up to this point involved market uncertainty and contingent decisions related to the resolution of that uncertainty. Many projects, however, face both market and private uncertainties, as discussed in Chapter 3. For an oil company, the market uncertainty surrounding the price of oil dictates the revenues from an unexplored oil field, whereas the yield from the site is subject to private uncertainty. The uncertainty related to the effectiveness of a new technology is private, and the probability of commercial success is market driven. Similarly, the efficacy of an experimental drug is subject to private uncertainty, whereas its sales are controlled by the market. In all these cases, it becomes necessary to account for the private risk along with the market risk in the ROA during project valuation. The following example illustrates how decision tree analysis (DTA) can incorporate private uncertainty into ROA, thereby providing an integrated framework for valuation of projects that exhibit both private and market uncertainties.

Example

Easy BooTox specializes in novel drug delivery techniques. It recently developed a skin patch that can deliver the drug BooTox transdermally, the-state-of-the-art delivery technique, and hence avoid the pain of injections. Before the product can be launched, the company needs to conduct large-scale clinical trials to prove the efficacy of the new technique and win FDA approval. There is private risk in both these steps that can lead to the abandonment of this project. The company estimates an 80% probability of success (p_1) with the clinical trials, which are expected to last for two years, and a 90% probability of success (p_2) in obtaining FDA approval, which takes an additional year. The costs are expected to be $10 million and $5 million, respectively, for the two phases. Even if FDA approval is secured and the product reaches the launch phase, its commercial success depends on market acceptance. Based on DCF analysis using a risk-adjusted discount rate of 20%, the value of the expected future free cash flows from this product at the time of launch (three years from today) is estimated to be $50 million with a launch cost of $40 million. The annual volatility of the payoff is 40%. The continuous annual risk-free rate over the next five years is 5%. What is the ROV of the project, given that Easy BooTox can launch the product anytime within five years once the clinical trials are successful and the product is approved by the FDA?

Solution

An integrated approach that involves both real options and decision trees is applied to solve this problem, since it includes both market and private risks. Two scenarios can be considered in valuation of this project:

1. Market risk is cleared only after, but not before, FDA approval. Once the project is initiated, the go/no-go decisions within the development phase are strictly related to the resolution of private uncertainty only. For instance, Easy BooTox would proceed with the FDA application as long as the clinical trials are successful, assuming that market risk cannot be cleared until after FDA approval.
2. Market uncertainty can be resolved during the development phase, and therefore the decisions in this phase are dependent upon resolution of both private and market uncertainties. For example, even if the product is successful in the clinical trials, the company may not pursue the FDA application process if the market uncertainty cleared and showed a negative NPV.

Depending upon the scenario, ROA and DTA are integrated differently in calculating the project ROV.

For the first scenario, assuming the product will pass the clinical tests and receive FDA approval, ROA is first applied to calculate the project ROV at the first possible launch time, time = 3 years (which makes the option life five years). The ROV is then discounted to time = 0 to account for the probability of technical success and FDA approval using DTA. The solution to the second scenario involves application of ROA to calculate the ROV at time = 0 using an option life of eight years, wherein the development phase success/failure probabilities are incorporated into the first three years to account for the private risk. A detailed step-by-step solution for the first scenario is presented next, followed by a brief discussion of the solution process for the second one.

Scenario 1

Real Options Analysis

Assuming FDA approval, you can treat the option available in the project as a simple option, the value of which can be calculated using the binomial method.

1. Identify the input parameters

S_o = \$50 million
X = \$40 million
T = 5 years
σ = 40%
r = 5%
δt = 1 year
p_1 = 0.8
p_2 = 0.9

2. Calculate the option parameters

u = exp($\sigma\sqrt{\delta t}$)
   = exp(0.4 $*$ $\sqrt{1}$)
   = 1.492
d = $1/u$
   = 1/1.492 = 0.670
p = $\dfrac{\exp(r\delta t) - d}{u - d}$
   = [exp(0.05 $*$ 1) – 0.670]/(1.492 – 0.670)
   = 0.464

3. Build the binomial tree and calculate the asset values at each node of the tree

Build a binomial tree, as shown in Figure 8-9, at one-year intervals for five years to account for the change in the underlying asset values. Start with S_o and multiply it by the up factor and the down factor to obtain $S_o u$ and $S_o d$, respectively. For the first time step, for example, $S_o u$ = \$50 million $*$ 1.492 = \$75 million; $S_o d$ = \$50 million $*$ 0.670 = \$34 million. Moving to the right, continue in a similar fashion for every node of the binomial tree until the last time step. In Figure 8-9, the top value at each node represents the asset value at that node.

4. Calculate the option values at each node of the tree by backward induction

The bottom italicized numbers in Figure 8-9 are the option values at each node calculated by backward induction. At each terminal node, you have the choice to either exercise the option by investing in the launch or let the option expire by discontinuing the project. Each intermediate node represents the value maximization of continuing to wait versus exercising by investing \$40 million.

A. Start with the terminal nodes that represent the last time step. At node $S_o u^5$, the expected asset value is \$369 million. If you exercise the option and invest \$40 million for the launch, the option value would be \$369 million – \$40 million = \$329 million. Since your objective is to maxi-

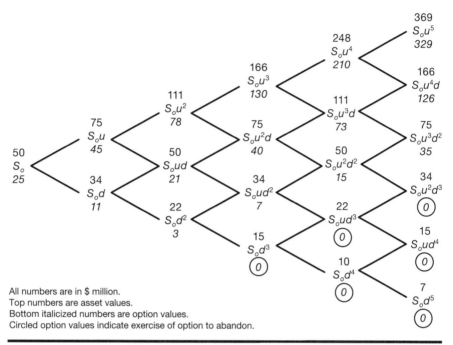

Figure 8-9. Binomial Tree for the Option to Wait for Easy BooTox

mize your return, you would invest in the launch rather than let the option expire. Thus the option value at this node becomes $329 million.

B. At node $S_ou^2d^3$, the expected asset value is $34 million. If you invest in the launch, the option value would be $34 million – $40 million = –$6 million. Since you want to maximize your return, you would rather let the option expire by not investing in the launch. Your option value at $S_ou^2d^3$ would, therefore, be $0 million.

C. Next, move on to the intermediate nodes, one step away from the last time step. Starting at the top, at node S_ou^4, calculate the expected asset value for keeping the option open and accounting for the downstream optimal decisions. This is simply the discounted (at the risk-free rate) weighted average of potential future option values using the risk-neutral probability. That value at node S_ou^4 is:

$$[p(S_ou^5) + (1 - p)(S_ou^4d)] * \exp(-r\delta t)$$

$$= [0.464(\$329 \text{ million}) + (1 - 0.464)(\$126 \text{ million})]$$
$$* \exp(-0.05)(1)$$

$$= \$210 \text{ million}$$

If, on the other hand, the option is exercised to invest $40 million, the expected asset value would be:

$$\$248 \text{ million} - \$40 \text{ million} = \$208 \text{ million}$$

Since this value is less than the $210 million corresponding to the alternative to continue, you would not exercise the invest option but would let it remain open, and the option value at this node would be $210 million.

D. Similarly at node $S_o u^2 d^2$, the expected asset value for keeping the option open, taking into account the downstream optimal decisions, is:

$$[0.464(\$35 \text{ million}) + (1 - 0.464)(\$0 \text{ million})] * \exp(-0.05)(1)$$
$$= \$15 \text{ million}$$

If, on the other hand, you exercise the option, the expected asset value would be:

$$\$50 \text{ million} - \$40 \text{ million} = \$10 \text{ million}$$

Maximizing $15 million versus $10 million, you would not exercise the option but would let it remain open. Therefore, the option valuation at node $S_o u^2 d^2$ would be $15 million.

E. Complete the option valuation binomial tree all the way to time = 0.

Decision Tree Analysis

Based on the ROA, the ROV of the launch phase at the time of the launch is $25 million. This is the ROV of the project if the first two phases of the project (clinical trials and FDA application) succeed. Now we calculate the ROV of the overall project at time = 0 using DTA.

We assume that Easy BooTox will terminate the project, resulting in zero payoff, if either the clinical trials or FDA approval fails. Figure 8-10 shows the decision tree for different decision paths, outcomes, and costs and payoffs associated with different paths. The success path implicitly represents a "go" decision to the next project phase, while the failure path indicates project abandonment. The steps involved in solving the decision tree and the solution are outlined in Table 8-1. The results show that the overall project ROV at time = 0 is $0.859 million.

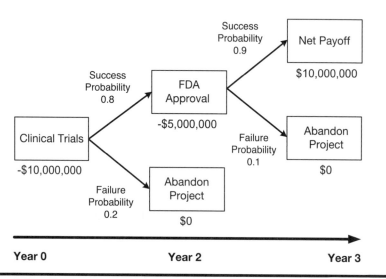

Figure 8-10.   Decision Tree for Easy BooTox

Scenario 2

In scenario 2, as was the case for the EnviroTechno example discussed in an earlier section of this chapter, Easy BooTox also exhibits two sources of uncertainty, which would require a quadrinomial solution. As shown in Figure 8-11, the lattice starts as a binomial and becomes a quadrinomial at year 2, when the clinical trial uncertainty is resolved. One set of up and down branches from each of the two nodes at year 1 are associated with the success and failure outcomes at year = 2. For example, $S_o u^2 x_1$ and $S_o u d x_1$ represent the success outcomes and $S_o u^2 y_1$ and $S_o u d y_1$ represent the failure outcomes from node $S_o u$, where x_1 and y_1 are the asset value adjustment factors related to the success and failure of the clinical trials, respectively. If the project is abandoned because of failed clinical trials and continues into the next phase because of success, y_1 will be 0 and x_1 will be 1.0. The nodes at year 2 that are associated with the failure outcome do not continue further, because the rational decision at these nodes would be not to continue the project and the asset value will be zero. Similarly, at year 3, the success and failure outcomes of the FDA process are denoted by x_2 and y_2, and the nodes associated with the failure outcome do not continue further. More mutually exclusive outcomes can be added into the lattice at any node with corresponding asset value adjustment factors. For instance, FDA approval may be obtained for the product for either the entire target general population or only a small niche segment. The new third state, repre-

Table 8-1. Easy BooTox Decision Tree Calculations with Real Options Analysis

Input Data		
Discount rate	8%	
Clinical trials duration	2 years	
Clinical trials cost	$10,000,000	
Probability of success with clinical trials	0.8	
FDA approval process duration	1 year	
FDA approval process cost	$5,000,000	
Probability of FDA approval	0.9	
Payoff at launch (end of FDA process)	$25,000,000	
FDA Process Phase		
Project payoff at the end of year 3	0.9($25,000,000) + 0.1($0)	$22,500,000
Present value at the end of year 2	$22,500,000/(1 + 0.08)^1	$20,833,333
Less FDA process phase cost		−$5,000,000
Project NPV at the end of year 2	$20,833,333 − $5,000,000	$15,833,333
Clinical Trials Phase		
Project payoff at the end of year 2	0.8($15,833,333) + 0.2($0)	$12,666,667
Present value at year 0	$12,666,667/(1 + 0.08)^2	$10,859,625
Less clinical trials phase cost		−$10,000,000
Project NPV at year 0	$10,859,625 − $10,000,000	$859,625

sented by, say, z, can be incorporated into the lattice, just as the other two are. If the asset value for the niche segment is expected to be only 40% of the value expected for the entire target general population, z would be 0.4. When there are more than two states, the lattice becomes increasingly complex and more difficult to solve.

In the Easy BooTox example, from the third year until the end of the option life, each surviving node would result in only two outcomes, because the private uncertainty has been resolved by that point and only the market uncertainty remains. Lattice branches beyond year 3 are not shown in Figure 8-11 because of the enormous structure that would be required. Once the branches related to the failure outcomes of private uncertainty are removed from the lattice, it becomes a recombining binomial, which makes the solution relatively simple. Figure 8-12 shows the resulting lattice where, for the sake of simplicity, notation of x_1 and x_2 has been omitted.

In building the lattice in Figure 8-12, you start with the expected value of the underlying asset value at time = 0. This would be $40 million after discounting the asset value of $50 million at time = 3 years with a rate (8%) slightly higher than the risk-free rate. (The reason for using this rate is discussed in question 7 in the section on the discount rate dilemma in Chapter 3.) You then compute the asset values (top values in Figure 8-12) using the up and down

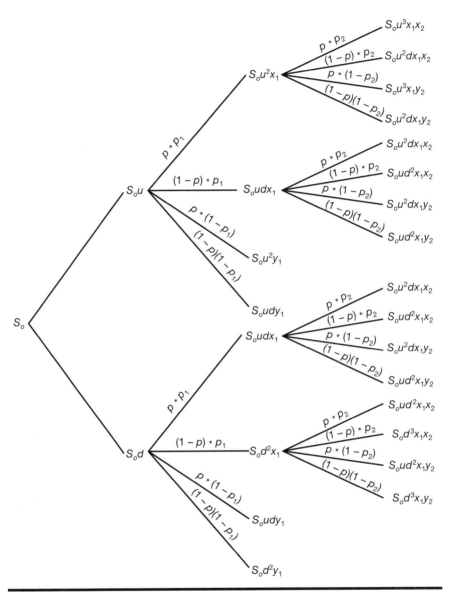

Figure 8-11. Partial Quadrinomial Tree for Easy BooTox Scenario 2

factors for a period of eight years. You apply the value maximization rule at the terminal nodes and calculate the option values at each node. By backward induction, you then calculate the option values for years 8 through 3 as illustrated in the previous ROA examples. In these years, only the market uncer-

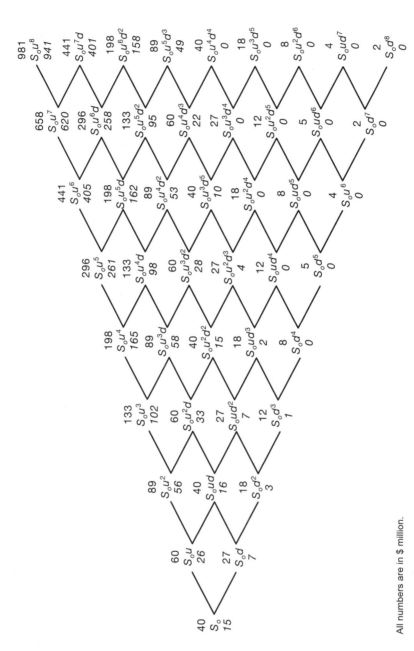

All numbers are in $ million.

Figure 8-12. Binomial Tree for Easy BooTox Scenario 2

tainty exists, because the private uncertainty was already cleared in year 3 according to the conditions assumed in this scenario. Therefore, only the risk-neutral probability is used in calculating the expected value of keeping the option open and accounting for the downstream optimal decisions. For example, at node $S_o u^5 d$, that value would be given by the following equation:

$$[p(S_o u^6 d) + (1 - p)(S_o u^5 d^2)] * \exp(-r\delta t)$$

$$= [0.464 * \$258 \text{ million} + (1 - 0.464)(\$95 \text{ million})] * \exp(-0.05)(1)$$

$$= \$162 \text{ million}$$

However, at the year 2 nodes, the product has not yet received FDA approval; therefore, the success/failure probability of that outcome has to be incorporated into the calculation of the expected value of keeping the option open at those nodes and accounting for the downstream optimal decisions. This is done by multiplying the risk-neutral probability by the objective probability of success of FDA approval. (The probability factors to be used are shown in Figure 8-11.) For example, at node $S_o u^2$, the expected asset value of keeping the option open and accounting for the downstream optimal decisions is:

$$[p * p_2(S_o u^3) + (1 - p) * p_2 * (S_o u^2 d)] * \exp(-r\delta t)$$

$$= [0.464 * 0.9 * \$102 \text{ million} + (1 - 0.464) * 0.9$$
$$* (\$33 \text{ million})] * \exp(-0.05)(1)$$

$$= \$56 \text{ million}$$

Similarly, at the year 1 node, during backward induction, the risk-neutral probability must be multiplied by the objective probability of clinical trial success, p_1. The probability factors to be used in the backward induction at the nodes for years 2 and 1 are included in Figure 8-11.

Analysis

A comparison of the project ROV from the two scenarios shows almost negligible difference: scenario 1 = $0.86 million and scenario 2 = $1.0 million. It seems that irrespective of the assumptions made relative to when the market uncertainty can be cleared, the ROV remains almost the same, and it is because of the specific inputs used for the problem. In scenario 1, the ROV from year 3 is discounted within the decision tree, which is constructed separately, whereas in the second scenario the decision tree is directly integrated into the options solution lattice. Both scenarios are considered to involve rainbow options because of more than one source of uncertainty. Scenario 1 shows compound options explicitly, whereas the other scenario does not. In scenario 2, although the compound options are embedded in the project, they are only implicitly shown in the solution process.

The option to invest in the clinical trials is an option to apply for and receive FDA approval, which, in turn, is an option to launch. However, the binomial solution used to calculate the ROV in scenario 1 did not involve a sequential compound option. This is because the clinical trials and FDA process represent private uncertainty, which we accounted for with a decision tree. In the Sweet 'n Sour Cola example presented earlier to illustrate sequential compound options, we used ROA but not the decision trees, because it involved only market, but not private, risk.

A practical scenario that involves both a sequential compound options solution and DTA for the Easy BooTox example would be to consider launching the project after FDA approval on a pilot basis first in a small market to clear market uncertainty before making a full-scale launch investment. In this case, you would first solve for the ROV at the time of the pilot test using the pilot test and full-scale launch as sequential options and then apply DTA with success/failure probabilities to solve for the ROV at time = 0.

Scenario 1 considered private and market risks separately by assuming that the market risk comes into the picture only after the product receives FDA approval. However, even before the launch Easy BooTox could get some limited market feedback from focus groups on their preference for transdermal products. Then again, it could be argued that because the focus groups cannot actually use the product before FDA approval, any such feedback would not accurately represent the market uncertainty. In view of these considerations, accounting for the private and market risks separately, as done in scenario 1, would probably give a better estimate of the true value of the project.

Although market risk is common in any industry, some analysts believe that it does not exist in the drug development business, because once a drug receives FDA approval, they contend that the payoff is always higher than the launch cost, even when the drug is considered a failure by industry standards. Therefore, they argue that there is no need for ROA in drug development project valuation and traditional tools will suffice. We believe that with the exponential increase in the launch and marketing costs of drugs in recent times, coupled with fierce competition, this may no longer be true.

In some scenarios, it is possible that market risk and private risk can coexist. For example, a retailer developing an e-commerce infrastructure is subject to private risk based on how well the project is managed and how robust the underlying technology tools are. At the same time, the project is also subject to market risk — whether shoppers will prefer to shop online. Although online shopping these days has become as ubiquitous as store shopping, this clearly was a market risk just a few years ago. A retailer developing an online infrastructure a few years ago would have also invested in some active learning to understand the market trends in order to clear the market uncertainty. The feedback obtained would have been used to re-evaluate whether to continue or abandon the project.

Let us now evaluate the ROV results at different decision points using the framework from scenario 1 of the Easy BooTox example. We started with the DCF-based project payoff of $50 million and a launch cost of $40 million and computed an ROV of $25 million at the time of the launch. Incorporating this value into the decision tree, we then calculated the ROVs at the time of the FDA application (that is, at the end of the clinical trials) and at time = 0 (start of the clinical trials). The results showed:

- ROV at the time of launch (time = 3 years): $25 million
- ROV at the time to apply for FDA approval (time = 2 years): $16 million
- ROV at the beginning of clinical trials (time = 0): $0.86 million

Since the project has a reasonably positive value at time = 0, the rational decision would be to invest in the first phase of the project and continue into the subsequent phases based on the results. Let us now compare the results and the decision facilitated by this integrated approach with those that would be arrived at with DCF and DTA, the traditional evaluation tools.

Discounted Cash Flow

Using the DCF method, we assume that every phase of the project, including the clinical trials, FDA approval, and product launch, will be successful. The future asset value is $50 million with a launch cost of $40 million, resulting in an NPV of $10 million at the time of the launch (at the end of year 3). Applying the same risk-adjusted discount rate of 20% to all the cash flows, including the costs for the clinical trials and FDA approval process, as is commonly done in this approach (although these costs are not subject to market risk and require a lower rate), the NPV of the project is –$7.7 million, as shown in Table 8-2. Therefore, the decision would be not to invest in this project. Many practitioners use the DCF method in combination with rigorous sensitivity analysis.

Table 8-2. Discounted Cash Flow Calculations for Easy BooTox

	Year			
	0	1	2	3
Discount rate	20%	20%	20%	20%
Outflows	−$10,000,000		−$5,000,000	−$40,000,000
Inflows				$50,000,000
Net cash flow	−$10,000,000	$0	−$5,000,000	$10,000,000
Discount factor	1.00	0.83	0.69	0.58
Present value of cash flow	−$10,000,000	$0	−$3,472,222	$5,787,037
NPV = sum of present value of all cash flows	−$7,685,185			

Decision Tree Analysis

In this approach, we start with a project NPV at launch time of $10 million, the same as in the DCF method. In both methods, after the launch, the asset value is driven by market risk, which is accounted for by a risk-adjusted discount rate; the higher the expected risk, the higher the discount rate. In the DCF analysis, the same risk-adjusted rate also is used to discount the cash flows during the development phase. However, in DTA, the risks are treated differently in this phase. Before the launch, the project NPV of $10 million is subject to private risk related to technical uncertainty about the product during the development phase. Therefore, in this phase, this cash flow as well as the development costs are discounted using a rate that is slightly higher than the risk-free rate. (The rationale for using such a rate is discussed in question 7 in the section on the discount rate dilemma in Chapter 3.) Furthermore, the cash flows are multiplied by the probability of success/failure of each path in the decision tree. Table 8-3 summarizes the discount rates that are used in the different valuation methods to deal with private and market risks in the overall valuation of the Easy BooTox project.

As shown in Table 8-4, based on DTA analysis of the Easy BooTox project, the expected project NPV at time = 0 is approximately −$7.7 million. Because of the high negative NPV, the project would be rejected. The decision tree approach coupled with detailed sensitivity analysis is the most commonly used method today for valuation of multiphase projects.

A comparison summary of the results from the two traditional methods and the integrated approach involving ROA is presented in Table 8-5. Whereas Easy BooTox would decide not to invest in the project based on the traditional tools,

Table 8-3. Private and Market Risks and Discount Rates in Overall Project Valuation Methods

Overall Valuation Method	Development Phase	Production Phase
DCF	Private risk is not considered. The same risk-adjusted rate as is used to address the market risk in the production phase is also used in discounting the cash flows.	The project payoff is calculated using a risk-adjusted rate to discount the free cash flows.
DTA	DTA with success/failure probabilities is used to account for the private risk. A rate slightly higher than the risk-free rate is used to discount all the cash flows inside the decision tree, which include the payoff from the production phase and the development phase investment costs.	Same as in DCF.
DTA and ROA	Same as in DTA.	The project payoff is first calculated using a risk-adjusted rate to discount the free cash flows, as in the other two methods. The payoff is then used to calculate the ROV using ROA, wherein a risk-free rate is used.

ROA would point the decision in the other direction because of the value it provides in terms of flexibility.

OTHER ADVANCED OPTIONS

So far in this chapter, we have discussed several advanced options, including compound and rainbow options. Other more advanced options are discussed below, but they are not presented in any detail because they are beyond the scope of this book.

Switching options — A switching option refers to the flexibility in a project to switch from one mode of operation to another. For example, a dual-fuel heater offers the option of switching from oil to natural gas and vice versa, depending on the relative market costs of these fuels. This flexibility has value and accounts for the price premium for dual-fuel heaters compared to single-fuel heaters.

Table 8-4. Discounted Cash Flow and Decision Tree Analysis Calculations for Easy BooTox

Input Data		
Discount rate	8%	
Clinical trials duration	2 years	
Clinical trials cost	$10,000,000	
Probability of success with clinical trials	0.8	
FDA approval process duration	1 year	
FDA approval process cost	$5,000,000	
Probability of FDA approval	0.9	
Payoff at launch (end of FDA process)	$10,000,000	
FDA Process Phase		
Project payoff at the end of year 3	0.9($10,000,000) + 0.1($0)	$9,000,000
Present value at the end of year 2	$9,000,000/(1 + 0.08)^1	$8,333,333
Less FDA process phase cost		−$5,000,000
Project NPV at the end of year 2	$8,333,333 − $5,000,000	$3,333,333
Clinical Trials Phase		
Project payoff at the end of year 2	0.8($3,333,333) + 0.2($0)	$2,666,667
Present value at year 0	$2,666,667/(1 + 0.08)^2	$2,286,237
Less clinical trials phase cost		−$10,000,000
Project NPV at year 0	$2,286,237 − $10,000,000	−$7,713,763

Exit options — As stated in Chapter 7, abandonment options are difficult to exercise due to political and psychological reasons. Abandonment option calls for abandonment of the project when the asset value goes below the strike price, but this reduction in asset value may be temporary and the asset value could bounce back above the strike price immediately thereafter. To avoid abandoning a project in such a situation, management may decide on a critical asset value that is smaller than the strike price before which the abandonment or exit option can be exercised. This critical value acts as a barrier below which the exit option will be exercised. Sometimes such an option is also referred to as a barrier option.

Complex compound options — Earlier in this chapter, we discussed the sequential compound option, which basically translates to a series of simple options. Exercising the first option creates the second one, exercising the second

Table 8-5. Comparison of Different Valuation Methods for Easy BooTox

Valuation Method	Project Value	Decision at Time = 0
DCF	−$7,685,185	No go
DCF and DTA	−$7,713,613	No go
DCF, DTA, and ROA	$859,625	Go

creates the third, and so on. In more complex compound options, the exercise of an option creates more than one option. For example, building the IT infrastructure for a retail store may create two options: building an online store and an online collaboration site for suppliers. In valuing such projects, it is important to take into account all the resulting options.

PROBLEMS

8-1. Hybrid Hydrogen, a new division of a major American auto manufacturer, is considering development of hybrid cars that can run on hydrogen fuel. Since there is market uncertainty regarding future sales, the company wants to use the options approach to value the project for a go/no-go investment decision. The project is divided into two phases: the design/engineering phase and the manufacturing phase. The first phase has to be completed before the second phase can begin. The design phase can start anytime next year, whereas the manufacturing phase can start anytime in the next three years. Design is expected to cost $200 million and manufacturing an additional $600 million. DCF analysis using an appropriate risk-adjusted discount rate values the present value of the future cash flows from this operation at $600 million. The annual volatility of the logarithmic returns of the future cash flows for the car is estimated to be 30%, and the continuous annual risk-free interest rate over the next five years is 6%. What is the value of the option to stage?

8-2. If there is no flexibility in the investments in Problem 8-1, what is the DCF-based NPV for this project assuming a 10% interest rate for discounting the investment costs?

8-3. Reconsider the Hybrid Hydrogen problem as a simple option where the company has the flexibility to make a single combined investment. The option life in this scenario is one year and the investment cost $800 million (the sum of the investment costs for both phases). What is the value of the option to wait to invest in this scenario? How does it compare with the ROV of the option to stage? Explain your answer.

8-4. AntiquesNow is a start-up company that is considering building a flagship brick-and-mortar store as well as an online e-business to sell antiques. It plans to use the flagship store as a warehouse from which to fill orders from the e-business. DCF analysis using an appropriate risk-adjusted discount rate places the NPV of the expected future cash flows at $50 million. The annual volatility factor for this payoff is calculated to be 25%. Based on the competition, AntiquesNow estimates that it has three years to make a go/no-go decision on this project. The continuous annual risk-free interest rate over this period is 5%. Construction of the flagship store is expected to cost $50 million and the development of the e-business is estimated at $20 million. AntiquesNow can start the e-business project at any time, but the flagship store must be built before the website is launched, thereby creating a parallel compound option. The company is interested in taking advantage of this option in project valuation to make a better investment decision that takes into account the payoff uncertainty. What is the ROV of the project?

8-5. Anti-Fossil Fuels is contemplating building a manufacturing plant to produce specialty fuel cells that generate power without emitting greenhouse gases. Since this is a novel approach to generating power, there is uncertainty regarding how well it will be received in the marketplace. The payoff for this project is also influenced by the price of oil, which determines the market for alternative sources of energy. Thus, the ultimate payoff for this project is affected by two sources of uncertainty: (1) uncertainty in the market for fuel cells and (2) uncertainty in the price of oil. The payoff volatilities due to these two factors are estimated to be 20% and 30%, respectively. Assuming that the two uncertainties are uncorrelated, Anti-Fossil Fuels is interested in valuation of the project using rainbow options. The present value of the expected cash flows from future fuel cell sales is estimated to be $250 million. Plant construction is expected to cost $300 million. What is the value of the option to wait to invest given an option life of two years, over which the continuous annual risk-free rate is expected to be 5%?

8-6. Recalculate the value of the option to wait for Anti-Fossil Fuels assuming that the volatility in the payoff due to the uncertainty in the market for fuel cells is 30% and the volatility due to the uncertainty in the price of oil is 20%. Is this value the same as or different than in Problem 8-5? Why or why not?

8-7. Smart Textiles, a specialty textile manufacturer, is considering an investment in a new plant that will manufacture a spill-proof fabric, but there is uncertainty about the market demand for the new fabric. The uncertainty will increase at the end of two years, when a regional trade pact goes into effect, resulting in a larger market but an increased number of competitors. Smart Textiles forecasts the present value of the expected future cash flows to be $200 million and the investment cost to be $250 million. The annual volatility of the logarithmic returns for the future cash flows is estimated to be 20% for the next two years and is expected to increase to 30% at that point when the trade pact goes into effect. The annual continuous risk-free rate for the next four years is 5%. What is the ROV of this project?

8-8. What is the sensitivity of the ROV to the expected volatility in the second half of the project in Problem 8-7? Recalculate the project ROV for each of the following scenarios:
   A. Second-half volatility = 25%
   B. Second-half volatility = 35%
   C. Second-half volatility = 40%

8-9. Shrinking Stomach specializes in weight-loss medication. It recently developed a pill that can produce substantial weight loss without major side effects. Before the product can be launched, the company needs to conduct large-scale clinical trials to prove the efficacy of the new pill and win FDA approval. Shrinking Stomach estimates a 70% probability of success (p_1) with the clinical trials, which are expected to take two years, and an 80% probability of success (p_2) in obtaining FDA approval, which takes an additional year after the clinical trials are proven successful. The investment costs are expected to be $20 million and $10 million, respectively, for the two phases. Even if the product receives FDA approval and reaches the launch phase, its commercial success depends on market acceptance. Based on DCF analysis using a risk-adjusted discount rate of 20%, the value of the expected future free cash flows from this product at the time of launch (three years from today) is estimated to be $70 million with a launch cost of $60 million. The annual volatility of the payoff is 30%, and the continuous annual risk-free rate over the next five years is 5%. Shrinking Stomach has determined that it can launch the product anytime within five years after the clinical trials are successful and the product is approved by the FDA. What is the value of the project using strictly the DCF approach (assuming no flexibility) if the appropriate discount rates for the investment and the payoff are assumed to be 10% and 20%, respectively?

8-10. Build a decision tree that depicts the clinical trials and FDA approval for Problem 8-9, and calculate the value of the Shrinking Stomach project based on DTA. Use the DCF-based payoff to represent the project value at the time of FDA approval and a discount rate of 8% to account for the private risk inside the decision tree.

8-11. Calculate the project ROV for Problem 8-9 at the time of the launch (three years from now) assuming that Shrinking Stomach has flexibility in deciding whether to launch the project based on market conditions. (This is an option to wait problem with a five-year option life.)

8-12. Calculate the project value as of today for Problem 8-9 based on DTA assuming Shrinking Stomach has the flexibility to react to both private risk and market risk. Use the project ROV from Problem 8-11 as the project payoff input to the DTA.

8-13. Calculate the project NPV as of today for Problem 8-9 using a discount factor of 8%. Using this NPV as the project payoff and assuming that the market risk exists throughout the project development phase until the launch (three years during the clinical trials and FDA approval phase and five years thereafter), construct a binomial lattice spanning eight years. Calculate the value of the entire project, accounting for simultaneous private and market risks during the first three years of the project.

9

REAL OPTIONS
IN THE REAL WORLD

"To invest or not to invest?" is a question pondered over every day by business executives across the globe. They are frequently faced with the dilemma of deciding whether or not to invest in developing a new product, introducing a new technology, testing a new drug, or launching a new service, to name just a few examples. Although the decision to invest in a project depends on several factors, it is primarily dictated by the expected financial return and risk associated with that project. The expected return is represented by the net payoff from the project, typically expressed in today's dollars as a present value, and the risk is represented by the uncertainty associated with that payoff. The most important and commonly used metric in the decision-making process is the net present value (NPV), which is the difference between the present value of the expected payoff and the project investment. If the project NPV is significantly positive or significantly negative (the expected payoff is significantly greater or smaller than the investment cost), the decision — to invest or not to invest, respectively — would be slam-dunk, especially when the payoff is deterministic and represented by one value. However, because of the uncertainty related to the commercial success of the associated product or service, the payoff is probabilistic, with a wide range of possible values. Even with a probabilistic payoff, the decision would be slam-dunk if the whole range of the expected payoff values is either far higher (Figure 9-1A) or far lower (Figure 9-1B) compared to the investment cost. However, there is a "gray zone" where the investment value may be within the range of the expected payoff values (Figure 9-1C), making the invest/no-invest decision somewhat difficult.

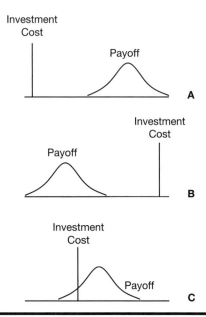

Figure 9-1.   Expected Payoff Distribution Versus Investment Cost

Discounted cash flow (DCF) analysis is a commonly used method which accounts for the market uncertainty with a risk-adjusted discount rate (the higher the uncertainty, the higher the discount rate) to calculate the present value of the payoff. While this approach focuses on the downside, the reward side is ignored. Conceptually speaking, the gray area on the left side of the investment value in Figure 9-1C is accounted for while ignoring the right side. Another limitation of the DCF approach is that it assumes a fixed path or one set of conditions in calculating the project payoff, and management is constrained to make the investment decision based on the analysis of these fixed conditions. However, in today's constantly changing environment, managers have the flexibility to alter the project outcome (for example, expand, contract, postpone, or abandon a project) in order to maximize the payoff or minimize the loss. This flexibility is not accounted for in the DCF approach.

When a project investment is equal or almost equal to the present value of the net payoff or in the gray zone and management has the flexibility to alter the scope of the project, real options analysis (ROA) provides additional information to facilitate the investment decision. While DCF is effective at the "extremes," ROA is valuable in the gray zone (Figure 9-1). Thus, it does not substitute the DCF method, but provides more information to help in the decision-making process when DCF cannot unequivocally point to either an invest or no-invest decision.

When the real options value (ROV) of a project is low, it suggests that the project's upside is low, and the investment decision might as well be based on the DCF results alone. A higher ROV, on the other hand, indicates that the project has great upside potential, which can be taken advantage of by management using its flexibility — but only after the market uncertainty is cleared by either passive or active learning. Passive learning means simply letting the uncertainty clear by itself with the passage of time, whereas active learning involves up-front management action. For instance, active learning may involve a market survey or release of a product in a test market. Once the uncertainty is cleared, depending on the results, the project may be launched at the same scale as originally planned, expanded, contracted, or even abandoned altogether. This delay helps avoid or minimize losses by clearing the uncertainty. With a small up-front expense to learn more about the market demand for your product, you can abandon the project if the results are unfavorable, thereby minimizing your losses associated with a full-blown investment.

Another type of uncertainty, known as private uncertainty, also must be considered in investment decisions. This uncertainty, which is commonly addressed by means of decision trees, is related to the probability of technical success and successful completion of the project on time and under budget. The former is generally referred to as technical uncertainty. Examples include efficacy of a drug in treating the target illness and effectiveness of a technology in providing the desired solution. Typically, this uncertainty is resolved by up-front investment to test the effectiveness of the solution involved. Sometimes you may simply wait (passive learning) until a competitor resolves the uncertainty, as may be the case with the introduction of new technologies. This may, however, stymie you from gaining the first-mover advantage.

In calculating the project's payoff, private uncertainty is accounted for by simply multiplying the net payoff by the probability of success of the project. For example, if the present value of the net payoff is $1 million and the estimated probability of successful project completion is 0.8, the expected net payoff is considered to be $800,000 (0.8 * $1 million), which is compared to the project investment in making the go/no-go decision. If a series of contingent decisions is involved, as in the case of drug testing for example, DCF alone is not an appropriate tool; therefore, decision tree analysis (DTA) is commonly used to estimate the project NPV. Decision trees can be integrated into ROA to create a more sophisticated framework in the overall decision-making process.

HOW DOES A PRACTITIONER USE REAL OPTIONS ANALYSIS?

Any project opportunity in an organization is typically evaluated on its own merit as well as how it stacks up against other projects competing for the same monetary and other resources. A balanced portfolio approach is commonly used to diversify among different types of projects using project size, growth, profitability, risk/return ratio, and other criteria. Every project opportunity typically goes through an initial management screening, where it is evaluated against basic qualitative criteria such as strategic fit. After this subjective screening, the practicing analyst is involved in project valuation using the quantitative financial tools. In the following paragraphs, we offer a simple integrated project valuation framework that includes the traditional NPV and DTA tools as well as the sophisticated ROA that will fit with the project portfolio approach.

1. Estimate the baseline investment cost and the present value of the payoff or the expected free cash flows of the project. Whereas the investment costs are more certain, free cash flow estimates involve uncertainty. You can use tools such as Monte Carlo simulation, scenario analysis, and tornado diagrams to understand the uncertainty and sensitivity of the free cash flows. One of the key parameters that determines the payoff present value is the discount rate, which you can estimate using the capital asset pricing model or weighted average cost of capital coupled with risk premium.

2. Conduct an initial analysis comparing the baseline project investment versus the present value of the payoff. If the difference between the two is far from zero or the investment is far outside the "gray zone," the go/no-go decision is easy. The project has financial merit if the present value of the payoff is far higher, whereas it is not worth the investment if it is significantly lower compared to the investment cost. This decision can be strengthened by other deterministic financial measurements, such as internal rate of return, return on investment, payback period, etc. If the investment falls in the "gray zone," you can evaluate the project characteristics to determine whether the project has high option value and deserves further consideration. The assessment tool in Appendix B can be used as a screening test to determine the ROA potential of a project. Although it is a simplistic tool based on subjective information, it provides you with preliminary insight into whether a project has real options potential. Detailed ROA can be conducted if the assessment indicates high enough potential.

3. Estimate the option value of the project using the binomial method. The first and perhaps most important step in this method is to frame the option application. Framing involves describing the problem in simple words, identifying the option, and stating clearly the contingent decision and the decision rule. The next important step is to identify the input parameters for the binomial model. One of the key inputs is the volatility of the underlying asset value, which you can estimate using the project proxy approach, market proxy approach, or simulations. You also need to determine whether there are different sources of volatility and whether the volatility changes during the option life, because this will define the exact lattice technique you will use to calculate the project's option value. Also, determine whether there is leakage in the underlying asset value, and if so, the characteristics of the leakage, so that proper adjustments can be made to the options value. Framing of a compound option is even more difficult; therefore, exercise caution in particular in defining whether a compound option should be sequential or parallel. Several assumptions are usually made in framing the application and in solving the options problem and should be clearly documented.

4. Analyze the option results to gain better insight into and better understanding of the project economics. First, compare the binomial results with the Black-Scholes solution or another closed form solution, if possible, to establish validity of the binomial method and gain confidence in the results. You can also use Monte Carlo simulation if the solution can be obtained easily without going through unreasonable computational complexity. Next, conduct a sensitivity analysis on the options value as a function of the key variables, including the exercise price, volatility, and option life. Calculate the probability for exercising the option at the end of the option life. With compound options, reframe the problem with different option dependencies (and also as a simple option) to see how the option value changes.

5. Prepare the results for presentation to management in an easily understandable format. In many organizations, management is known to reject ROA as a valuation tool not because they think it is flawed or ineffective but because they do not understand it. Therefore, it is paramount that the option valuation results are presented in a simple and easily understood format, without delving into the complex theory and intricate computations. This is a vital step in gaining buy-in from management on the use of real options as a valuation method. Communicate the options results to management using tools they are familiar with, like bubble diagrams, pie charts, and histograms. In presenting the results, start with the DCF results that management is familiar with. Then explain the options embedded in the project by clearly framing the application. Communicate all the key assumptions. Explain how, by creating an option, you are buying a right — without any obligation whatsoever — to invest in a project and hedging the risks. Wherever applicable, draw parallels from the financial options examples with which management is most likely familiar.

Explain the concepts of volatility and the managerial flexibility, and demonstrate how the options value changes as volatility changes. You can show the binomial tree, which is similar to a decision tree that most managers are familiar with, to depict where it is best to exercise the option versus keeping it open. Avoid discussions on the calculation of the asset and option values across the binomial tree, because this is where management most likely will be lost.

Demonstrate that ROA is not a substitute for the traditional tools such as DCF and DTA, but simply an extension of them. This step is especially important in organizations where ROA is misconstrued as a totally different and complicated tool that replaces the traditional methods. Illustrate how ROA yields the same results as DCF when the volatility of the underlying asset is zero, and drive home the point that ROA is an extension of DCF but not a substitute. Use decision trees that management is familiar with as an overall strategic map to depict the contingent decisions and options value at each decision point.

After discussing the options results from individual projects, the focus can turn to relative merits of projects competing for investment in the context of a portfolio. You can start with a comparison and ranking of projects based on their baseline project NPVs calculated using the DCF method. Then you can show the reprioritized list of projects based on their ROV and discuss the changes. Competing projects may differ in characteristics relative to investment, such as size, resource needs, risk profiles, etc. You can categorize them into different groups, use ratios, etc. Furthermore, other relevant criteria can be added for comparison purpose.

WHAT IS THE STATUS OF REAL OPTIONS IN THE CORPORATE WORLD?

Several authors (Copeland and Keenan, 1998; Amram and Kulatilaka, 1999) have documented potential applications of real options in various industries, including aerospace, automotive, banking, chemicals, consumer goods, electronics, insurance, medical products, oil and gas, pharmaceuticals, technology, telecommunications, transportation, etc. Table 9-1 lists a few recent examples of real options applications in selected industries. Today's corporate world, in general, seems to take either a "love it" or "hate it" attitude toward ROA. Those who truly understand the principles behind real options appreciate the value ROA brings to project valuation and have embraced it. The energy, oil and gas, and pharmaceutical sectors are the leaders in successfully adopting the real options framework. They recognized the value of the real options approach and adopted it quickly. Being the early pioneers, they have been able to accumulate the historical input data that are so vital to the successful application of real options tools.

Table 9-1.   Real World Examples of Real Options Applications

Airlines
Buying aircraft, especially new models, in today's uncertain world is risky business for airlines. When the market demand is uncertain, performance of new products is unknown, and the investment is huge, many airlines use ROA in their strategic decisions. In April 2005, Air Canada placed firm orders with Boeing for 32 of its new 787 airplanes and took options to buy 64 more in the future. In the same month, Air India placed firm orders for 35 of the same plane and acquired options to purchase 15 more later. Buying options to purchase additional aircraft in the future while placing firm orders is a common practice in the airline industry. Since the investments are significant and the market demand is uncertain, airlines prefer to hold an option rather than buy all the aircraft they need outright. As the uncertainty clears over time, and if the expected payoff from expanding their operations is higher than the purchase price of the aircraft (strike price), they will exercise the option and expand their operations. This call option is, in effect, an expansion option, the value of which can be calculated using ROA. The payoff from expansion depends not only on the market risk dictated by passenger demand but also on the private risk related to performance and maintenance of the new aircraft. This private risk is small for well-established models like Boeing 747s, but is not known for the 787, a new product.

Automakers
Global competitiveness in recent years has forced the automobile industry into continuous restructuring, increasing plant closings, and massive consolidation, not to mention higher productivity. With enormous investments and risks involved with every strategic initiative, the auto industry needs real options tools to help make the right decisions. In 2000, when the industry was on the verge of sweeping consolidation, Detroit-based General Motors (GM) bought a 20% stake in Italy's Fiat Auto in exchange for a 5.1% stake in GM, as part of a master agreement worth $2.4 billion. This deal included a put option for Fiat — the right, but not an obligation — to sell the remaining stake of the company to GM before 2010 if and when Fiat got into serious trouble. In early 2005, Fiat wanted to exercise its put and sell its money-losing business to GM for the strike price of $8 billion, because it was losing money by the billions and was loaded with massive debt. But GM argued that the put option was unenforceable, because Fiat had violated the master agreement by restructuring its finances the previous years. After going through mediation, GM ultimately agreed to pay out nearly $2 billion to terminate the put option once and for all. It seems that GM underestimated the value of the put option it granted to Fiat in their master agreement.

Pharmaceuticals
As drug development costs soar into the $1 billion territory and the R&D pipelines are becoming empty, Big Pharma is turning to strategic alliances, partnerships, joint ventures, and other such initiatives with smaller start-up companies. While the innovative start-ups focus on the initial development efforts, the giants get involved in the later development stages and commercialization of the drugs as they are proven effective after going through clinical trials and FDA approval. Using the real options approach, a project can be abandoned or go to the next phase as the private uncertainty related to the effectiveness of a drug is resolved. In essence, this is acquiring a call option, the underlying asset of which is the payoff from future drug sales. This is a sequential compound option wherein exercising one option generates another option, and the strike price of a given option is the investment needed to exercise that option. In 2002, GlaxoSmithKline reached an agreement with Exelixis, an upstart genomics-based drug discovery company, where the pharmaceutical giant will develop, manufacture, and commercialize

Table 9-1. Real World Examples of Real Options Applications (continued)

the drugs that the upstart has discovered and tested through Phase II clinical trials. The total size of the deal is $439 million, which includes an up-front lump sum payment and purchase of stock coupled with a loan, development funding, and milestone payments tied to successful completion of different phases, among other incentives.

Telecommunications
Just a few years ago, five carriers from the United Kingdom spent close to $36 billion to obtain third-generation (3G) spectrum licenses. Obtaining a 3G license provided these carriers the option to roll out high-speed wireless data services to their customers. Some of the carriers have already started rolling out the 3G service to their customers, after making additional investments in upgrading their network infrastructure.

There is huge uncertainty in the market demand for 3G services, and many analysts think that the telecom companies paid too much for these licenses and that it may take them up to 10 years just to break even with their investments. The upside potential, however is also very high. The availability of high-speed wireless capability may result in novel products and services developed by technology companies and content providers.

In spite of the huge uncertainty in the market demand for the 3G services, these companies are going ahead with the rollout. If they had waited for the uncertainty to clear, they could limit the potential downside, but they would also lose out on the huge upside potential. The wireless marketplace is highly competitive, and no company can be waiting it out while its competition is moving forward. This is a scenario where a company cannot afford to wait out the uncertainty and needs to make some risky bets and go ahead with its investments right away.

Oil Industry
The oil industry has long used ROA to value oil field leases. Significant investments are required for the drilling operations, and it usually takes years before the production of oil begins. Obtaining a lease for an oil field provides a company the right, but not an obligation, to drill for oil, thereby creating a call option. But just like any other option, the right to drill has value and needs to be determined. ROA is a common tool for such valuation.

Oil prices are volatile and depend on market demand as well as the demand-supply equilibrium in the oil markets. Therefore, a company that acquires the lease for an oil field may want to wait until the uncertainty on the oil prices clears before making the decision to drill. Apart from the market risk of oil prices, the drilling operation is also subject to the private risk of the reserve quality and quantity. The cost of the oil extraction process varies depending on the terrain. This private risk can be accounted for by making smaller investments in active learning to gather more information on the terrain. The private risk can be reduced by investing in the development of more efficient extraction techniques.

Oil sands (also known as tar sands), found extensively in the Canadian province of Alberta, are estimated to contain 1.6 trillion barrels of crude oil. For decades, extraction of this oil was considered uneconomical due to the difficulty in getting oil out of these tar sands. The recent increase in oil prices (reduction in market risk) coupled with the latest breakthrough improvements in the extraction process (reduction in private risk) have turned the attention of major oil companies toward Alberta. In the last two years, Shell and ChevronTexaco invested in the Athabasca Oil Sands Project in Alberta, and ChevronTexaco opened a new plant in Venezuela, another country with huge tar sand reserves.

Despite its potential for broad-based application, the real options framework has been applied and accepted to a limited extent only. According to Bain & Company's 2000 survey of 451 senior executives in more than 30 industries, only 9% used real options as a management tool and one-third of those abandoned use the same year. Potential first-time users have shown resistance because of the real or perceived limited success of real options in the real world. There are several reasons why the real options framework has received lukewarm support in the finance community.

First, ROA is a relatively new tool compared to the traditional methods such as DCF analysis that have been around for decades. Even DCF took decades to become a staple in the financial world. As with any new tool, it may take a few years before ROA gains wider acceptance. ROA is a more sophisticated and complex technique compared to the traditional tools and requires a higher level of understanding. Some organizations seem to shy away from ROA because of the higher level of mathematics involved in solving the real options problems, as well as lack of a clear understanding of the principles and benefits of the method. We believe that many in-house analysts as well as outside consultants have promoted a "black box" approach to ROA, instead of opening the black box to demystify it and explain what is inside in simple terms easily understood by upper management and decision makers. Unfortunately, Black-Scholes, the most well-known options model, although it is not the most appropriate for many real options problems, easily lends itself to the black box approach because of its outward simplicity (the solution involves just one equation) and the enormous theoretical complexity behind it.

We also believe that the current real options literature has been primarily academic, whereas practical "how-to" guides, easy-to-use computer tools, and publications on real world success stories have been rare. The latter are more likely to appear in the future as more organizations embrace ROA. Real options proponents believe that it is just a matter of time before ROA becomes widely accepted and integrated into the standard project valuation framework of the finance world.

HOW TO MAKE REAL OPTIONS WORK IN YOUR ORGANIZATION

Notwithstanding the limited acceptance to date, the real options approach has an important place in the project valuation framework. It can be one of several tools that practitioners have in their valuation toolboxes. The technique is theoretically sound and technically feasible. The real challenge for a practitioner is not so much convincing yourself whether or how the technique applies to the project initiatives in your organization as persuading management to embrace and support it. In today's technology-driven, hyper-competitive world, organizations are filled with strategic and growth project opportunities with enormous uncertainty and flexibility — the right conditions for real options application. Rejecting long-term strategic opportunities simply on the basis of unattractive NPV would certainly be a competitive disadvantage. ROA provides an objective framework to evaluate a project for its own merit as well as its relative merit compared to other competing projects and helps senior management make better decisions to gain competitive advantage in the long run.

Analysts as well as management can implement the following ideas to promote ROA within their organizations:

- Introduce ROA as part of a comprehensive framework designed to promote effective strategic decision making. Make ROA a critical piece of the overall valuation puzzle, because its value lies not just in itself but in the context of the bigger picture.

- Initiate, evaluate, and select projects as part of a portfolio, and apply portfolio management principles to maximize the overall portfolio value. Integrate ROA into the overall project selection process.

- Break the myth that ROA is a substitute for DCF and there is no need for a new, complex technique when the current methods are proven and simple.

- Highlight the limitations of the DCF approach and how ROA addresses the gaps that DCF cannot fill.

- Frame the options problem in simple and clear terms that senior management can easily understand. Present the results using well-accepted and easily understood tools, such as decision diagrams, bubble charts, pie charts, and so on.

- Avoid the black box approach to ROA and demystify the black box. Use the more transparent binomial method for solving the options problem and communicating the results. This is not to say that Black-Scholes has no place in the real options world. Use the ground-breaking, Nobel Prize–winning model for verification of the binomial results, wherever possible.

- Underscore the significance of management executing the right decisions at the right time. Irrespective of the ROV of a project calculated by an analyst, if management is not willing to exercise the flexibility and execute the decisions, the true option value will diminish to zero. The timing of the exercise also is critical in capturing the potential value of a project. Early or late exercise can significantly decrease the value of the options.

- Emphasize the importance of the input data, and do the necessary upfront homework to collect the information needed not only to merely solve the options problem but also to study the sensitivity of the results to the input data in order to gain better insight.

- Build historical information on input parameters, especially the uncertainty of the underlying asset, that drive the options value. "Garbage in, garbage out" is a well-known axiom, but unfortunately, if it is "garbage in" and you don't know it, you may treat the results as "gospel out!"

- Communicate clearly the assumptions on which the options solution is built, and bring to light the caveats that dictate the limitations of the application. Real options is not the panacea to project valuation. It is only effective under the right project conditions. The constraints and limitations of the tool for a given application must be openly discussed to avoid misuse of the tool for promoting selfish interests.

- Avoid becoming a zealot to the point where you may lose objectivity and become an evangelical supporter of the tool irrespective of its validity for a given application. Abuse and misuse of the method can ultimately lead to rejection of the tool as a whole in your organization.

- Document and share your success stories with peers in your organization to gain support for further successful use of real options.

In conclusion, we hope that this book gives you a better understanding of the principles behind ROA and, more importantly, the practical tools you need to solve your options problems. The spreadsheet-based solutions to the examples and the end-of-chapter problems presented in the book are available at www.jrosspub.com and www.kodukula.com. The spreadsheets are flexible, so that you can obtain answers to the scenarios of interest to you by changing the input parameters. We hope that the book and the websites will serve as excellent resources for you to become proficient in applying ROA to evaluate project opportunities in your organization and ultimately lead to the right strategic decisions.

REFERENCES

Amram, M. (2002). *Value Sweep: Mapping Corporate Growth Opportunities*, Harvard Business School Press, Boston, Massachusetts.

Amram, M. and Kulatilaka, N. (1999). *Real Options: Managing Strategic Investment in an Uncertain World*, Harvard Business School Press, Boston, Massachusetts.

Amram, M. and Kulatilaka, N. (2000). "Strategy and Shareholder Value Creation: The Real Options Frontier," *Journal of Applied Corporate Finance*, Volume 13, No. 2.

Brach, M.A. (2003). *Real Options in Practice*, John Wiley & Sons, Hoboken, New Jersey.

Canada, J.R., Sullivan, W.G., and White, J. (1996). *Capital Investment Analysis for Engineering and Management*, 2nd edition, Prentice Hall, Saddle River, New Jersey.

Copeland, T. and Antikarov, V. (2001). *Real Options: A Practitioner's Guide*, Texere, New York.

Copeland, T. and Keenan, T. (1998). "Making Real Options Real," *The McKinsey Quarterly*, No. 3.

Damodaran, A. (2002). *Investment Valuation: Tools & Techniques for Determining Any Asset*, John Wiley & Sons, New York.

Dixit, A. and Pindyck, R. (1994). *Investment Under Uncertainty*, Princeton University Press, Princeton, New Jersey.

Mun, J. (2002). *Real Options Analysis — Tools & Techniques for Valuing Strategic Investments and Decisions,* John Wiley & Sons, Hoboken, New Jersey.

APPENDIX A: REPLICATING PORTFOLIO

Replicating portfolio theory is the foundation of the ground-breaking Black-Scholes equation originally developed to value financial options. This theory is also the basis for the binomial method developed for the same purpose by John Cox, Stephen Ross, and Mark Rubinstein.* The advantage of the binomial method is that it is a transparent, efficient, numerical method that uses elementary mathematics to value not only the simple European options but also the more complex American options, where premature exercise may be optimal. In its special limiting case, the binomial method reduces to the Black-Scholes equation. This appendix briefly presents the theory behind the replicating portfolio approach and the derivation of equations for the binomial method to solve financial as well as real options problems.

A call option provides the owner of the option the right to buy the underlying asset (normally a stock) at a predetermined price (strike price) on or before the expiration date. The replicating portfolio method uses a portfolio that consists of a certain number of underlying stocks and risk-free bonds that correlates perfectly with the option value — irrespective of whether the stock prices go up or go down in the future. Since the portfolio correlates perfectly with the value of the option, the current price of the call option is calculated as the current value of the replicating portfolio.

---

* Cox, J.C., Ross, S.A., and Rubenstein, M. (1979). "Option Pricing: A Simplified Approach," *Journal of Financial Economics*, 7, 229.

To better illustrate the principle, let us assume that the current price of a stock is S_o. Also assume that in the next time period (say, one year) it can either go up to S_u with a subjective probability q or go down to S_d with a probability $(1 - q)$. Note that different players in the market may have different estimates for this subjective probability, q. Let us consider a call option that is written on this underlying stock with a strike price of X. Since the stock price can take one of two values, the call option value (C_u or C_d) can also be one of these two values:

Up state: $C_u = \text{MAX}[0, S_u - X]$ with probability q

Down state: $C_d = \text{MAX}[0, S_d - X]$ with probability $1 - q$

Let us assume that the replicating portfolio consists of m shares of the underlying stock, and B risk-free bonds, each valued at $1. The values of the portfolio (P_u and P_d) at the two states are:

Up state: $P_u = mS_u + B(1 + r)$

Down state: $P_d = mS_d + B(1 + r)$

where r is the risk-free rate and hence represents the returns on the bonds. Since the replicating portfolio accurately tracks the option value in both states, the following equations should hold true:

$$P_u = C_u$$

$$P_d = C_d$$

$$mS_u + B(1 + r) = C_u$$

$$mS_d + B(1 + r) = C_d$$

Solving for m and B, we get

$$m = \frac{C_u - C_d}{S_u - S_d}$$

$$B = \frac{S_u C_d - S_d C_u}{(S_u - S_d)(1 + r)}$$

Let us assume that the stock returns follow a multiplicative binomial process over discrete time periods, with u being the up factor and d being the down factor. In this case, the two possible values for the stock prices reduce thus:

$$S_u = uS$$

$$S_d = dS$$

Applying these equalities to the above equations for m and B, we get:

$$m = \frac{C_u - C_d}{S(u - d)}$$

$$B = \frac{uC_d - dC_u}{(u - d)(1 + r)}$$

The current value of the call option is easily calculated by substituting these equations for m and B:

$$C = mS + B$$

$$C = \frac{C_u - C_d}{u - d} + \frac{uC_d - dC_d}{(u - d)(1 + r)}$$

This equation can be simplified to:

$$C = \frac{pC_u + (1 - p)C_d}{1 + r}$$

where

$$p = \frac{(1 + r) - d}{u - d}$$

and

$$1 - p = \frac{u - (1 + r)}{u - d}$$

In other words, the current call option value is the expected future call option value discounted back to today using the risk-free rate. The factor p has the characteristics of probability and is called risk-neutral probability. The risk-neutral probability is independent of the subjective probability, q, which represents the probability that the stock price will go up. By removing the subjectivity, this equation provides an easy way for both buyers and sellers to agree upon the current option price and hence is considered risk neutral.

You can replace $(1 + r)$ with $\exp(r)$ in the above equations for the risk-neutral probability and call option price if a continuous risk-free rate is used. In that case, the equations become:

$$C = [pC_u + (1 - p)C_d] \exp(-r)$$

where

$$p = \frac{\exp(r) - d}{u - d}$$

and

$$1 - p = \frac{u - \exp(r)}{u - d}$$

The binomial lattice method of valuing financial or real options is based on taking a current asset value and constructing an asset tree over multiple time periods, determining the option values at the end nodes of the lattice, and calculating the current option price by backward induction. The value of the option at any node is the expected value of the option at the future nodes discounted back to the given node using the risk-neutral probability.

APPENDIX B:
REAL OPTIONS
ANALYSIS
APPLICATION
ASSESSMENT TOOL

The objective of this tool is to help you quickly assess whether a project has significant real options value. Depending upon the results, you may decide to conduct a detailed real options analysis or just use the traditional tools such as discounted cash flow to make your investment decision. This assessment tool has four steps. Depending on your answers in step 1, you may stop at the end of step 2 or go all way through step 4.

STEP 1

Select the most appropriate answer to each of the following four questions by circling the number in front of it.

Question 1: What is the level of uncertainty related to your estimated payoff?
  6 High
  3 Low
  0 None

Question 2: What is the investment cost in relation to the estimated payoff?
6   About the same
3   Much different but between the pessimistic and optimistic payoff estimates
0   Below the pessimistic or above the optimistic payoff estimate

Question 3: Do you have contingent decisions in your project definition?
6   Many
3   Just a few
0   None

Question 4: Do you have flexibility in changing project direction to maximize its value?
6   High
3   Low
0   No

STEP 2

If you circled "0" for any of the questions in step 1, the project does not have any real options value. The investment decision can be made based on results obtained by using discounted cash flow and other traditional methods, and there is no need for detailed real options analysis. You can stop here on this assessment tool. If you circled any number other than "0" for every one of the questions in step 1, proceed to step 3.

STEP 3

Select the most appropriate answer for each of the following six questions by circling the number in front of it.

Question 5: What is the potential for this project to create future growth opportunities?
6   High
3   Moderate
0   Low

Question 6: Can the project be broken down into a sequence of logical small projects, each requiring its own investment?
  2   Yes, the initial project(s) requires small investments
  1   Yes, the initial project(s) requires large investment
  0   No

Question 7: What is the source of your payoff uncertainty?
  2   Only or mostly market risk
  1   About equal levels of market and private risk
  0   Only or mostly private risk

Question 8: How long does it take for the payoff uncertainty to clear?
  2   Three to five years
  1   One to two years
  0   Very long, in which case the competition will erode the asset value

Question 9: What is the investment needed to clear the uncertainty relative to the estimated payoff?
  2   Small
  1   Moderate
  0   High

Question 10: How many other projects is the candidate project being evaluated against for investment as part of a project portfolio?
  2   Many
  1   Just a few
  0   None

STEP 4

Add up the numbers you circled in both steps 1 and 3 and compare the total with the following ranges to find the real options value of your project.

Less than 10	Little value
Between 10 and 30	Moderate value
More than 30	Significant value

NOTATION

B	Barrier price
β	Risk measure factor under the capital asset pricing model
C	Call option value
C	Cost of the capital component in the weighted average cost of capital
CAPM	Capital asset pricing model
d	Down factor
DCF	Discounted cash flow
DTA	Decision tree analysis
ε	Simulated value from a standard normal distribution with a mean of zero
EV	Expected value
FV	Future value
MARR	Minimum acceptable rate of return
n	Number of time increments
NPV	Net present value
p	Probability
P	Put option value
PV	Present value
r	Interest or discount rate
ROA	Real options analysis
ROV	Real options value
S	Underlying asset value
σ	Standard deviation of the natural logarithm of cash flow returns
σ^2	Variance (standard deviation squared)
t	Time increment

T	Option life
u	Up factor
W	Weight of the capital component in weighted average cost of capital
WACC	Weighted average cost of capital
X	Strike price
y	Dividend yield

A GLOSSARY
OF TERMS

Active learning — Learning about the market uncertainty by actively investing up front in market surveys, focus group studies, etc.

Aggregate volatility factor — A single volatility factor that accounts for the cash flow uncertainties related to several variables, such as unit price, quantities expected to be sold, margins, etc.

American option — An option which can be exercised at any time on or before its expiration date.

Arbitrage — Inefficient market conditions that allow you to buy an asset at one price and simultaneously sell it at a higher price.

At the money — A call or put option is at the money if the underlying asset value is equal to the strike price.

Barrier call option — A simple call option where a barrier price is set at a value higher than the exercise price, and the option goes into the money when the asset value exceeds the barrier price.

Barrier price — The price that dictates whether a barrier option is in or out of the money. The option is in the money if the asset value is above (for a call) or below (for a put) the barrier price.

Barrier put option — A simple put option where a barrier price is set at a value lower than the exercise price, and the option goes into the money when the asset value dips below the barrier price.

Binomial method — An option valuation method that uses a binomial lattice. *See also* Lattice.

Black-Scholes — The famous equation originally developed to price financial options. It is named for Richard Black and Merton Scholes, the two MIT economists who in 1973 published the ground-breaking paper on financial options pricing theory.

Buy option — *See* Call option.

Call option — Also known as a buy option. An option to buy a specified number of shares of a security (or an underlying asset) within a specified period at a predefined price.

Capital asset pricing model — A method to estimate a publicly traded company's cost of equity. According to this model, the expected return of a security equals the risk-free rate plus a risk premium proportional to the company's risk relative to the market.

Compound option — An option whose value depends on the value of another option rather than the underlying asset value.

Decision tree analysis — A project valuation method that portrays alternative decisions, their outcomes, probability of the outcomes, and the cash flows related to the decisions and the outcomes in the form of a branching tree and calculates the project value using "expected values."

Deferral option — *See* Option to wait.

Discounted cash flow method — A method for converting future free cash flows into today's value using an appropriate discount rate.

Discount rate — The interest rate used to convert future cash flows to today's value.

European option — An option which can be exercised only on a fixed date, its expiration date.

Exercise price — Also known as the strike price. The price at which the option owner can buy or sell the underlying asset.

Expected value — The product of the probability of a cash flow and the value of the cash flow.

Financial option — A right — not an obligation — to take an action (buy or sell) on an underlying financial asset (e.g., a stock) at a predetermined cost on or before a predetermined date.

Free cash flows — Net revenues after accounting for depreciation, interest, and taxes.

Future value — Value of money at a given time in the future.

Hurdle rate — Also known as minimum acceptable rate of return. A benchmark return rate a project is expected to yield before funds are committed for investment. This rate usually is set by corporate finance departments.

In the money (call option) — A call option is in the money if the underlying asset value is greater than the strike price.

In the money (put option) — A put option is in the money if the underlying asset value is less than the strike price.

Lattice — Decision diagram that basically lays out, in the form of a branching tree, the evolution of possible values of the underlying asset during the life of the option. A solution is obtained by optimizing the future decisions at various decision points and folding them back in a backward recursive fashion into the current decision. Lattices can be binomial, trinomial, quadrinomial, and so on.

Leakage — A positive or negative dividend such as a cash flow that affects the underlying asset value either positively or negatively.

Learning option — A compound option that involves resolution of either private or market uncertainty.

Logarithmic cash flow returns method — A method to estimate the volatility factor based on the variability of the same cash estimates that are used in calculating the underlying asset value.

Market risk — Risks related to the volatility of the expected future payoff driven by market forces, such as market demand, competition, etc.

Monte Carlo simulation — A method in which the input variables of any model can be simulated based on their respective probability distributions in order to solve for the model output.

Net present value — The difference between the sums of present values of revenues and costs.

Opportunity cost — The rate of return that would have been earned by selecting another alternate project rather than the one under consideration.

Option — A right — not an obligation — of the owner to buy or sell the underlying asset at a predetermined price on or before a predetermined date.

Option life — The remaining time left on an option to buy or sell it before it becomes worthless.

Option price — Also known as option premium. The price paid to acquire an option.

Option to abandon — A real option that gives you the right, with no obligation, to abandon a project.

Option to choose — A real option that gives you the right, with no obligation, to choose among abandoning, scaling up/down, or continuing a project.

Option to contract — A real option that gives you the right, with no obligation, to scale down a project.

Option to expand — A real option that gives you the right, with no obligation, to scale up a project.

Option to stage — *See* Sequential compound option.

Option to wait — A real option that gives you the right to wait, with no obligation, to invest in a project.

Out of the money (call option) — A call option is out of the money if the underlying asset value is less than the strike price.

Out of the money (put option) — A put option is out of the money if the underlying asset value is greater than the strike price.

Parallel compound option — Simply referred to as a compound option. Both the dependent and independent options are available at the same time, as opposed to a sequential option, where the independent option must be exercised to create the dependent option.

Pascal's triangle — A branching arithmetic triangle where the branches recombine to form a so-called recombining binomial tree and where each row begins and ends with a 1 and all internal digits are formed by adding up the nearest two digits in the upper row.

Passive learning — Learning about the market uncertainty as it clears through the simple passage of time without actively investing in the learning process.

Present value — Today's value of future money.

Private risk — Risks related to the efficiency and effectiveness of an organization in executing projects.

Put option — Also known as a sell option. An option to sell a specified number of shares of a security (or an underlying asset) within a specified period at a predefined price.

Rainbow option — A simple or compound option that exhibits multiple sources of uncertainty.

Real option — A right — not an obligation — to take an action (e.g., defer, expand, contract, abandon, stage) on an underlying nonfinancial asset at a predetermined cost on or before a predetermined date.

Real options analysis — A project valuation method for real options that is based on financial options pricing theory.

Real options value — Value of a project based on "real options analysis."

Replicating market portfolio approach — An approach to solve the binomial (or other) lattice and calculate the options value. Considered a rather difficult approach, it involves setting up a portfolio of a number of nontraded assets in the market to replicate the existing asset's payout profile. Assuming that the value of the asset and the portfolio are the same given that the payout profiles are identical, the asset value is derived.

Risk-adjusted discount rate — The discount rate used in converting future cash flows to present value which includes a risk premium on top of the risk-free rate to account for the risk related to the cash flows being considered.

Risk-free rate — Interest rate with no risk. The interest rate offered by the U.S. Treasury is considered risk free because the investment is guaranteed by the full faith and credit of the U.S. government.

Risk-neutral probability method — An approach to solve the binomial (or other) lattice and calculate the options value. In this approach, the probabilities of the cash flows are adjusted and the risk-free rate is used to discount them, instead of using risky cash flows and discounting them at a risk-adjusted discounted rate, as is done with discounted cash flow analysis.

Sell option — *See* Put option.

Sequential compound option — Also known as an option to stage. Simply referred to as a sequential option. It requires that one option be exercised to create another one.

Simple option — An option whose value depends directly on the value of an underlying asset, but not the value of another option. Options are commonly referred to as simple options when the calculation of their value is relatively simple. Examples include options to wait, abandon, expand, contract, and choose and barrier options.

Strike price — *See* Exercise price.

Terminal value — The total value of the remainder of a project after the terminal year. The terminal year is the time through which the project cash flows are calculated.

Volatility — Also known as uncertainty. A measure of the variability of the total value of the underlying asset over its lifetime. It signifies the uncertainty associated with the cash flows that comprise the underlying asset value.

Volatility factor — Volatility of the rates of return, which is measured as the standard deviation of the natural logarithm of cash flow returns, not the actual cash flows.

Weighted average cost of capital — Weighted average of the cost components of issuing debt, preferred stock, and common equity.

INDEX

La Nina